COUNTRY WOODCRAFT

Shaping a bucket stave.

COUNTRY WOODCRAFT

DREW LANGSNER

Rodale Press Emmaus, Pennsylvania

1978

Printed in the United States of America on recycled paper.

Library of Congress Cataloging in Publication Data

Langsner, Drew.
Country woodcraft.

Bibliography: p.
Includes index.
1. Woodwork. 2. Agricultural implements.
3. Implements, utensils, etc. I. Title.
TT200.L34 684'.082 78-780
ISBN 0-87857-200-7
ISBN 0-87857-201-5 pbk.

2 4 6 8 10 9 7 5 3 1

CONTENTS

Foreword—Wm. S. Coperthwaite vi

Acknowledgments ix

Introduction x

Part I: THE FOUNDATION OF COUNTRY WOODCRAFT

1. The Basic Tools 3
2. Materials 15
3. Felling 25
4. The Woodshed 37

Part II: THE WORKSHOP

5. Sawbuck 55
6. Shaving Horses 59
7. Clubs, Mauls, and Mallets 73
8. Bow Saws 81
9. Tool Handles 89
10. Wedges 101
11. The Workbench 107
12. A Spring-Pole Lathe 123

Part III: AGRICULTURAL IMPLEMENTS

13. Hay Rakes 135
14. Pitchforks 145
15. The Wheelbarrow 163
16. Swiss Milking Stool 171
17. A Hauling Yoke 177
18. Sleds 181
19. Bull Tongue Plow 191
20. Spike-Tooth A-Harrow 197
21. Drags 201
22. Poke 205

Part IV: HOUSEHOLD CRAFTS AND FURNISHINGS

23. Broom Tying 211
24. Bark Boxes—Louise Langsner 217
25. White Oak Basketry—Louise Langsner .. 225
26. Spoons 241
27. Dough Troughs 253
28. A Farmhouse Table 263
29. A Dining Bench 269
30. Pine Whisks 273

Appendix I. MORTISE AND TENON JOINERY .. 281

Appendix II. WOOD FINISHES 290

Appendix III. USES OF USUALLY USELESS WOODS 293

Appendix IV. TOOL SUPPLIERS 295

Annotated Bibliography 297

Index 301

White oak basket.

FOREWORD

MY FIRST MEETING with Drew and Louise Langsner came shortly after the publication of their book *Handmade*. Overjoyed to see their concern for simplicity and beauty in everyday life, I wrote to them, and we have been in close contact ever since.

It has been a pleasure reading this new production of Drew's on uses of wood, and I hope it will be followed by many others.

The Langsner cabin is a place that expresses well the simplicity and meaningfulness of their lives. The radiant warmth of the wood stove sets the tone when you enter it in mid-February. Signs of handwork are everywhere—in the kitchen things, in the clothing, in the baskets, and in the workshop. My pleasure and profession is to seek out people who live in voluntary simplicity—those who believe in bread labor and to whom such things as power lines are questionable blessings. So finding the Langsners in their cove in the Carolina mountains was a special treat.

Drew Langsner is an exceedingly energetic and enthusiastic man. We are fortunate that he chooses to apply his talents to the use of wood in more primary and lovely ways for daily living—for it would be a great loss for society had he chosen to use his abilities to advance the martial arts or one of the other much respected and highly lucrative ways of exploiting ones fellows.

Pouncing is a rather uncommon way to refer to a human being—but Drew Langsner pounces. Whenever a new technique of using wood comes within his range, he pounces on it with all of his eager nature. Then he tumbles it over in his hands and brain, appearing much like a raccoon with a new-found morsel. He explores the techniques and its possibilities fully and then proceeds to apply what he has discovered in his workshop. Fortunately he writes as well so that we can share in the fruits of his experience.

There is a great treasure of knowledge stored in the folk cultures of the world. And folk wisdom is, of course, mixed with folk ignorance—even as today our "civilization" is made up of a mixture of ignorance and wisdom. If we are ever to attain the height and splendor of a society in which *all* people have the opportunity to grow and flower to their fullest, it will be due to our ability to sort the wisdom from the ignorance of all cultures in all times and to blend what we find into better ways of living.

We badly need more people gleaning this wisdom of how to live more beautifully and simply in our daily lives. This knowledge is one of the primary productive wealths of the world—primary in that its possession enriches all and impoverishs none, as opposed to the commonly sought-after tertiary forms of wealth (material goods, position, etc.) that by their very nature "enrich" some while making others poorer.

The Langsners are gleaners of this folk-wisdom treasure and as such are part of a vital body of pioneers seeking to create a society in which it is possible for all to live gently and joyously on this planet.

Wm. S. Coperthwaite
Director
The Yurt Foundation
Bucks Harbor, Maine
May, 1977

Splitting a white oak.

ACKNOWLEDGMENTS

I WISH TO THANK Rudolf Kohler for initiating me into country woodcraft during the summer of 1972 when I studied Swiss cooperage under his patient guidance. I have also learned a great deal from local craftsmen, particularly Peter Gott. During the preparation of this manuscript we had a surprise visit by Swedish woodworker Wille Sundqvist, which resulted in the chapters on spoons and dough troughs. John Chiarito did the mortise and tenon frame for the spring-pole lathe. My wife Louise has contributed two chapters, Bark Boxes and White Oak Basketry. She has been quite tolerant with my obsession for making more shaving horses, hay rakes, and wooden mauls than we could ever use.

The manuscript was reviewed by William Coperthwaite, of the Yurt Foundation, Bucks Harbor, Maine; and J. Baldwin, soft technology editor for *The Whole Earth Catalog* and *The Co-Evolution Quarterly*.

Editor Bill Hylton of Rodale Press had the initiative to take on my proposal and then follow through with all the details that authors are unaware of. Glenn Johns, the publisher, has been tolerant toward my ideas of author participation in the production stages of this book. Most of the photographs are by Bob Griffith and myself. The photographs by Doris Ulmann appearing on pages xvi, 52, 132, and 208 are used with the permission of the Doris Ulmann Foundation and Berea College. Drawings were collaborations between Sally Onopa and me. I'm responsible for the basic design, Barbara Field honed the edges and worked out numerous details.

Spoon carving in Switzerland.

INTRODUCTION

. . . If the boring of water pipes (in solid elm wood) by hand strikes us as a laborious and uneconomic process, our present practice of digging up coal and iron ore, transporting them great distances to blast furnaces and ironworks, and then carrying the finished cast-iron pipes to their final resting place, would have appeared equally absurd to the old carpenters, who could produce pipes from trees growing on the spot. . . . Pipes laid down in London in the New River Scheme of 1613 were found to be perfectly sound when unearthed at Holborn in 1930.

—H. L. Edlin
Woodland Crafts in Britain [1]

WE ARE HOMESTEADERS, living on a patch of cleared farmland surrounded by forest. Wood plays an important part in our life. We begin each day warming the kitchen and cooking on a wood stove. The old cabin itself is all wood, as are our furnishings. The barn and corncrib are also wood, as well as many agricultural implements—sleds, wagons, and such—and the fences that enclose the fields defining the boundaries of pastures, garden, and woodland.

I am also fond of handmade wooden objects, particularly functional implements whose beauty lies in the

1. Herbert L. Edlin, *Woodland Crafts in Britain* (London: David & Charles, 1949), p. 56.

nature of wood, purity of form, and care in construction. I am willing to devote a good many hours to making one wooden bucket. The work is challenging—its own fulfillment and reward. Through the fusion of myself and the wood, an object is born that is useful and beautiful—a joy to make, to see, and to use.

The woods around us are the wellspring of this joy and our partners on the land. Oak, maple, locust, poplar, dogwood, hickory, beech, birch, holly, pine, wild cherry, ash, and many others make their home here. To them I take my needs and my respect. Which tree shall make Louise's spinning wheel, my workbench, our firewood? How shall I fell it to cause the least damage and problems, and then transport it through the forest to our home? How shall the trunk be cleft or hewn? What is the nature of the wood? How to answer these questions is my passion and the subject matter of this book.

I prefer to find the answers through simple technology (with apologies to my chain saw). Such methods use tools rather than machines. This is a "soft technology," one that is "gentle on its surroundings, responds to it, incorporates it, feeds it." [2] To grow food, make an object, or build a shelter with primary materials and basic tools is my idea of good living. Work that is tangible and personal, that develops skills that feed a flow of activities and relates to the many rhythms of nature, enhances my own aliveness.

I am not claiming that country woodcraft or farming with horses (another personal interest) will solve all of the world's problems. However, I do propose that these are aspects of our heritage that deserve to be looked at with more than nostalgia. Rather, intimacy with traditional crafts can reveal patterns of eminent practicality of value in a modern world. In "The Preservation of Old Buildings," Wendell Berry writes:

> The question is whether we are to be tourists or participants in our heritage. I am interested in the question because I believe it to be an eminently practical one: I do not believe that tourists can preserve anything, including themselves, for very long. And one of the tragedies of the modern world is that it has made us tourists of our own destiny. It has taught us to turn to the past for diversion rather than instruction. It has taught us to look into our inheritance for curiosities rather than patterns.[3]

Several good books have been published on woodland crafts; however, they are restricted in the sense that they take an "armchair" approach. I have found that to participate in these crafts is to receive the full benefit of their instruction and so I present this book not as a "collector's guide" but as an introduction to traditional techniques both useful and aesthetically rewarding.

One of the first lessons learned upon hefting an axe

2. Stewart Brand, *The Whole Earth Epilog* (Menlo Park, Calif.: Point, 1974), p. 526.

3. Wendell Berry, "The Preservation of Old Buildings." *The Co-Evolution Quarterly*. Spring, 1975, p. 50.

The season of this book, a good time for woodworking.

is that the woodworker's craft demands a true fusion of mind and body. One will not get by with brawn alone. Many of the skills that the wood extracts require the combination of strength—sometimes maximum strength—and accurate employment of subtle, sophisticated technique. In our culture, force is often equated with clumsiness and a fair margin of error. But concentration, physical effort, and a great deal of practice are necessary to master a skill such as hewing with a broadax.

My pursuit of the mental challenge does not in any way detract from the physical pleasure of woodworking. In fact, my preference for hand tools and hewn or cleft timber comes as a result of enjoyment in this physical interaction of tools and materials. Through feel our relationship is deepened. My hands sense the nature of the wood-grain strength, irregularities, durability, workability. The body must respond to this personality in wood.

This enjoyment is increased by the knowledge that I am providing for many everyday needs—fuel, shelter, furnishings, utensils, and tools—mostly on a primary basis.

Simple hand tools are made without great expenditure of energy and have no need of further fossil fuel supplies to keep running. Efficiency and productivity are in accord with the user's acquired skill, not a manufacturer's financial development scheme. Given proper care, hand tools should serve well for generations of regular use. Using such tools, one finds a modern trend reversed: instead of continually developing more machines to do man's work, one constantly discovers the capacity of doing more yourself.

Another type of "discovery," a private treasure of the woodworker using hand tools, is the beauty found in newly cut wood. First comes the pungency of fresh shavings or sawdust, then revelations of what lies beneath thick bark. I am often entranced by the fleeting moment when wood fibers are first touched by light. As successive layers are pared away with drawknife or plane, the magic repeats, but with infinite variations.

The questions come: Is the wood usable for the intended purpose? How does the grain run? Are there imperfections within? Shall I work with or around this twist or that knot? My hands and the wood itself provide the answers.

Shaping of wood shapes my relationship with the world at large as well. Dealing with tools, skills, and materials in a simple, direct manner contributes practical solutions to the problems of everyday living. Beyond the creation of an object of intrinsic beauty and functional value is the attitude of a craftsman. More than the wood itself, that which drew me to woodworking was a meeting with a seventy-five-year old Swiss cooper who, after fifty years of coopering, shaped a dairy bucket with the same vigor and enthusiasm as might be expected for his first. Quite clearly, this repetitive chore was for Herr Kohler continual creation. His interest and joy was in the wood and his workmanship, as much as in the product that would result.[4]

4. Drew & Louise Langsner, *Handmade* (New York: Harmony Books, 1974), pp. 178-88.

Splitting holly for spoon making.

In a sense, this book is a continuation of that meeting. It is my wish to pass the energy along in response to the interest and enthusiasm shown by visitors to our own crafts and workshop. People are intrigued by the many uses and forms of wood. They want to learn details and have the satisfaction of making something themselves. Children, in particular, are fascinated by the shaving horse (though it's missing rockers, it has four legs, a head, and a jaw that works!) and are anxious for the chance to use a drawknife. Some of the material included in this book would make excellent projects for young people—particularly the bent-wood saw, mallets, brooms, baskets, bark boxes, and pine whisks.

All of these projects derive from homestead life. But the material is not meant exclusively for back-to-the-land folk. The woodworker who also gardens, for example, will find useful such projects as the wheelbarrow and wooden rakes. The dough trough belongs in every kitchen. The tools and skills, of course, may be applied to other special projects, as well.

After the foundation discussions of tools, materials, harvesting, and woodshed, the book divides into three project areas. We start with handmade tools and devices for woodworking. These range from simple mallets to a spring-pole lathe. I have lavished attention on the shaving horse as I feel that using this implement is a key to success with most of the other projects. The next section is devoted to farm and garden implements. The wooden rakes and forks should prove very useful. They also have historic and aesthetic appeal. A plow, a sled, and several harrows have been included for those who

work with draft animals. This is followed by a section devoted to household crafts: basket-making, kitchenware, and some furniture. The book concludes with appendices on mortise and tenon joinery, wood finishes, and unusual materials.

It has been necessary to limit the range of this book, omitting some related projects. Log and timber-frame architecture is too vast a subject to even review in a book such as this. However, splitting techniques explained in the chapter on hayforks and basket-making are identical to the methods for making shingles. Similarly, the rudiments of broadax work are outlined in the instructions for hewing sled runners. With the exception of a bench and table, I have omitted projects dealing with home furnishing.

In making up plans I have generally avoided the conventional approach of listing materials, listing steps, and presenting flat, measured drawings. Rather, I have taken a conversational approach illustrated with multiple sketches, exploded drawings, and photographs.

Many of the projects are shown in several variations. I am not particularly interested in differences such as dimensions or decoration. That is a personal matter for each craftsman to decide. Rather, I have included examples that illustrate a variety of technical approaches solving the same problem. For instance, the chapter on hay rakes illustrates different geometries and joints for securing the rake head to the handle. These solutions can also be grafted to other projects.

All of the projects are intended for use. These are practical implements whose beauty derives from their functionality. The material has been garnered from various sources including travel, mountain traditions, and library research. I have made and used all of the wooden tools, devices, and objects offered.

Finally, a note on using this book. An attempt has been made to present a wholistic approach to woodworking, set in the context of a living situation. As there is no objective organization to this material, different skills and tools are called for throughout the book in no particular order. I suggest looking over the complete book and becoming familiar with the contents before beginning any of the projects.

Be patient. Be careful. And have fun!

Riving boards or shingles with a froe and maul.

Used by permission of the Doris Ulmann Foundation and Berea College.

PART I
THE FOUNDATION OF COUNTRY WOODCRAFT

Basic tools.

CHAPTER I
THE BASIC TOOLS

COUNTRY WOODCRAFT has its origins in the tradition of the peasant woodworker—the farmer who could fill most of his own needs for wood products. Everybody needed wood; for fuel, shelter, furnishings, household utensils, and agricultural implements. A high degree of home-craftsmanship for the peasant's own use, or for barter, was inseparable from a self-supporting agricultural community. This link is intrinsic to a discussion of the tools employed.

The tools themselves were homemade, with the help of a local blacksmith if the farmer did not do his own metal work.[1] Knowledge of tools and techniques were passed from one generation to the next. Due to isolation, rural craftsmen were generally restricted to the local level of technology and customary design. These limitations also reflected the economic level of the community. Tools such as saws and planes were in use by artisans in the employment of the aristocracy long before becoming commonly available in the outlying countryside. There they did not find much use until the devel-

1. Rural Industries Bureau, *The Blacksmith's Shop* (Wimbleton, Eng.: Rural Industries Bureau, 1952).

opment of mass production creating a trade economy and merchant class.

So, prior to the industrial age, a country woodworker applied his skill with a limited selection of tools. These were of three basic types—striking tools (such as hammers), cutting tools (like knives), and scrapers (usually flint or other sharp-edged stones). The variation found within the limits of these basic tools is one of the fascinating aspects of country crafts, and testimony to the inventiveness of indigenous craftsmen throughout the world. Not only were tools specialized for different types of work, but craftsmen in different locations developed preferences for certain styles or modifications to the extent of using totally dissimilar tools for accomplishing very similar tasks. In addition, the individual craftsman often adapted tools to satisfy his own needs, hands, and imagination.

Continued personal, as well as technological, adaptation applied to ancient principles and traditional knowledge has contributed to the myriad types and designs of hand tools used by craftsmen through the ages. The history and scope of these tools is covered quite thoroughly in several works listed in the Annotated Bibliography. The following discussion is limited to the most basic tools: mallets, knives, axes and adzes, cleavers, and finally saws.

Cutting tools. A knife of some description is found among the tools of all who work with wood. For some it may be the only tool used. Prototypal knives, well documented by archeologists, were made from chipped stone (such as flint and obsedian), bone, and shell. In the bronze age, two-piece knives consisting of a blade and handle were developed. This has been the pattern ever since.

Most carving knives have rather generous handles (of a size giving a good, comfortable grip to one's hand) and relatively short, stubby blades. It is this relationship of large handle to small blade that results in leverage, resulting in power and control for the craftsman. Shapes vary according to specialized function and local tradition.

My first experience with the versatility of knives was in the shop of Herr Kohler, the Swiss cooper with whom I studied. Jobs performed with knives included debarking limbs for hoops, carving out the handholds of buckets, beveling the staves, spoon-making, and decorative schnitz (chip) carving. All of the Master's knives were used with a "critically" sharp edge.

While the knife is useful to the cooper, it is indispensable to those craft-workers whose range of tools is more limited. This has led to the development of some highly specialized knives designed to make efficient use of shape and leverage.

Such needs are of special concern to nomadic people, who work without heavy accessories (workbenches, shaving horses, vises). Among these woodworkers one finds a variety of knives that are manipulated with one hand, leaving the other free to hold the material. One example is the crooked knife, common to the Lapps, Eskimos, and Indians of North America, as well as others.

Crooked knives have handles designed for a comfortable, firm grip. A short, curved blade is attached at the lower end. The knife is generally held backward (opposite the manner in which knives are usually gripped), with the blade curving up beneath one's little finger. The grip increases arm leverage, as well as control of the tool. The crooked knife is very effective for hollowing and carving across the grain of wood. Canadian Indians and other northerners depend on the crooked knife for carving canoe ribs, snowshoes, eating utensils, and other woodenware.

A unique development (as far as I know) in tool technology is a crooked knife developed by the Lapps. To increase the power of their tool, these craftsmen use a long-handled knife (called a *ch-chak*) which is linked to a leather thong looped around the woodcarver's neck. The intersection is at the knife hilt. Pushing the handle against the thong creates a fulcrum, increasing the leverage.[2]

Another leverage technique is utilized by the Welsh spoon maker, who calls his crooked knife a *twca cwm*. This knife, used to hollow the spoon quickly, has a short, curved blade and a handle about 18 inches long. The *twca cwm* is held tightly under the spoon carver's arm, against his body, while being manipulated from a point near the blade. With the handle tip acting as a fulcrum, considerable strength is achieved in the stroke of the blade.[3]

2. Information on crooked knives has been garnered from William Coperthwaite (of the Yurt Foundation, Buck's Harbor, ME 04618).

3. J. Geraint Jenkins, *Traditional Country Craftsmen* (London: Routledge and Kegan Paul, 1965), p. 61.

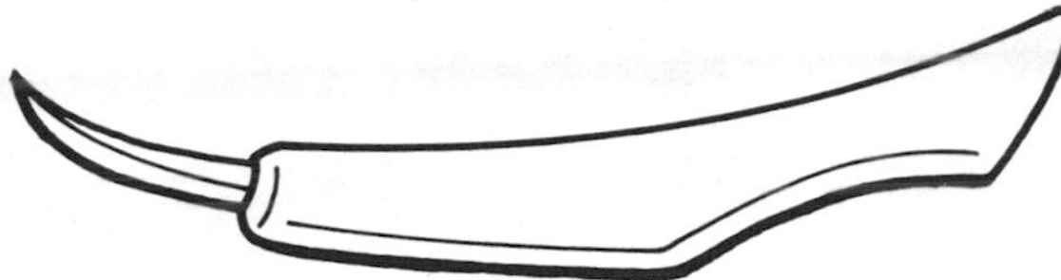

Indian crooked knife, 7½ inches.

Swedish *skedkniv*, 6½ inches.

Swedish sloyd knife, 7½ inches.

Swiss *schnitz messer* or chip-carving knife, 6 inches.

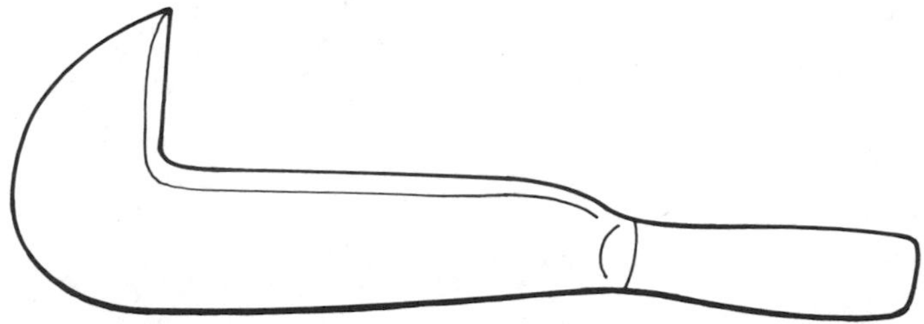

Billhook or spar hook, 15 inches.

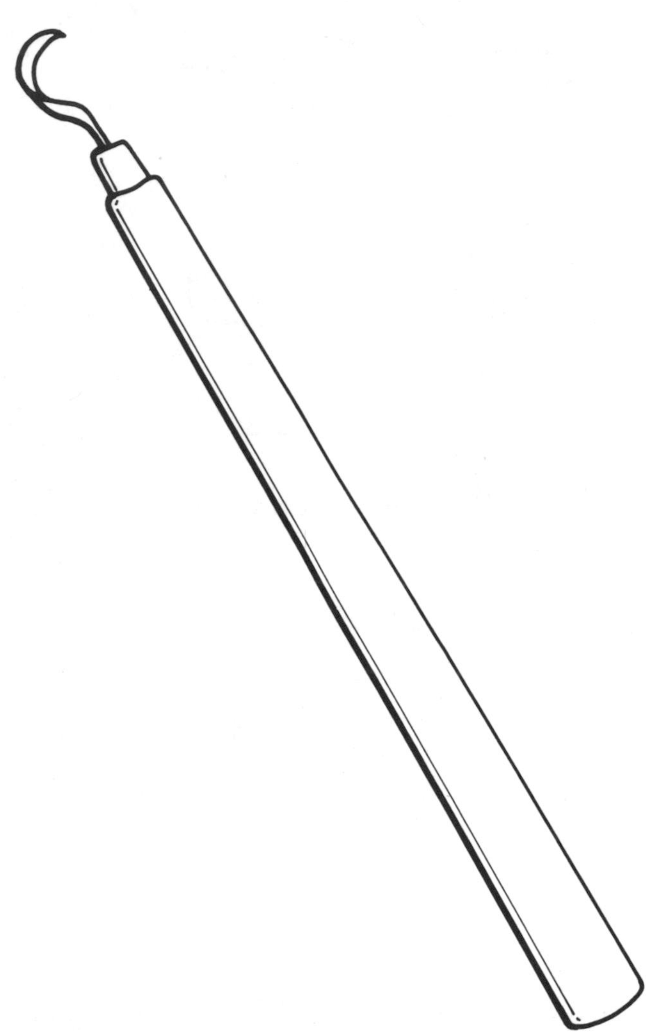

Welsh spoon carver's *twca cwm,* 18 inches.

A third example of applying the principle of leverage to increase the effectiveness of a knife is found in the tools used by clog and *sabot* (Dutch wooden shoe) makers. This is the "block" or "stock" knife: a tool consisting of a long handle and stout, straight blade forged from a single piece of steel. A hook at the end of the blade is inserted through a screw eye set into the craftsman's carving block. Holding his work on the block with one hand, he bears down on the knife handle with action similar to that of using a tabletop paper cutter. The blade is loosely hooked so that it can be worked at most any angle.[4]

The drawknife represents a variation developed by those whose work is stationary (e.g., a large log, wagon, or other heavy object) or held so by some device. The basic drawknife has a straight, flat blade, about 10 inches long, and two handles with which to pull the cutting edge over the wood set perpendicular to the blade. This tool is easily made by a blacksmith and commonly is used by rural craftsmen for such jobs as removing bark, shaping broom handles, chair-making, forming rake parts and similar items, working basket splits and cleft wood, roughing out some objects, and finishing others.

The principle of the drawknife was applied to further uses when modified by a variety of blade shapes. Drawknives with moderate to considerable curves (round shave or inshave) are used for both rounding and hollowing. The cooper, in particular, makes use of any number of these curved drawknives. There are also miniature drawknives for fine work (such as hollowing cream

4. Jenkins, *Country Craftsmen,* pp. 18-21.

skimmers), including a single-handed version in which the blade makes a full loop (scorp).

Swedish woodworkers have their *spantkniv,* a drawknife variation with handles in line with the blade. This is a push or pull tool, useful for bench work where conventional drawknife handles might bump into the workbench or vise. The *spantkniv* is harder to control as there is no mechanical advantage of leverage with the straight handles.

As technology permitted, other cutting tools, all highly specialized knives, evolved to provide a degree of precision and mechanized control in woodworking. These include chisels and gouges, planes, spokeshaves, augers, and saws.

Striking tools. Prehistoric striking tools were of two types: rocks and sticks. Rocks had weight and a flat end to pound with. The length of sticks gave the magical effect of increasing power through leverage. Man also learned that a thin shaft with a bulge, knot, or burl at one end combined some qualities of weight and leverage with a slight whip or spring-like effect. The cudgel developed into mallets and mauls that woodworkers and other craftsmen still use. (Chapter 7: Clubs, Mauls, and Mallets further elaborates on the development of these useful tools.)

The idea of attaching a stone head to a wooden shaft must have occurred to many of our remote ancestors. The big problem was how to do this. A stone could be imbedded in a hole in a stick. Or it might be fastened to a forked stick with wet leather thongs which would shrink and tighten up when dried out. Reversing

Dutch sabot-maker's block knife, 30 inches.

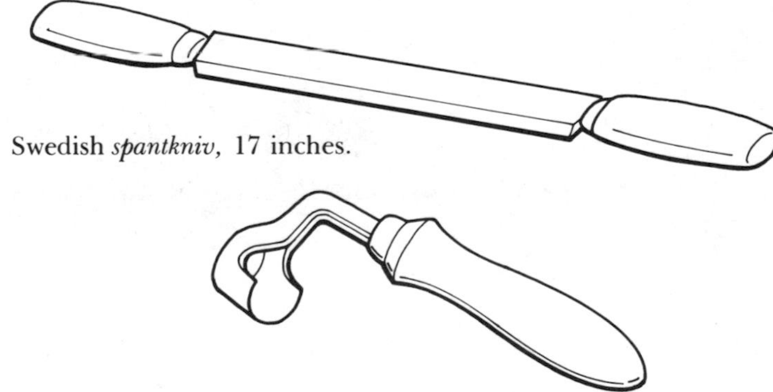

Swedish *spantkniv,* 17 inches.

Scorp, 7 inches long, blade 1¼ inches wide.

Axes (l. to r.): broadax, polled axe, hatchet, double-bit; (bottom left): Japanese shaping hatchet.

the system, boring an eye through the head, was certainly a flash of brilliance. It must have taken great effort to drill a hole in one stone with another. To do this, the "head" had to be softer than the "drill." The resulting tool was a hammer, useful for pounding stakes into the ground and striking wedges for splitting logs. Many early tools also served as weapons.

The idea of combining the cutting edge of a knife with the shaft length of a hammer was also conceived during the Stone Age. Wooden sticks with a sharp flint imbedded at one end have been found at various neolithic sites. Such a tool may have been useful, but it should not be considered a true axe. However, shaping the sides of a stone hammerhead something like a heavy knife blade resulted in a tool that could shape or split wood by combining impact (hammer), with a cutting edge (knife) working on a wedge principle. This is an axe.

As with knives, axes made a great leap forward with the discovery of smelting.[5] Using bronze, and then iron, it became possible to cast or forge an axe head having a sharp cutting edge and an efficient wedge shape with an eye through the center. Axes were made for special purposes, such as felling, splitting, hewing, small shaping work, and so on. The peak of axe specialization came during the feudal ages before saws became prominent tools. In more recent times development of axes has mainly been a function of marketing.

The handmade axe was traditionally made by a

5. Georgious Agricola, *De Re Metallica* (New York: Dover Publications, 1950).

blacksmith using several components. The sides forming the eye and including the poll ("hammer"—if it had one) were of soft iron, to absorb the blows of continuous hard use. The cutting edge was a separate strip of high-carbon steel, tempered to take and keep a sharp edge. The last shop to produce handmade axes in the U.S. used steam-powered trip-hammers to shape the heads, which were manufactured, one at a time, by skilled craftsmen. These were made by the Emerson & Stevens Manufacturing Company of Oakland, Maine.

Modern axes are made by drop-forging. A red-hot alloy blend is set in a mold, and BANG! a form comes down producing an axe head that requires only a little grinding and polishing around the edges. The alloy is formulated to be both tough and edge-holding. Some are quite serviceable, and they are the only choice that the new axe buyer has. I recently bought a brand-name axe that bent into an S-curve along the bit the first time it was used. However, a more common fault of new axes and hatchets is that many are tempered so hard that they are impossible to sharpen with a machinist's mill file, which just slides over the steel without any effect on the cutting edge.

A tool as ancient as, if not actually predating the axe, is the adze. While the axe has a blade in line with the handle, the adze blade crosses the line of the handle at a right angle. The blade is slightly curved, generally to follow the circumference of the swing when in use. Some adzes are curved in the width as well as length, with variations in form found peculiar to many different crafts. Like axes, long-handled adzes are worked two-

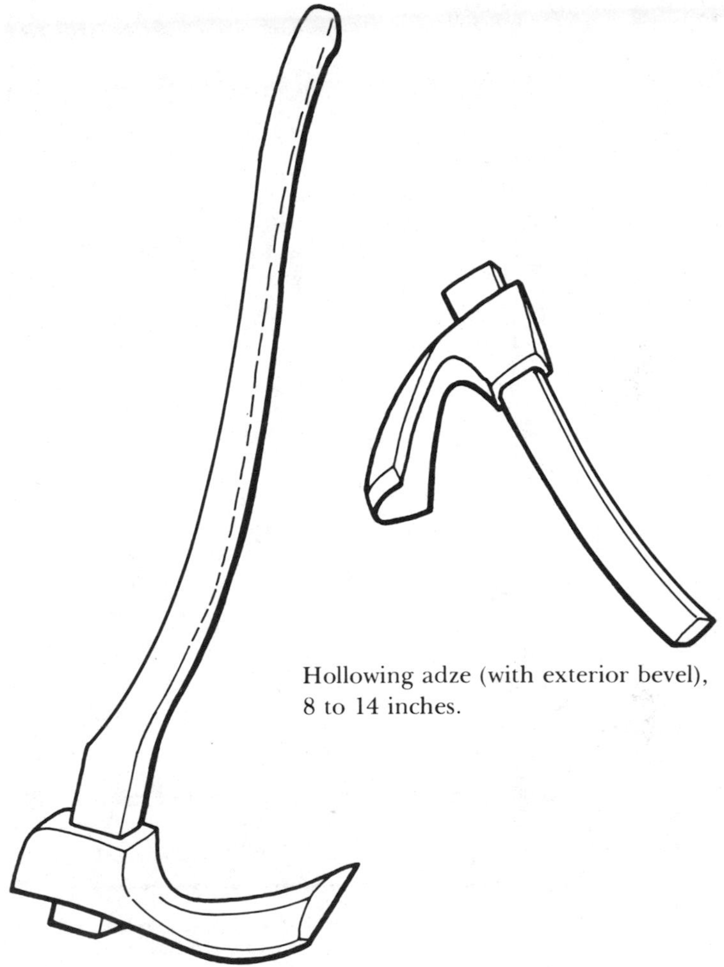

Hollowing adze (with exterior bevel), 8 to 14 inches.

Hewing adze (bevel in), 28 to 34 inches.

Froe, blade 7 to 10 inches, handle 12 to 18 inches.

handed, while short-handled adzes (generally much lighter versions) may be deployed with one hand.

Basically, the adze is a carving tool. A skilled craftsman can adze with a high degree of control to shape wood from a rough block to very nearly completed form. Historically, adzes have been used by wheelwrights, carpenters, coopers, and furniture makers (to shape the seats of Windsor chairs and level off slab tabletops). The curved adze is well suited for hollowing bowls and troughs of all sizes. Some woodworkers prefer an adze over the broadax as a hewing tool, and adzes are still in use by builders of wooden ships. Heavy adzes were used for leveling out railroad ties and floor puncheons (hewn-log flooring).

Cleaving. Axes are fine as hewing and splitting tools. But as with hammers, the power behind an axe is the swing that results in a strike of sudden impact. Such a concentration of energy is effective for chopping, but provides minimal control over the direction a split will take once it has begun. Both accuracy and control are requirements of good cleaving techniques.

Various methods are employed to meet these requirements by controlling the direction of a split through manipulation of the tool or material. For rough work, wedges and a maul or sledgehammer may be used. For smaller poles or splits, a stout knife is the basic cleaver. Once inserted in the wood, the split is opened by twisting the knife handle or tapping on the blade with a club. The leverage that may be applied against the blade is improved with a froe—basically a knife with a handle attached at a right angle to the blade. (The use of froes is further discussed in Chapter 14: Pitchforks and Chapter 25: White Oak Basketry.)

Cleft wood has qualities superior to sawn lumber due to the fact that all the pieces run with the grain and are therefore stronger, as well as more supple (imperative for bentwood or handles subject to impact). More wood may be wasted when employing cleaving techniques, because generally only the best sections of clear, straight-grained wood are used. But what is produced is of the highest quality.

While cleaving is desirable for many purposes, its greatest importance is in the making of baskets, shingles, chair legs, and tool handles.

Saws. The eventual adoption of saws opened vast new opportunities for woodworkers, almost turning traditional technology inside out. Many specialized tools, such as hewing axes, became practically obsolete.

Large crosscut saws replaced axes for felling and bucking logs. Pit saws were used to make boards with a fraction of the waste in hewing. Countless families moved off tamped dirt and onto board floors. Carpentry and furniture-making became leading trades.

The use of modern saws was also linked to the takeover of the industrial cash economy that resulted in the demise of subsistence agriculture and a barter society.

Saws were not often made by a village smith. Saws were bought from peddlers or merchants who required money to carry on their business activities. At the same time, other factory-made products were also introduced, such as iron stoves, plate glass, machine-made textiles,

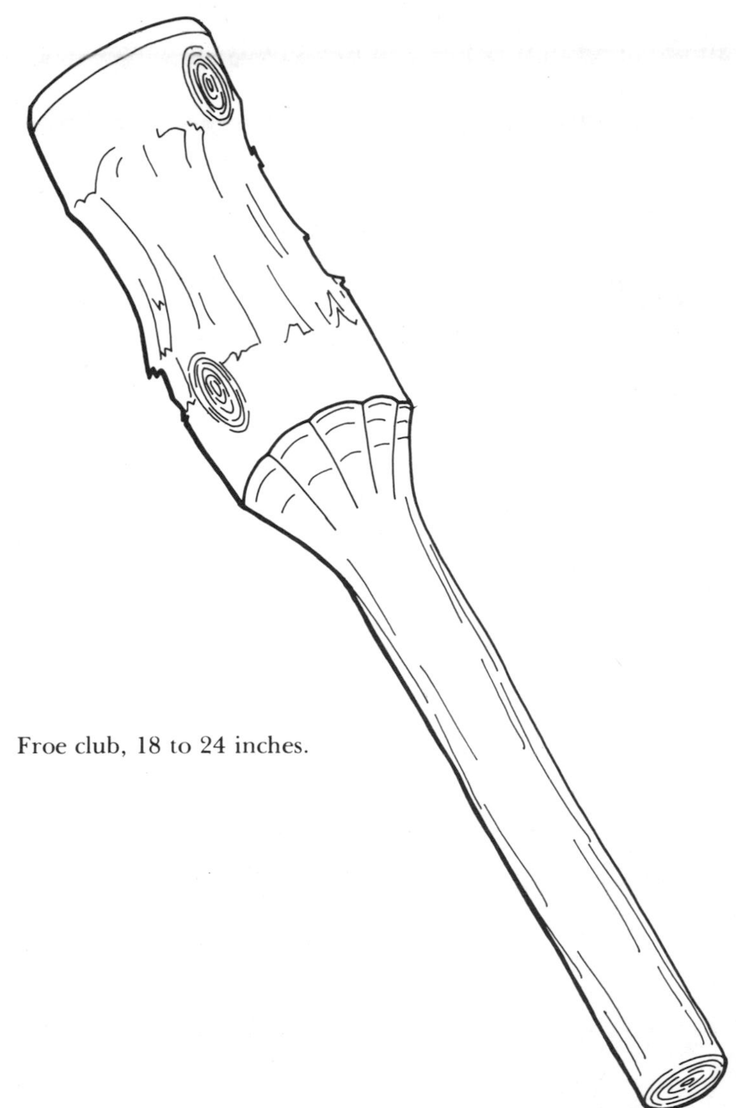

Froe club, 18 to 24 inches.

and so on. Country folk had to find ways to earn money and this limited the time available for general farming and crafts work. In some areas the old ways fell into disfavor and were regarded as inferior. The well-proven subsistence economy fell apart and many peasant farmers/craftsmen found themselves enslaved by a new type of poverty. (Saws are further discussed in Chapter 8: Bow Saws.)

SHARPENING KNIVES

Knives for wood carving should have a very acute, flat bevel. The common practice of whetting the lower 1/8-inch results in too obtuse an angle for woodworking. Small chip-carving knives (1½-inch blades) are beveled from the back of the blade straight to the cutting edge. Swedish sloyd knives (2½- to 3½-inch blades) are beveled in a flat band beginning just below the midpoint where the tang enters the handle.

If grinding is necessary, use a sandstone wheel passing through a water trough. Do not attempt such a fine angle on a high-speed electric wheel. Hold the knife handle in the right hand with the fingers of the left against the blade, controlling the bevel angle. The wheel is treadle operated, or turned by an assistant or by a motor with speed-reduction belts. Face the bevel into the direction of the turning wheel. Do not hollow-grind; finish up on the side of the stone to ensure a flat bevel.

Whetting is started on a clean, fine India stone. The best arrangement is to mount the stone in a wooden box that is then held in a vise. Apply a few drops of thin oil to the stone. (Kerosene and new S.A.E. 30 motor oil mixed equally are excellent.) Hold the bevel flat against the stone and rub towards the edge. To reverse direction rotate the knife in a back flip so that the edge cannot contact the stone at any angle other than flat across the bevel. As in grinding, work two-handed.

When the blade is very sharp, stop and wipe it clean. Then continue whetting on a clean, oiled Arkansas stone. The Washita grade is fine for general work. The soft Arkansas (white) creates an even better edge. Hard Arkansas stones (black) must be used in combination with softer stones; these give the best edge of all. Always rub the bevel flat against the stone.

The perfect edge is finished on a leather strop dressed with a paste of crocus powder (red ferrous oxide) and oil, or plain household porcelain cleanser. Work away from the edge, with the bevel flat against the strop. When reversing direction, rotate the blade backwards, as in whetting (not against the edge). A final polishing can be done across another strop kept free of paste. (Old-timers used their palm or trousers.) This last step eliminates any very fine wire edge along the bevel.

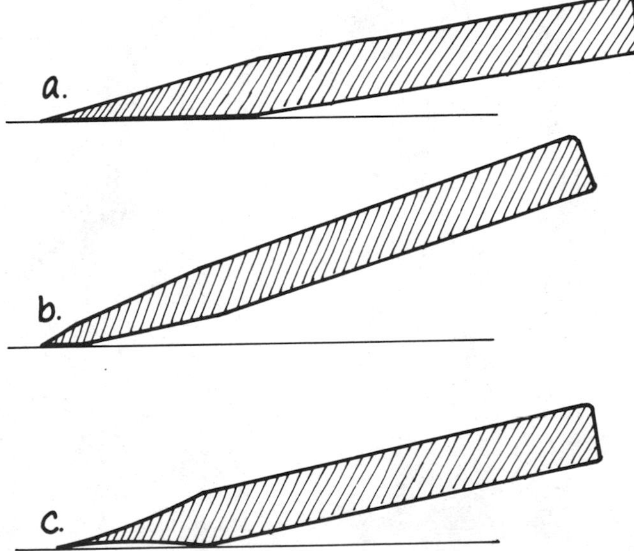

Sharpening a carving knife. Bevel must be flat for good control of the knife; (a) is correct. Obtuse bevel (b) lacks sharpness and results in edge lacking control. Hollow-ground bevel (c) is too thin (weak) and doesn't provide bevel surface for controlling the cut.

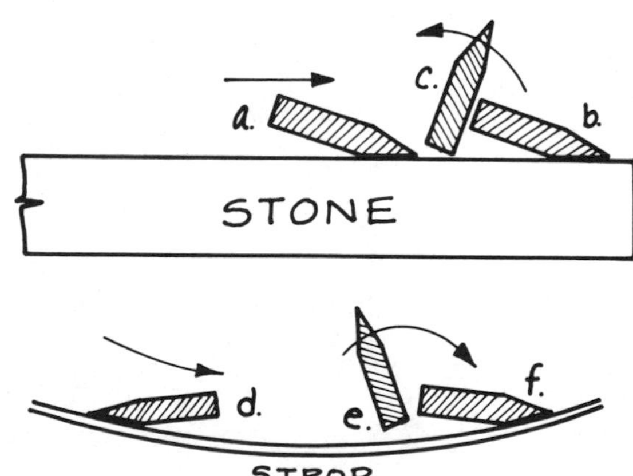

Whet toward the edge (a,b). To reverse direction flip the knife backward (c).
Strop away from edge (d). Somersault the bevel (e,f) to reverse direction.

Skidding a 22-foot poplar with Hat, our old mule.

CHAPTER 2
MATERIALS

THE COUNTRY CRAFTSMAN, especially the woodsman with access to a mixed forest, has available a very diversified palate of materials.

"Wood" is defined as "the hard, fibrous substance which makes up the greater part of the stems and branches of trees or shrubs."

In our context this definition is somewhat expanded. Roots generally are not included as they are difficult to work and don't easily adapt to profitable production techniques. However, the traditional craftsman found special uses for these tough, twisted subterranean forms. The natural curvatures of roots are used for hooks, handles, and other special uses. Roots are also tough and can be used for maul heads (hickory and dogwood) or bearings for turning machinery (pine).

The Swiss Alpine butter-churn stand is traditionally made of cured pine roots.[1] Spruce roots, cut with the lower trunk, are used in shipbuilding.[2] Finer spruce roots can be pounded and split into lacing thongs or basketry material.

---

1. Langsner, *Handmade,* p. 168.
2. Edlin, *Woodland Crafts,* p. 129.

Bark, generally a waste material of industrial technology, has many uses for the woodland crafts worker. Birch bark has extremely fine lasting qualities when wet. It can be easily peeled in early summer, then used for the hull of a canoe or underlayer of a sod roof. Birch bark baskets are made throughout Scandinavia and northern Europe. Tulip poplar bark can be scored and folded into containers such as berry-picking boxes. Basswood bark was used for shingles in Russia. The inner bark of hickory (called "bast") can be cut into strips to make a very tough, durable lacing material. Traditionally, tanners used bark from oak, birch, and alder as their source for tanin.

Even twigs can be useful. Fine fences can be woven from many pliable varieties; willow and hazel are considered best. Young willow growth is the standard basketry material in many areas. Young pine limbs may be shaved down and used for bucket hoops. Birch twigs and many kinds of brush make fine broom sweeps.

"Trees" are generally considered to be single-stemmed woody plants that attain a height of at least twenty feet. Shrubs, which are often multistemmed and which generally grow less than twenty feet high, are likely a nuisance to commercial woodsmen. For special purposes, certain shrubs contain excellent-quality wood. Like roots, the irregular sections can be used to advantage in specific situations. For instance, the Finns consider lilac to be the best material for rake tines. Rhododendron makes fine spoon wood, shelf brackets, and clothes hooks. Peasants of many cultures use dry brush and shrubs to fire their traditional bake

ovens. Holly, generally planted as an ornamental, will grow into a fair-sized tree with excellent-quality hardwood.

Trees are divided into two classes. Conifers, or everbearing needle-leafed trees, are known as softwoods. Deciduous trees, which are broad-leafed, are called hardwoods. However, there are some hard "softwoods" such as yellow pine and yew (which is extremely hard). And there are soft "hardwoods" like willow and bass. Most hardwoods shed their leaves each year. But not all. Exceptions include the citrus family, some oaks, rhododendron, and my favorite, the holly, which even puts out winter berries.

Such factors as toughness, durability, and workability are not always related to weight or hardness. Walnut is heavy but easy to work, even when seasoned for many years. With age, Douglas fir becomes very hard. Redwood is light, but takes weather and dampness very well. White oak and ash are hard and heavy, but both bend easily. Handles can be shaped from seasoned ash, but hickory handles are best worked green.

The cross section of a tree trunk generally reveals two types of wood. Just beneath the bark is a ring of sapwood, which is the lighter, more porous, and younger wood. This is living tissue, actively participating in the activities of the tree as an organism. The heartwood, or darker, inner section, is older wood, no longer physiologically alive. Heartwood forms the skeletal support as the tree grows.

Within a species, in fact within one tree, there is

a great deal of variety in wood quality. A few years back I made over two hundred white oak hayforks. Each fork had its own story. Some seemed to "make themselves." Others had imperfect sections that required special attention. Occasionally, a fork that worked very well suddenly broke when set into the bending jig. I've had many adventures within one tree, making replicas of the same object.

Along the butt (the lowermost log cut just above the stump) the sapwood might be punky or "doughty" in appearance. Such wood is weak and undependable. Heartwood tends to be sound, but towards the center it is often twisted and gnarled, unsuitable for many purposes. Above the butt one may often cut another log or so. Such wood is seldom punky, but it is more likely to contain knots.

Choice of felling time traditionally "determined" the workability and lasting qualities of the wood product. Time of year and phases of the moon were often considered factors for felling timber by peasant woodsmen. Contradictions of opinion on this subject collect as "data" accumulates. According to Jenkins, the British wattle-hurdle maker cut hazel only during winter. Alder for clogs was always cut in spring or summer.[3] Viires reports that the natives of the Estonian mainland cut coniferous trees with the new moon, and deciduous trees during the old moon. However, the nearby islanders believed just the opposite.[4] Investigators from the Foxfire Project asked informants in the southern Appalachians about the correct time to cut white oak for making basket splits. Some said early spring, but others preferred midwinter, or even summertime.[5] The Cherokee Indians, who are among the best white oak basket makers, cut their trees any time of year.

It is hard to be objective in such matters as every tree is different, and one seldom cuts a large number of trees of the same age from the same location and for the same purpose. We have cut white oak saplings throughout the seasons and have made no practical observations that could be linked to the time of year.

In answer to my inquiry on this matter, Karl E. Wolter, a plant physiologist at the USDA Forest Products Laboratory, writes:

"The movement of sap (moisture) in trees is a complicated phenomenon, and not all aspects are completely understood. I would strongly recommend that you consult *Tree Structure and Function* by M. H. Zimmerman and C. L. Brown (Springer Verlag, 1971) for specific details. More than half the book is devoted to this subject. Briefly, there is always water in living trees; however, its state (frozen vs. liquid), movement, pressure, amount, and constituents (e.g., sugars) vary considerably during the different seasons and ambient conditions.

"Exuded sap, especially in species such as *Betula* and *Vitus* are most likely due to high root pressure in spring. Maple sap flow, however, appears to be more

3. Jenkins, *Traditional Craftsmen,* pp. 18-21.
4. A. Viires, *Woodworking in Estonia* (Washington, DC: The Smithsonian Institution, 1969), pp. 6-9.
5. Elliot Wigginton, ed., *The Foxfire Book* (New York: Anchor Books, 1972), pp. 115-18.

complicated. As a *general* rule, there will be more pressure, hence surface moisture, in spring.

"Oleoresins from *Pinus* species are the result of wounding living cells in the xylem (wood) which respond by producing resins which are then collected.

"Bark peeling is feasible when the cambial cells, producing wood in spring and early summer, are dividing very rapidly, producing many thin-walled cells between the xylem (wood) and phloem (bark). These thin-walled cells are easily broken, and the bark separates from the wood. Later in the year, the growth slows down, and these cells become mature, adding cellulose and lignin to their wall surfaces, and can no longer be easily cleaved."

There are some seasonal factors that one should pay attention to. Bark (from tulip poplar, birch, and hickory) must be peeled while it is pliable and easily detached from the cambium layer. Late spring and early summer is the best time for this work. Oak cut in summer is likely to be attacked by ambrosia beetles if not removed from the forest or worked right away. These minute critters drill pin holes in the sapwood, leaving tiny piles of sawdust above. A fungus grows in the fresh holes, this being what the ambrosia beetle feasts on. Wood riddled with this fungus becomes brittle and easily breaks under stress. Other fungi seasonally discolor or weaken felled timber.

The location of growth has a definite relationship to a tree's qualities as a craftsman's material. Climate and soil conditions affect any plant. Trees found in the open, relatively isolated from one another, tend to spread out and develop massive branches. The same species, growing in a crowded forest where there is severe competition for sunlight, grows tall and straight, with its few branches located mainly at the crown. In practice, this means that most sawlogs and timber for cleaving comes from forest trees. However, trees grown in the open are preferred for a few specialized uses. For instance, the massive bent trunks and branches of isolated oaks can be used for boat building. In old England, curved timbers formed the basis for curved framework and half-timbered building construction.

There are good reasons why many handmade wooden objects outlast factory or machine-made counterparts. The craftsman working with hand tools is in intimate relationship with his materials at all times. A careful machine operator closely watches his work, but the handcraftsman constantly *feels* his progress. The slower speed allows for more attention to detail. A knot, check, or imperfection in the wood is immediately noticed. As every piece of wood differs from another it is possible to make continual, often very subtle adjustments, making a handle a little thicker or reversing the direction of planing to match a curly grain.

There is also a difference in basic technique between hand and machine work. Machine production is not the automation of hand-tool methods, although it is sometimes imitative of hand-tool results in final appearance.

The traditional woodworker almost always works with or across the grain of his material, not against it. Hand tools do not work very well going against wood grain—they tend to dig in and go out of control. Handmade wooden objects (such as tool handles) are shaped following the actual grain of the material and are therefore stronger than machine-made counterparts. High-speed machines work irrespective of the way wood grain runs. Machines shape whatever is put to them, without regard to the integrity of the material.

Diagram (a) indicates boards sawn at a conventional sawmill. The center sections are sawn across the grain and called "cross-grain." They make strong, stable lumber. (Except for the piece with the central pith running down the middle.) But note that many of the boards are sawn almost parallel to the grain; these are

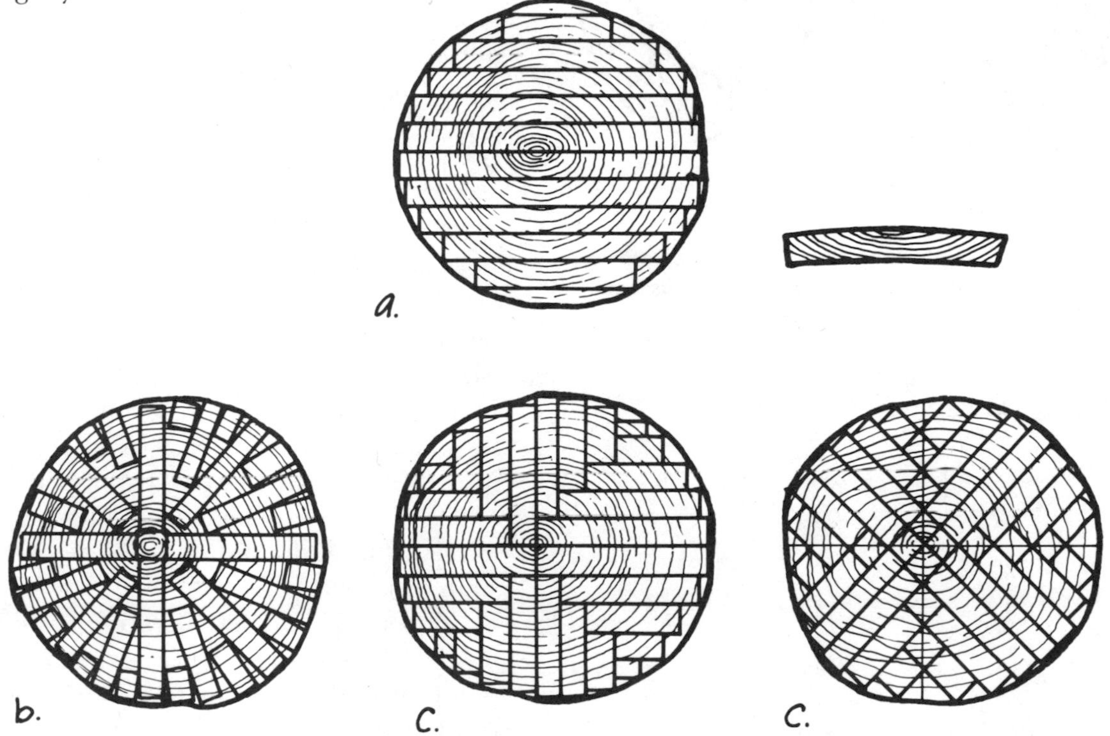

Diagram (a) shows plain-sawn boards as made by most sawmills. Slash-grain boards tend to warp. Quartersawn (b) produces highest grade but is most time-consuming and wasteful. Commercial quartersawn (c,c) are compromise methods with minimal waste.

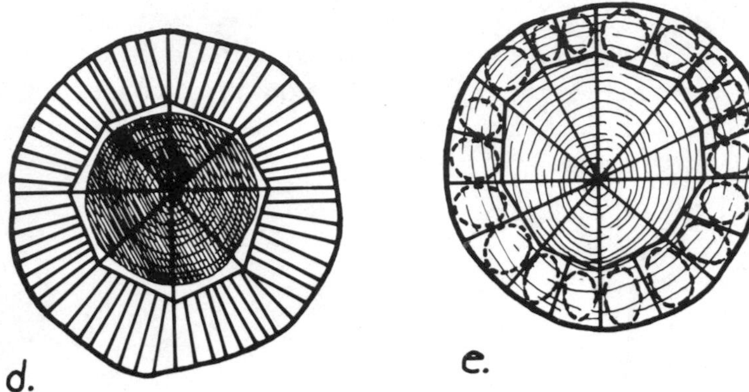

Diagram (d) indicates shingles split from pine. Shaded center is heartwood. In (e) bolts are rived from hickory for various handles.

called "slash-sawn." Such boards warp easily, and are weaker and more difficult to work.

In the old days, when carpenters knew more about wood, were fussier and took their time to do good work, the mills sometimes sold "quartersawn" lumber. This was a time-consuming way to saw wood, but superior to making plain slabs. Diagrams (b) and (c, c) show methods of quartersawing a log. Note that these methods allow for only a few wide boards. But there was more giant timber to harvest back then.

In splitting out wood for shingles, wheel spokes, or barrel staves, all of the wood used must have perfectly straight grain. More wood is "wasted" in cleaving, but everything used is superior quality. Diagram (d) shows how shingles are split out of a typical log. The heartwood in the shingle log has been entirely discarded (actually, set aside for firewood). On the log representing tool handles (e), the outer part was used, but the inner core was too twisted, knotty, and uneven for working. Some hardwoods, such as hickory, have heartwood unusable for axe or peavey handles, this portion having a tendency to warp badly. Almost an entire section of ash can be used. With oak, the heartwood is the desirable material.

There is a method of taking slab-sided lumber and sawing out material that runs with the grain. This technique was developed by boat builders, who steam and bend ribs and other pieces of framework. Clear logs (usually butt sections of white oak) are selected at a mill and specified for sawing at the particular thickness needed. Plain slabs are sawn. The edges are not squared as in conventional lumber. The craftsman saws out strips following the growth pattern of the tree. The inner heartwood is discarded. This method is most successful with cross-grained lumber, but it may be adapted (with clear, straight pieces) to slash-sawn wood also.

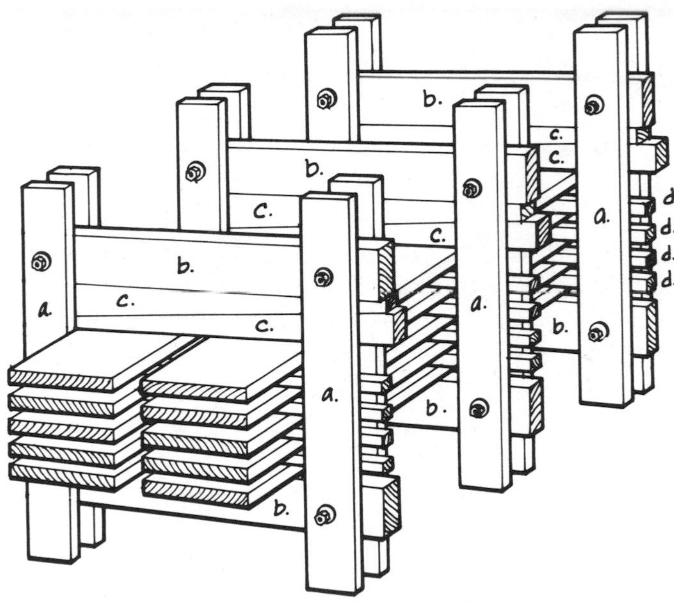

Jig for air-seasoning small quantities of green lumber. Space between frames should be 30 inches or less. (a) 1 x 4 uprights; (b) 2 x 4 crosspieces; (c) pairs of narrow wedges ripped from 2 x 4s; (d) 1 x 2 stickers.

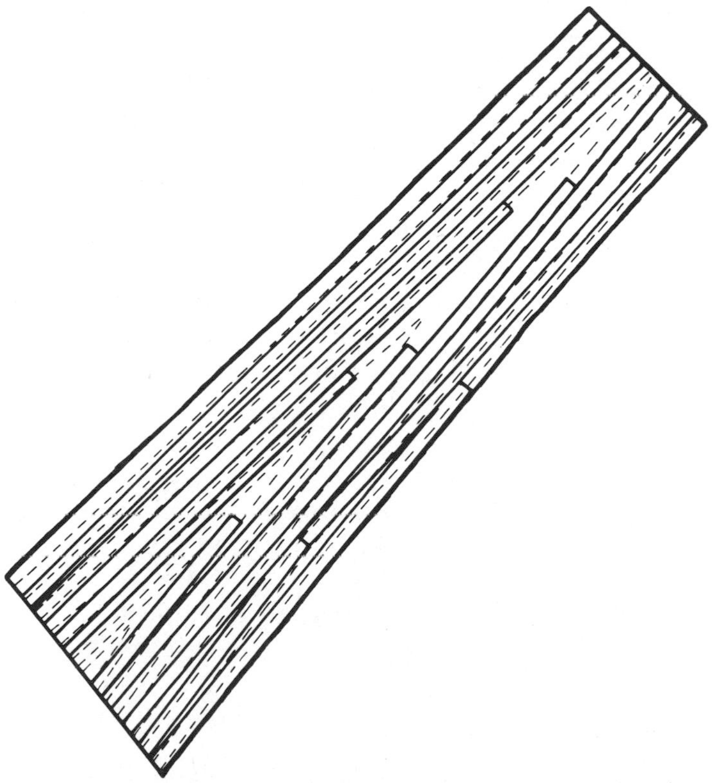

Straight-grain laths may be ripped from plain-sawn boards with untrimmed sides. Such lumber is excellent for steam bending or making long handles. (Dotted lines indicate growth pattern.)

WOOD WEST OF THE MISSISSIPPI

Some of the projects in this book call for hardwoods that are rare or unavailable in the western states. Finding suitable wood may be a problem compared to the situation here in southern Appalachia. However, by searching one should be able to locate suitable materials in most any part of the country. This has, after all, always been an attribute of the "indigenous craftsman."

The western craftsman does have an outstanding selection when it comes to conifers, especially redwood, spruce, pine, and cedar. This is of great advantage in the building crafts—log hewing, shingle making, rail splitting, and so on.

In some instances it is possible to switch from hardwoods to softwoods. Bucket staves can be made from a variety of woods ranging from oak and ash to pine and cedar. In the Southern Highlands fence posts are usually made from black locust, one of the hardest, most durable native woods. Westerners can use cedar and redwood, very soft woods that are equally suitable.

There are western hardwoods, but one may have to search them out. Some species to look for include:

Big-leaf maple.

Box elder (*Acer negundo*); also called ash-leaved maple and three-leaved maple. Native of spotted areas through the Pacific coast, Southwest, and Rockies.

California laurel; also called myrtle. A good carving and cabinetry wood.

Golden chinquapin; also called golden leaf chestnut. Used in furniture making.

Holly. A very dense carving wood.

Mesquite. Said to be suitable for mauls.

Mulberry. Suitable for rake teeth, wheel cogs, and the like.

Oak. Most California oaks are good mainly as fuel wood but tan oak (a California coastal tree) has been used for furniture making and canyon live oak (sometimes called "maul wood") was formerly used for making wagons and agricultural implements.

Oregon white oak.

Pacific dogwood.

Pacific madrone.

Red alder. The leading hardwood of the Pacific Northwest and scattered into southern California.

Pacific yew and box (*Boxus*) are conifers having close-grained hardwood.

Another good source of wood is orchard trees cut down by developers and other builders. These trees include: apple and pear—both good, fairly heavy carving woods suitable for fine tool making; cherry—a good turning wood; olive and walnut.

It is also possible to establish a coppice (a woodland yielding a continuous harvest of poles and other light materials) quite quickly. The most common fast-growing species (discounting bamboo) is willow. According to Edlin,[6] stems may be taken from a parent tree in winter. These are cut into 12-inch lengths, then planted 10 inches deep, 18 inches apart in good, rich soil, preferably high in nonstagnant water (such as along a stream or ditch). Willow thrives in such conditions and the roots help bond the bank together. There will be some shoots available for basketry the first year, and a full crop the third.

Another species that may be easily established is hazel.[7] Fresh nuts are kept over winter in damp sand. Come spring they are planted in nursery flats. The next year seedlings are transplanted to the new woodland. These are cultivated to minimize competition from weeds. Hazel eight to ten years old may be harvested, with second growth repeating continuously. Oaks may be planted, with good spacing from one another, in the hazel coppice for future harvest.

---

6. Edlin, *Woodland Crafts*, pp. 100-105.
7. Edlin, *Woodland Crafts*, pp. 63-75.

Felling tools.

CHAPTER 3
FELLING

IT IS OBVIOUS that a woodworker needs wood; often special kinds and of a particular quality, too. In some cases limbs can be used (such as pine branches for bucket hooping or crooked dogwood for spoon carving). Fallen trees should be salvaged for timber or firewood before rot sets in. But as one sets out to accomplish specific projects, developing techniques and accumulating knowledge regarding tree harvesting takes on importance.

Not too long ago I was enthusiastic about mastering the traditional skills of the felling axe. Harvesting trees by axe all but died when the rolled steel, two-man crosscut saw was popularized. But cuss that I am, I wanted to experience woodworking from its elemental stage. I was fortunate to acquire a never-used, handmade, 4½-pound double-bit axe. I sharpened the axe and hiked into the forest to fell a tree. The sacrificial victim was a hemlock, about 12 inches in diameter at felling height.

I studied the tree, decided where *I* wanted it to fall and set to work chopping away. Clean chips and the aroma of freshly cut wood spurred me on. After hack-ing out a notch about one-third of the tree's diameter, I stopped to review progress.

Once rested, I set to work on the opposite side of the trunk, making my felling notch. The 4½-pound head seemed to gain weight. I had read the old-timers preferred 6-pound axes. I'd like to see them fellers.

Chipping away, I realized that most of the wood to be removed is in the middle third of the trunk. Beginning those notches was easy compared to the final effort. But never mind. The tree wasn't big, and it soon began to creak and groan. A few more whacks and I would see it on the ground. But the tree started to sway in the wrong direction. With the tree tipped at perhaps a 5-degree angle, there was nothing left but to finish the job.

TIMBER!

My tree was down, but at a right angle to where I had planned the descent. And to make matters worse, the trunk now hung over a gully; a very difficult position to work from in the next stage of bucking out logs.

The work showed my trouble. The lower edge of a felling notch must be level; a tilted base twists the fall towards the lower end. Both notches had slanted bases, in line with my diagonal swing.

Examining the situation I made some other observations. Besides being hard work, felling with an axe means wasting the bottom and thickest section of the tree. It is almost impossible to swing an axe horizontally into a notch close to the ground. One generally begins at least 30 inches above ground (or snow) level, but it is possible to kneel. Work is accomplished by chipping out a good fat wedge-shaped section of wood, which is also wasted. Finally, the log itself must later be sawed straight across, as the felling results in a pencil point-shaped butt. This was handy in the old days, when logs were skidded by horses or mules. The "nosed" logs had less tendency to dig into the ground on their way out of the woods.

All told, I realized that felling with an axe is a special craft in its own right. But besides being hard work, it wastes a great deal of valuable wood and leaves a large unsightly stump. Still, it's a great fantasy—building a log cabin with only an axe and one good horse.

Now for saws. Two-man crosscut saws are manufactured in lengths from 5 to 7 feet. (Back when the virgin forests were harvested, crosscut saws came in lengths exceeding 12 feet.) Basically, there are two different styles, with seemingly endless variations in teeth details. There are usually two to four cutter teeth, followed by four raker teeth to clear the kerf. In general, the pointier-tooth saws are meant for felling softwoods. The teeth of saws meant for hardwoods have less rake. The old-timers who used these saws ten hours a day knew what they needed, but I haven't discerned any practical difference in the teeth patterns. Mainly, keep them sharp.

The most common crosscut saw has a straight or slightly curved back, and is about 6 inches wide at the blade center, curving gradually to about 3 inches at each end. This is a rugged saw, easy to guide in a straight cut. The other style is in the shape of an arched ribbon, about 3 inches wide from end to end. The advantage of this type is that there is less friction and weight to deal with when sawing. And it's less likely to get pinched.

The saw must be in good condition; otherwise, its use is sheer torture. Many an old saw can be refurbished. This means filing the teeth, and possibly setting them. The Nicholson File Company still manufactures crosscut saw files.[1] A good way to remove rust is to first apply thin oil (such as a 1:1 mixture of SAE 30 and kerosene) across the blade, then work away with 80-grit garnet or aluminum oxide paper. Kinks in the blade must be straightened out before attempting use.

To use a two-man saw effectively, the workers must be coordinated with each other. Each sawyer pulls, then glides back. If one pushes, the blade buckles, leading to friction within the kerf.

The biggest difficulty in using a crosscut occurs if the trunk begins to sink halfway through a cut pinching the saw in place. The best way to deal with this situation is to avoid it. In felling a tree, a properly cut initial notch will often relieve pressure from the final cut. One can sometimes support a fallen log in such a way that sawed-off sections drop away from the blade, thereby automatically opening the kerf. It is worth going to some effort to prop up a trunk before taking the chance of a pinched blade. A peavey should be kept on hand so that the log may be easily rotated.

When a blade might pinch, it becomes necessary

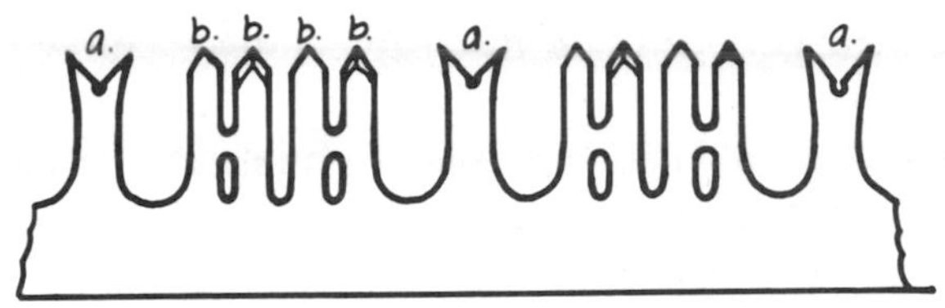

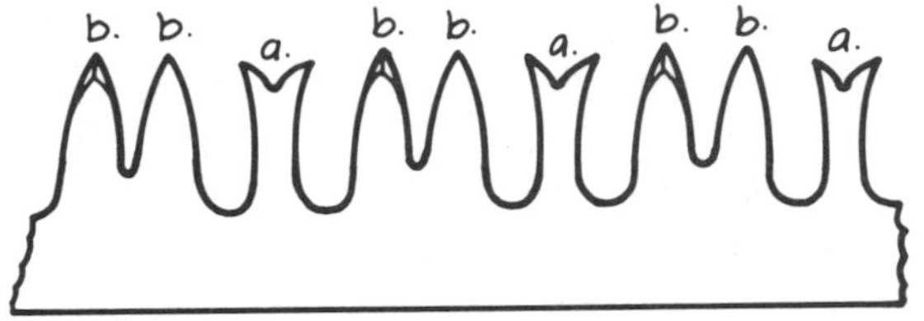

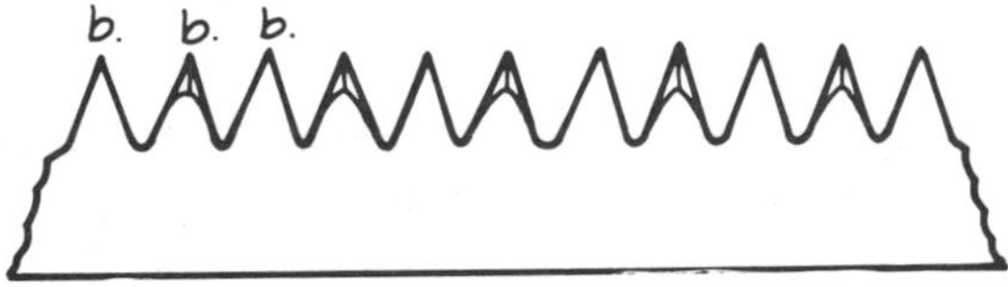

Crosscut saw patterns: (top to bottom) lance tooth, champion tooth, peg tooth. (a) indicates raker teeth; (b) indicates cutter teeth.

1. J. K. Coggin, *A Manual on Sharpening Hand Woodworking Tools* (Danville, Ill.: The Interstate Printers & Publishers, n.d.), pp. 31-34.

to open the kerf with a thin wedge. These can be made on the spot by chopping a hardwood limb or sapling along the grain. Drive into place with an axe or hatchet head. A flat iron "timber wedge" used to be sold specially for this purpose. (This iron wedge is not to be used with chain saws!)

A problem with two-man saws results from the approximate six-foot length of the saw. Add a minimum of 2 feet of space for each sawyer and you need at least 10 clear feet to work in. This is sometimes impossible on slopes or awkward locations jammed with tree limbs, boulders, shrubbery, or debris.

A solution is to have a second saw, a one-man crosscut. These are generally 3 or 4 feet long. The blade is heavy enough to work with push and pull strokes. Such a saw cuts almost as quickly as a two-man crosscut, but with more effort from the single worker. The obvious advantages are that it can be used in tight locations and it needs only one operator. Some are sold with an extra handle that can be attached just above the standard grip for two-handed sawing. The handle may also be fastened at the blade toe for use by an additional worker.

Other woodland saws include bow saws and bucksaws. I often carry one of these smaller saws in the woods, especially if we're after saplings or other small stuff. They're light and easy to carry, and for some work, better than a hatchet or light axe. These saws are sold with wicked, razor-sharp teeth that can quickly leave a row of cuts across the hand of an unwary user. To avoid this problem, start sawing with your left

thumb placed across the back of the blade. This will stop the saw from jumping at the beginning of the cut.

Before going into details on felling technique, I have another short story to tell. When we first started homesteading, Louise and I were avid chain-saw haters. We had a fine old Disston alligator-tooth crosscut saw and were really quite happy with it. It was work to use, but generally not too difficult. However, there were limitations to what we could handle, and we were putting in a lot of time getting together our winter firewood supply.

One day a neighbor volunteered to help us out. He had a chain saw and a tractor that could pull a wagon into the woods. In about three hours we had filled the trailer with stove-sized firewood.

The job was not only fast but efficient. We were salvaging a commercial logger's leftover tops and limbings —working in a jungle of crisscrossed limbs and fallen cull trees. We could barely move about, let alone find space for our 6-foot crosscut.

A chain saw is about 30 inches long, and that is all the space required to use it. It can be used in the most awkward places and positions. One can cut very close to the ground, thereby saving many stumps of good firewood. (Be sure to watch out for possibilities of fence wire in the wood, and clean away dirty bark on the surface where you're working; both will damage any type of saw quickly.) It is also possible to avoid pinching the blade when sawing horizontal timbers resting between two supporting points: first saw from the top. Before the wood starts to cave in, remove the bar of the saw from the kerf. Finish by sawing from the bottom going upward. (You can saw with either side of the bar, holding the saw in any position.) As the cut is completed, the wood will part on either side of the chain. At this moment quickly withdraw the saw.

Considering our need of timber, for firewood and materials for our hayfork "business" and other woodworking projects, the decision to buy a chain saw suddenly became quite easy. We also felt that there are many woodworking skills and homesteading jobs to master that are more interesting than sawing firewood. So, although this book is about traditional woodworking, I must state that we are very happy with our chain saw.

A chain saw with a 14-inch bar can theoretically fell a 28-inch-diameter tree. In practice, 18 to 22 inches is about the limit. At that point, the small engine is working pretty hard and maneuvering the saw around becomes quite awkward. With a small saw it's harder to buck than to fell. However, chances are that the amateur logger will seldom fell trees larger than 20 inches. The smaller saws are less expensive to buy and are easy to haul around. Many beginners complain that the smaller chain saws lack power. For heavy work this is certainly true. But the real problem is often dull chippers. With a sharp chain, my small (top line) saw will easily handle any oak or hickory that's not too big. Learn to sharpen the chain exactly as the manufacturer suggests. Heavy work requires sharpening at least once a day.

Felling very small stuff like saplings is no particular trick. A small axe or bow saw are effective tools to use. First cut a notch on the side where you want the tree to fall. The lower kerf must be horizontal. Make this about one-third the diameter of the tree. Then work from the opposite side, slightly above the initial cut. With saplings there isn't much to cause concern, but be careful not to pinch the saw or chip an axe while working close to the ground. If the tree starts to fall in the wrong direction, simply pull or push it over. With such light work the main reason for making two cuts is to avoid ripping the wood when the the tree falls.

Larger trees, 6 or 8 inches up to several feet in diameter, demand care and skill for safe, accurate felling. In this work one is dealing with tremendous forces of weight, mass, and leverage. A white oak averaging 1 foot in diameter for 40 feet weighs well over a ton, discounting the top and heavy limbs, which may weigh half as much. It is not hard to imagine the impact of such a tree crashing to the forest floor, or the problem one faces if this trunk pinches your saw. Or if for one reason or another, the tree becomes lodged—that is, cut through but unwilling to come down.

Lodging can occur several ways. Occasionally the cuts are made, but the tree just balances on its stump, refusing to fall. Usually by looking up, one sees some upper limbs gently supported by a neighboring tree. Sometimes a wedge driven into the felling cut will tip the tree over. You can also try prying with a crowbar or peavey or bumping the butt with a heavy sledge. Another tactic is to wrap a chain or cable around the butt, then give a good pull with a tractor, truck, or team of horses. It's important to be careful as one doesn't have much control in this situation. Going away to wait for a good wind is perhaps more prudent. (I've done this.)

The other type of lodging is more dangerous to deal with. The tree starts to fall, but gets caught by the trunk or limb of another tree and there it stops at a precarious overhead angle. To get tree *A* on the ground one now has to cut tree *B*. Because of the force exerted on *B*, there's no question of which direction *B* will fall. But, to cut *B*, one has to work underneath *A*. To make matters worse, *B* is under great stress and may rip or "pop" unexpectedly. It is best to cut *B* with an axe or one-man crosscut as the noise from a chain saw might overpower the tell-tale popping sounds of *B* starting to break and fall. Work only on the tension side of the trunk, and in small increments. Step aside often to evaluate the situation. Always remember that *A* may start to fall before *B* is fully cut through.

I have jumped ahead in our tree harvesting to warn that this is serious work. Now we'll backtrack and fell a fair-sized tree. Instructions are for using a crosscut saw or a chain saw. Felling with an axe is quite different, and in my opinion generally unwarranted.

The first step after deciding to fell a particular tree is to make a survey of the situation. Examine the tree to decide in what direction it naturally leans. This is determined by the angle of the trunk and location of any particularly heavy limbs that have strong leverage on the mass. If the trunk looks straight, you can often detect some lean by comparing it to the plumb line formed by an axe held at the handle end by thumb and first finger.

Examine the surrounding area. Is there a clear bed for the tree to drop to? What sapling growth might be damaged? How will the wood be removed from the location? Is there a stout tree to stand behind when your tree begins to fall?

Look for "widow makers." These are suspended loose or dead limbs that may fall unexpectedly. It's a good idea to wear a hard hat. Chain-saw users should use ear plugs.

Prepare the tree for felling. The best wood on a tree is in the butt section; stumpage left in the woods should be minimal. If under 20 inches in diameter, plan to cut the stump 8 inches above ground level, or even flush. Flush-cutting leaves a neat-looking forest floor without obstructions that may hinder skidding or trip grazing livestock. For clearing, mowers can be taken over flush cuts to remove second growth and brambles that tend to grow around old stumps.

Remove imbedded rocks or dirt from the bark with an old hatchet. Any kind of abrasive matter intercepted by a saw will quickly dull the blade. Saw off protruding buttresses that will interfere with work later on.

If the tree looks like it may fall in the wrong direction, several steps can be taken. With a very small tree, one can toss a rope over a limb, securing it with a noose. The loose end is tied to another tree. As the tree begins to fall, pull on the rope to swing the tree in the desired direction.

Another method is to use a spring pole. Cut a stout

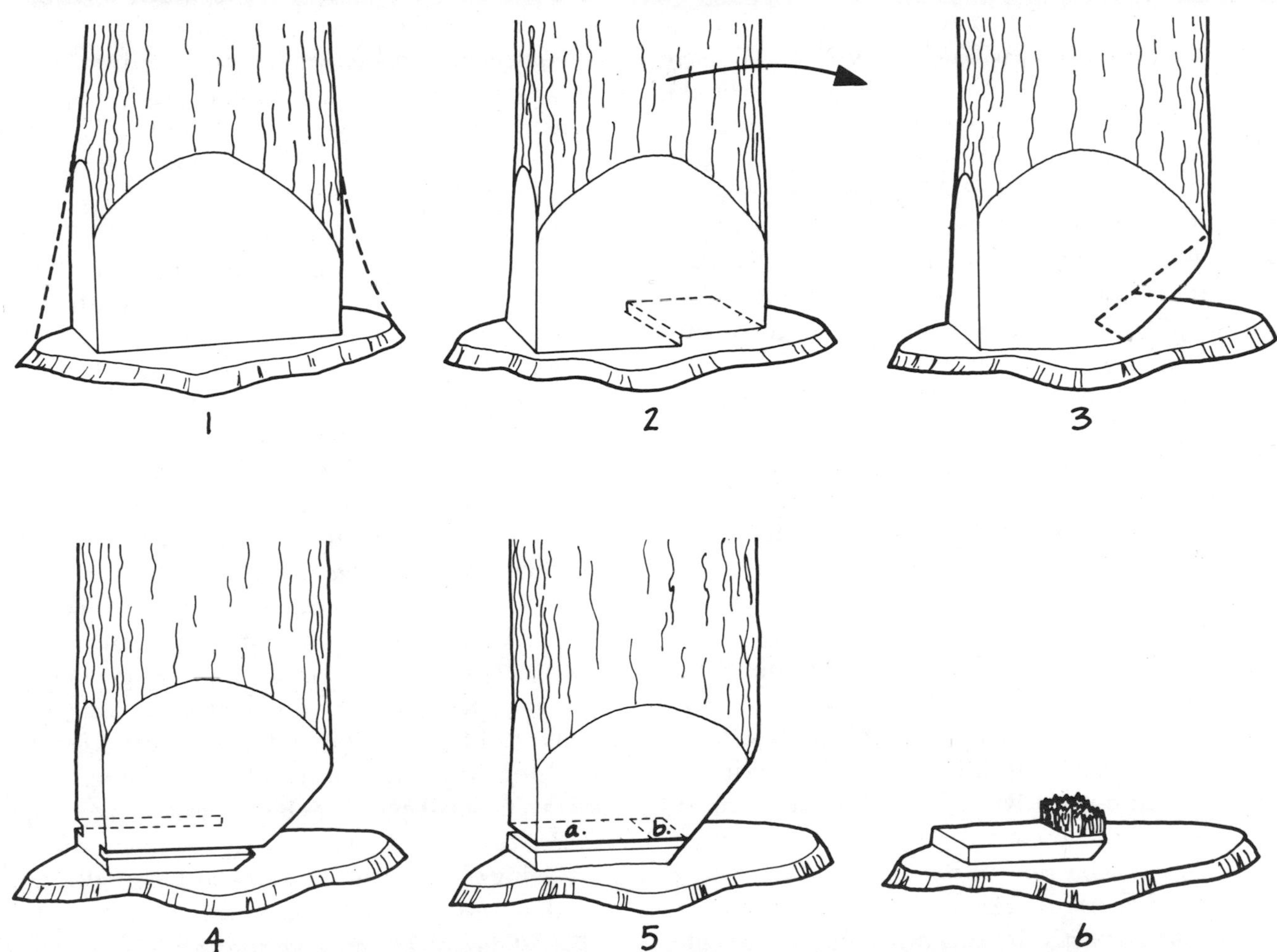

Clean stump felling: 1. Remove buttresses (optional). 2. First cut. 3. Notch. 4. Splint cuts (optional). 5. Felling cut (a), hinge (b). 6. Stump with hinge.

sapling. Jam one end under a limb or into a notch some distance up the trunk. Bend or draw in the sapling. Secure with a stake driven into the ground. I have never done this, but the spring is supposed to tilt the fall towards the opposite direction.

One could also climb the tree to remove the top growth or particular limbs, but this is probably best left to professional toppers.

Other methods of modifying a fall are discussed further on as part of the technique for the felling cut.

The tree is felled by a series of cuts, executed in a specific sequence, with special attention given to each detail. *Persons not actually involved should leave the area before work begins.*

First the undercut is made. In normal situations it is exactly perpendicular to the falling direction, carefully sawn horizontally on the falling side. Different authorities recommend that this undercut extend from one-fifth to one-third of the tree diameter. A wedge-shaped section is then sawed or chopped out just above the undercut to form the *notch*. (A variation, the Humbolt undercut, is notched out below the horizontal kerf.)

Splint cuts should be made to avoid the possibility of cracking or ripping wood during the fall. Splint cuts are recommended especially when cutting oak, elm, or hickory. These shallow cuts are made on each side, a few inches above the base of the notch.

The main cut or felling cut is made directly opposite the notch, exactly in line with the splint cuts. Work from the back edge towards the notch. If friction is detected, it may indicate that the tree is beginning to

lean backwards and about to pinch the saw. Stop and insert a timber wedge behind the saw blade. Iron or homemade wooden timber wedges are used with cross-cut saws. Plastic, aluminum, or wooden wedges must be used with chain saws.

Using a small chain saw to fell a large tree requires a series of fanlike cuts, all in the same plane.

Just before the notch, STOP CUTTING. Do not attempt to cut through the notch. Always leave a hinge, or control of the fall will be lost! Without the hinge, the falling tree can twist and topple in the wrong direction. The butt, with nothing to hold it, could kick up off the stump.

When the tree begins to fall, remove the saw and step aside, not backwards, and preferably behind another tree. If felling wedges are used with a crosscut saw, one partner quickly unfastens his handle and the other man slips the saw free as he steps away. Don't panic and drop the saw. The tree could fall on it.

To drop a tree against its natural inclination, several steps may be taken during sawing. The direction of the notch can be moved somewhat to compensate for the effect of lean or a heavy limb. The notch can be made a little deeper than usual. When making the felling cut, leave a small piece of the log as a support opposite the direction of fall. The last step is to cut off this support leaving only a small hinge towards the fall. The tree will fall towards the bulky hinge.

Once on the ground, the tree is limbed and bucked. Limbing is the removal of branches, leaving a clean log for skidding. Limbing can be done with an axe or chain saw. A few precautions should be taken: Always have a good stance on the ground. Don't balance on the log or underfoot debris. Clear away brush and limbs that will interfere with the axe swing. A good safety precaution is to limb the opposite side of the trunk from which one stands. Watch out for sprung limbs. They can be vicious when released. Consider temporarily leaving limbs that hold the trunk above the ground. These may release weights in a tricky manner, and they may be convenient supports during bucking, or useful handles for rolling the log over. Also, examine the limbs and crotches with an eye for usefulness, e.g., for maul wood, furniture legs, hooks, brackets, and so on. Most limbs join the firewood department. Start with the smallest limbs and work towards the trunk.

Bucking the trunk into logs of suitable length and weight is necessary before skidding to a truck, wagon or work area. Thoroughly examine the log before beginning. Different grades of material can be segregated for various uses. Buck logs at least 6 inches longer than intended use will require. Skidding and mill operations usually damage the ends of logs. Watch out for saw pinching.

Traditional craftsmen often avoided the problem of hauling bulky materials out of the forest by bringing their tools in and working on the spot.[2] An example is the English wattle-hurdle maker. Wattle hurdles are portable, modular fence sections made by weaving saplings or splits together. These were traditionally used by sheep farmers who had need for temporary enclo-

2. Jenkins, *Traditional Craftsmen,* pp. 21-25.

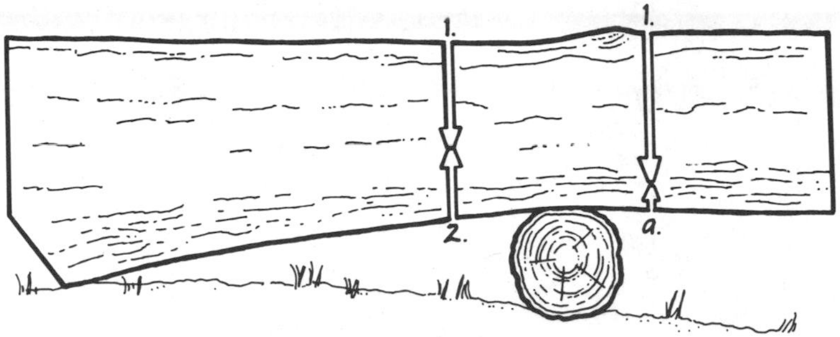

Bucking a log. Work from upper limbs toward the butt. The overhung section can be sawed straight through, but could rip at the bottom. If this is a problem, start with a short cut from (a). A supported log will pinch saw as it compresses downward. Start sawing from the top, but quickly remove the saw when the kerf begins to close. Finish cut working upward. The log will part around the saw. When the blade won't fit below, it is necessary to roll the log over 180 degrees. The best way to remove an accidentally pinched blade is by driving a narrow timber wedge into the kerf.

sures. They also make attractive and flexible garden fencing. The only tools used are a hatchet, a froe or billhook, and a jig in which the upright standards are set during weaving. The hurdles are made green, seasoned in the woods, and later hauled out—much lighter in weight and without the need for dealing with the waste wood, which decomposes into humus right on the forest floor.

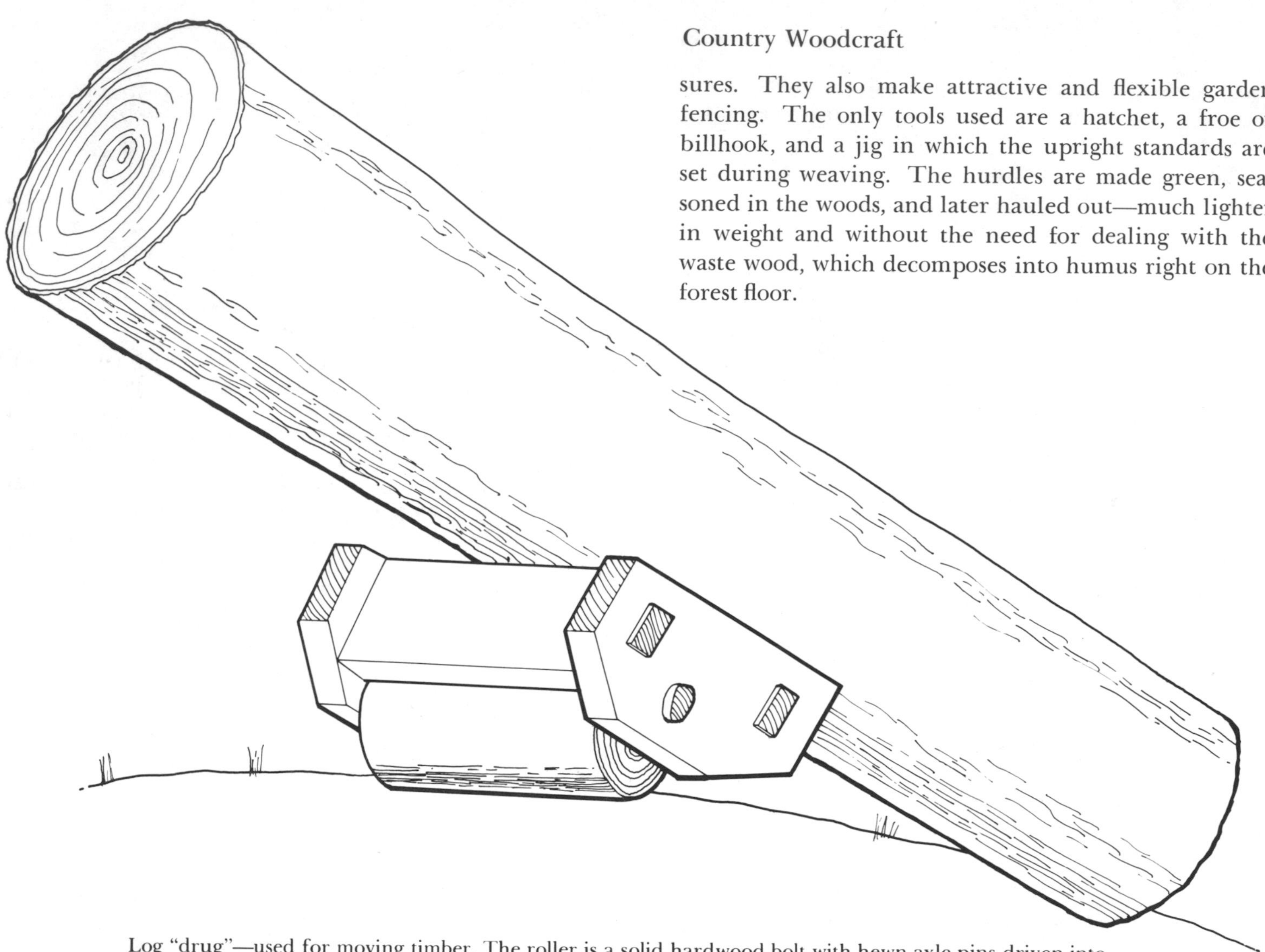

Log "drug"—used for moving timber. The roller is a solid hardwood bolt with hewn axle pins driven into each end.

Moving or rotating logs is facilitated by a cant hook, peavey, or hookaroon. These are stout-handled pinching tools that grab a log, giving a good grip and the needed leverage. Lacking the above, a pole can sometimes be substituted to good effect. It is often impossible to muscle around large logs with bare arms. Always be careful, especially on slopes where heavy logs have a tendency to move unexpectedly. If one must lift a heavy weight, keep the back straight, putting the strain on larger leg muscles with their strong bone levers. Make use of peaveys, rollers, log carriers, winches, and other mechanical devices. During skidding never ride a log. Always keep on the uphill side, as logs may roll or swing sideways without warning.

Actual methods of skidding depend on terrain and power available. Although it sounds obvious, try to cut timber uphill from the loading or work area. It's vastly harder to haul logs uphill than down. If possible, plan skidding operations during winter over well-packed (but not icy) snow cover. Work will be much easier and there will be few scars or other damage to the terrain. On snow, be extremely cautious hauling downhill or on even slight inclines.

The woodworker is not a logger in the commercial sense, so a fair amount of improvised technique is often called for. Be careful.

Woodlot at the Yurt Foundation, Bucks Harbor, Maine, in December.

CHAPTER 4
THE WOODSHED

THE COUNTRY WOODSMAN often gathers building and crafts materials along with firewood in a combined operation. Wood heat and woodcraft fit together like hand and glove. A tree, no matter how "perfect," combines a conglomerate of woods suitable for different purposes. The clear, lower trunk is the only wood that might be suitable for splitting into shingles, handles, bucket staves, or basket weavers. Farther up, knotty wood may be sawn into board lumber. Some limbs are useful for fashioning into mauls, gluts, furniture legs, handles, etcetera. A few crooks may be set aside for making wall hooks or clever odds and ends. But in general, limbings make excellent firewood.

The fundamental skills of country woodcraft have their origin in the woodlot, backyard shed, and barn shop. Here, one masters the axe (in its simple, but fundamental uses), hatchet, and carving knife. Before the Industrial Era, these were the basic tools available to the subsistence peasant farmer/woodworker. As mentioned earlier, individual tools were hand-forged by a blacksmith who worked with relatively scarce materials. Factory-made tools were gradually adopted as the new

Woodshed tools (l. to r.): polled axe, iron wedge, go devil (wedging or splitting maul), glut (wooden wedge).

cash economy created a merchant class of traveling peddlers and storekeepers.

The woodshed is a good place to first learn about the quality of different kinds of wood, how they split, chip, and alter with seasoning. The woodpile is also the source of material for many woodcraft projects. Splitting firewood, one has an opportunity to look through raw material, setting aside likely pieces for making dowels, fence posts, utensils, spinning wheel spokes, handles, or whatever.

Woodshed tools include a selection of axes, a splitting maul, and a hatchet. We occasionally use wedges. A bucksaw, bow saw, or one-man crosscut saw is handy to have. It is important to have several good hardwood stumps for chopping on. These are often knotty or crotch sections of a trunk that would be difficult to split. A sawbuck also is needed.

Actually, one doesn't need a real "woodshed." We generally work outdoors on a small, level area under the cool shade of an apple tree. We stack our wood in "ricks" scattered around the cabin, between trees, etcetera. We're always hoping to get a year ahead in seasoned firewood, but that is an ideal we haven't approached yet. (Our third homesteading winter required more than twice the firewood of the previous years. Be prepared! We weren't.)

The basic woodshed tool is an axe, which is potentially a very dangerous tool. A good axe is kept sharp. In use, one's movements are swift, often long and powerful. Accidents can occur quickly. The cutting power of an axe is a function of leverage, speed, and the sharpened, wedge-shaped, weighted head.

Always work in a safe area with good tools. Work with minimal overhead and underfoot clutter or obstructions. Small children and animals should be kept away from woodshed activities. If more than one person is working, there should be a safe radius around each work place. Be sure that tools are sharp, with sound handles and heads that fit tight and are free of any wobble. Don't attempt to tighten a loose axe head with a bent-over nail or by soaking overnight. Wedge it.

Good hard stumps, level and solidly placed, make the best work surfaces. We have held onto three oak stumps. One, 12 inches high and 15 inches in diameter, is used for the initial busting of log sections with a splitting maul. Another stump is 15 inches high and 12 inches in diameter. I like this extra height for splitting down bolts of stove and heater wood with a polled axe. The third stump is 24 inches high, 13 inches in diameter, and is used for light hatchet work, such as splitting kindling, roughing out bucket staves, dowel wood, etcetera. The taller stump frees us from having to bend over when using a small hatchet.

Concentrate. If the mind is wandering, put the axe away. A shin or finger could be butchered before it is realized that a slip has occurred.

Logs for firewood are first sawn to convenient length, generally 12 to 24 inches, depending on expected use. Uniformity makes nice looking ricks, the logs easier to keep dry, and the stacks more solid. Saw wood the maximum length for intended use and there will be less sawing to do. It is important that saw cuts

A double wood rick with one cord capacity, 16 feet long, 2 feet wide, and 4 feet high. The bottom course of firewood is on stringers, keeping the wood off the ground.

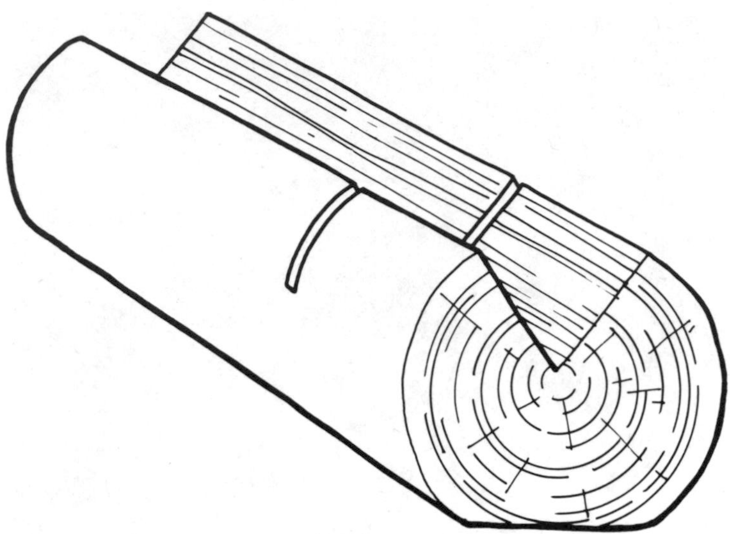
Miter-buck for crosscutting short logs.

be straight across, perpendicular to the log. Otherwise, bolts won't balance on the chopping stump.

For busting thick logs, you will need either wedges and a sledge, or a splitting maul (also known as a wedging maul or go-devil in the Southern Highlands). This go-devil is a hybrid derived from axe, sledge, and wedge. In other words, it's a monster. Splitting mauls are made in weights ranging from 6 to 16 pounds. I use a 10-pounder, perfect for my size and physique. I think that 6 pounds is too light for a go-devil. An 8- to 10-pounder will probably serve anyone. (Wedging mauls with metal handles have poor weight distribution and lack the spring of hickory handles.)

The best way to learn is by working with an experienced axeman. There are many tricks to this craft, and often bad habits prove to be dangerous. Make use of local talent, particularly old-timers.

Place the log segment on a low stump, generally small end up. Stand directly in front of the work, legs apart, the right leg slightly forward. At first, set the maul head where you intend to hit. Aim along a radial line, like a pie slice, not at the center. Gauge the distance. Lift the maul straight above your head (not around and over your shoulder). Begin the blow with a driving force, but about halfway through, let the momentum of the heavy maul lead the impact. This saves a great deal of energy and needless shock on your body.

Splitting wood is hard, sometimes exhausting work. There are a few "secrets," besides the skill that comes from practice, that can make the work enjoyable and

Splitting white oak firewood with a 10-pound go-devil.

The go-devil is brought straight down in a vertical plane.

not too difficult . . . even fun. There is an attitude, expressed by Thoreau in his journal where he wrote that splitting wood "heats us twice; and the first warmth is the most wholesome and memorable, compared with the other is mere coke. . . . The greatest value is received before the wood is teamed home." There is a sense of satisfaction in seeing, hearing, and even feeling a log split apart from well-placed blows. Quite quickly a good woodpile accumulates for cooking and cold weather ahead.

Developing a personal rhythm will also help to save much fatigue and avoid strained muscles. First, one's stance is set, distance is gauged, and preliminary aim is taken with the axe bit resting on the log exactly where one intends to split it. The breath is out. As the axe is lifted directly overhead, full inhalation is taken. Axe above head, there is a brief pause, retaining the breath. When the axe is brought straight down, the vigor of the action is accompanied by a strong exhalation. Breath and movement are coordinated into a cyclical rhythm. Raising the axe becomes a complementary action of the downward swing that follows. Body, axe, and wood are aligned. The muscles in effect are sprung and fueled prior to a release of synchronous energy. The importance of good exhalation is that it rids lungs and muscles of CO_2 build-up, making inhalation more efficient and keeping one's self fresh and alert rather than becoming exhausted and dull.

This woodchopper's rhythm is one secret of the Japanese woodsman. The technique is also practiced, often intuitively, by back-hills woodsmen in this country. This approach to axemanship makes splitting wood far easier and more enjoyable than simply whacking away. Splitting wood becomes yoga.

Most woods fly to pieces under this treatment, but several blows are sometimes necessary with hardwood or knotty chunks. With the go-devil, aim to crack the log in several places, so that it divides into halves, quarters, etcetera, depending on size and intended use. Sometimes a bolt will crack straight through but still resist breaking in half because fibers cross from one section to another. (This commonly occurs in splitting oaks.) A hatchet is useful for cutting the pieces apart. When the chunks are broken down to a width of 4 to 6 inches, cast them aside for further splitting (if necessary, i.e. for small stove wood) with a lighter polled axe.

Splitting should be done in a specific sequence. Begin on the opposite side of the log, not at the center. For some wood this only needs to be a light scoring stroke. Then swing down on the close side, with the axe bit crossing the bark. The split automatically opens on the radius towards the center, then crosses the log following the first marks. Blows at the center are the cause of most damage to axe handles and leave no control over the direction of the split.

Knots and crotches mean trouble. With the softwoods, knots emerge perpendicular to the grain as spikes, growing from the core outwards. These are often tough and can be the cause of chipped bits, accidents, or broken handles. It's a good idea to work around softwood knots. The powerful crotches of hardwood trees structurally originate many feet below the actual joint. Cross sections of the trunk develop into two sets of rings, side by side, with a kind of tough, granular cement binding the trunk together. One way to split such wood is to consider each set of rings as a separate log, dividing it into two adjacent "pies." The most difficult section is the cement between the circles. Sometimes it's possible to make a split from center to center, right across the joining area. With branch knots (as opposed to crotches, where the tree divides into more or less even sections), try to chop through the knot itself.

Some hardwood crotches seem to resist all attempts aimed at destruction. Try splitting the bolt in different locations. Sometimes a piece will bust easier if turned upside down. While it should be possible to split anything, there is a point of diminishing returns. It is senseless to sweat with no progress towards success when you could split up a whole pile of "reasonable" wood in the same work time. But before giving up, we try to get very tough pieces down to a size that will just fit into our wood heater. Often a bolt that is very hard to halve will split into smaller side segments. If all else fails, get out the saw.

The procedure for working with wedges is similar, but more time-consuming. Have at least two wedges on hand, as they tend to get stuck in difficult sections of some woods. Do not use the poll of a single-bit axe for driving wedges. It is too light, will quickly mushroom, and may fracture. Use a sledgehammer or go-devil. (The advantage of the go-devil is that no time is spent placing wedges, and that it very rarely gets caught in the wood.

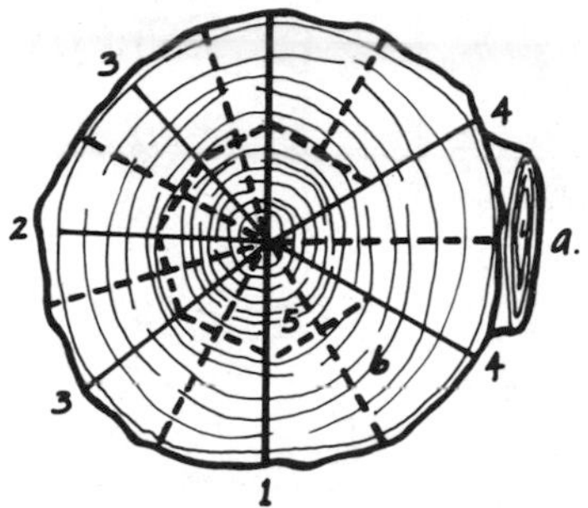

Typical sequence for splitting a hardwood log with a large knot. Split (a) may be attempted after splits (1) and (4,4). Splits (5 and 6) are optional, depending on size firewood needed.

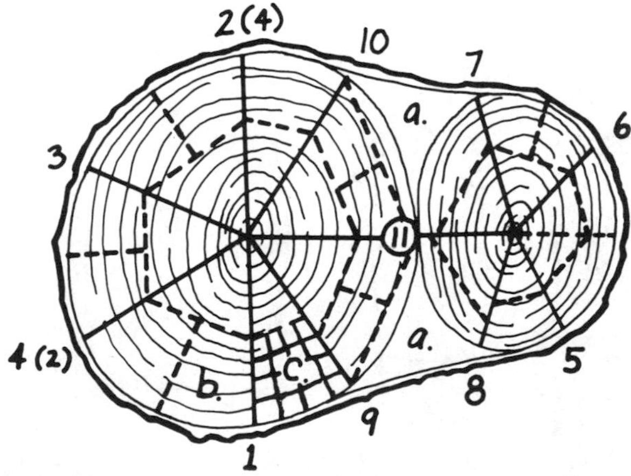

Splitting a tough hardwood crotch. Numbers in parenthesis indicate options (2,4). Split (11) creates two large pieces of heater wood (a,a). Dashed lines indicate how major splits can be subdivided into stove wood (b) or kindling (c).

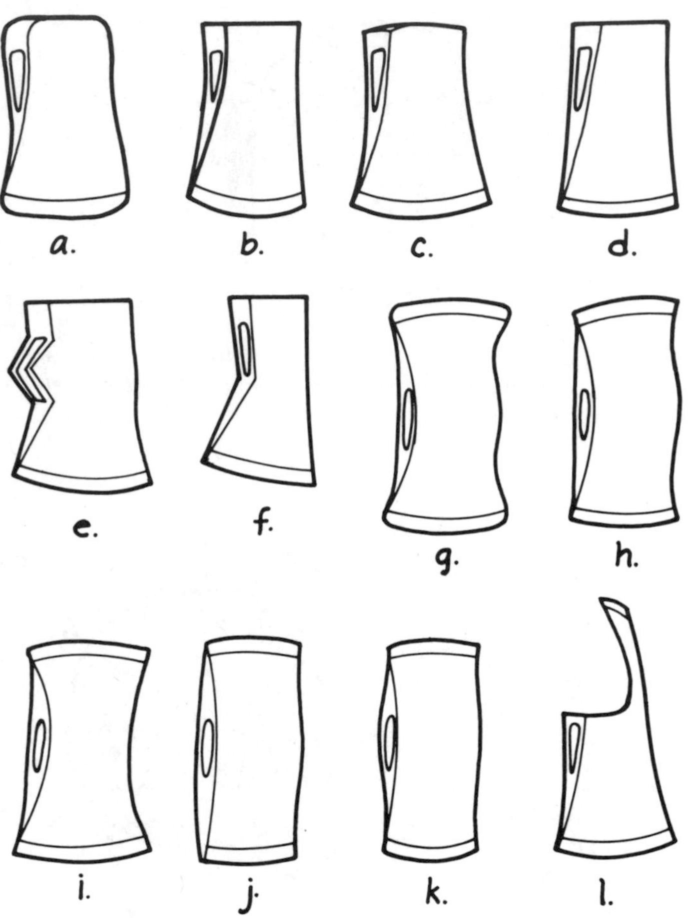

Common axe patterns: (a) Michigan; (b) Yankee; (c) Connecticut or Dayton; (d) Wedge; (e) Rockaway or Baltimore Jersey; (f) Hudson Bay; (g) Crown or Michigan; (h) Western or Pennsylvania; (i) Peeling; (j) Wedge; (k) Puget Sound; (1) Foresters' or Pulaski.

The head angle is rather obtuse, the effectiveness being from the impact of heavy blows.)

The common splitting wedge is forged iron or steel, ranging in weight from 3 to 6 pounds. The smaller wedges will serve for most purposes; however, it is handy to have a 5- or 6-pound wedge on hand.

Another type combines a wedge and glut in a single device. The wedge itself is cast steel and is hollow. Into this is inserted a large wooden extension section. An iron ring is fitted at the pounding end to help prevent the wood from disintegrating. Altogether, it's comparatively lightweight, tough, and very effective.

Further splitting for stove wood is generally done with a single-bit (polled) axe. The single-bit is preferred over a double-bit as the wide poll has a wedging effect during the splitting blows. The poll is useful for hammering (but not for driving iron wedges). I also believe that the polled axe is safer for general use. (However, our neighbors use double-bit axes for just about everything, even hog butchering and some hewing work.)

Stance and swing using an axe are the same as in using a splitting maul. Take careful aim. Again, a direct overhead swing is most efficient and accurate.

In conventional splitting an enormous amount of time and energy goes into bending over to pick up wood for splitting, resplitting, and loading into a wheelbarrow for stacking. One friend who is a very experienced axeman prefers to split firewood on a 2-foot stump. His polled axe, with the end of the handle sawed off at 24 inches, can be used one- or two-handed. A wheelbarrow of stuff to be split is placed just beneath the left side of the chopping stump, and a second empty wheelbarrow on the right side. The first splits generally require resplitting (for stove wood) and most fall into either wheelbarrow. During resplitting, he holds the chunks in his (heavily gloved) left hand and most pieces automatically drop into the wheelbarrow on the right, ready for wheeling to the wood rick.

Polled axes are manufactured in different "patterns" with names such as the Michigan (slightly flared with rounded corners), Dayton (straight sides), and Baltimore (exaggerated flair with extended eye flanges). I like the Baltimore, which seems to protect the handle somewhat. For general use, the bit should be slightly curved and pointed at the corners.

In really cold weather, axes become brittle and may possibly chip or fracture at the eye. In such conditions it's a good idea to warm an axe before using it. This would probably happen to an axe left in the open during prolonged subzero weather. I have never seen this, but stories are common.

Really small splitting, such as for kindling, can be done with a hatchet on the 30-inch stump. If the pieces to be split balance on edge, simply set them up and chop away. But with much small stuff, a technique of holding the wood while the split is started is necessary. The method I use is a little tricky at first, but avoids the need for balancing props and lowers the chances of slicing fingers.

Hold the piece in the left hand, about 10 inches above the stump. The hatchet is positioned above the

A safe technique for splitting kindling.

Left hand is pulled away just before impact.

wood, where the split is desired. Both arms are brought down in unison towards the stump. In mid-stroke the left hand slips away, allowing the axe head to follow the wood downward and begin penetration on impact. This should be practiced with easily split wood, using light strokes at first.

Another technique is used for making firewood out of long branches or saplings. Use a lightweight axe, such as a 2½-pound double-bit, a long-handled hatchet, or a Hudson Bay axe. The wood is held in the left hand at about 45 degrees across the far side of a wide, low stump. The axe, which must be sharp, is swung down on the sapling where it crosses the stump. The bit must enter the sapling at an angle, and the cut should take a single stroke.

Some woods, such as elm, certain birches, and hickories, resist all efforts at radial splitting. In such cases try slabbing: splitting parallel to the growth rings.

Use a polled axe. Place the block directly on the ground. Score the slab with a few light strokes in a line about 2 inches from the left edge. To make the split, swing straight down to the scored line; but at the exact moment of impact twist the axe clockwise popping the slab off to the left. The twist bursts off the slab and stops the axe from contacting the ground. For the next split rotate the log 60 to 90 degrees, score, and split off another slab. Continue forming an irregular polygon, slabbing round and round to the center of the log. (Practice with the log being split placed on a stump dug in flush at ground level.)

An alternative method for dealing with small stuff

is the use of a bow saw or bucksaw. (Instructions for making these saws are in Chapter 8: Bow Saws.) A good sawbuck is a necessity. (See Chapter 5: Sawbuck.) Sawing is somewhat slower than axing, but also safer and results in uniform, neat firewood.

Sharpening axes. Maintaining an axe is rather simple, reasonable care during use and storage being the main requirements. To function properly the bit must be sharp. The head must be securely fastened to a stout, comfortable handle. I'll repeat that loose heads should never be cobbled down with a bent-over nail or soaked in water overnight. These makeshifts result in many accidents. If an axe head is slightly loose, it is first tightened by bumping the heel of the handle on a log or other solid surface. The inertia of the head seats it on the handle. This works better than pounding on the head with a hammer. Then insert a notched steel axe wedge into the eye. Very loose heads may require the fitting of a large, new wooden wedge, or possibly, two or three steel ones. (To make wooden wedges see Chapter 10: Wedges.) Drive in wooden wedges with a mallet; a hammer can splinter them.

To sharpen a dull axe, secure the head so that one's hands are free for working. A double-bit axe may be driven into a log. I have found a shaving horse to be excellent for holding polled axes and hatchets. Axes can also be held in a vise or clamped to a workbench. An old woodsman's method is to chop a narrow V-groove into a fallen log, then drive in the axe, poll downward.

Begin sharpening with a fine mill file, working perpendicular to the edge. The file should be handled

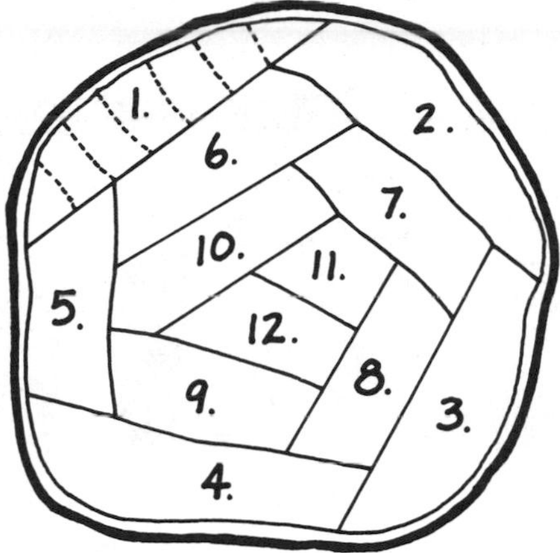

Some firewood that resists radial splitting can be easily slabbed. Numbered segments show progression of the work. Dotted lines indicate additional splits for stove wood or kindling.

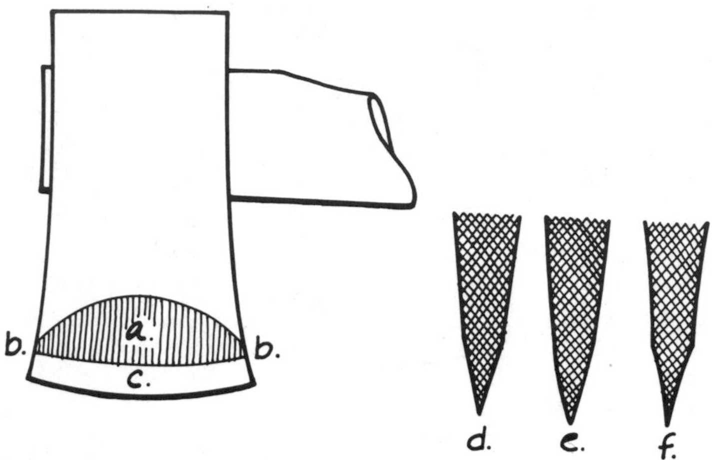

When grinding a damaged or well-worn polled axe, work for a fan shape (a), leaving adequate reinforcement (b,b) at corners. The bevel (c) should be flat (d), or slightly convex (e), never concave or hollow-ground (f).

and fitted with a guard. (Refer to Chapter 9: Tool Handles.) The angle of filing should not be too acute or too obtuse. This is difficult to define, but an obtuse bit will have inferior cutting power, and an overly acute edge is likely to become chipped. Complicating factors include different grades of bit steel, the type of jobs to be done, and the user's work habits and preferences. File both sides alternately. Occasionally stop and inspect the edge by viewing it from one end into the light. Stop filing when the line down the center disappears.

The file tends to make a fine serrated edge that feels sharp, but dulls quickly. Finish up with an abrasive stone. A hand-stone finish smooths out these serrations.

Secure the head as before. Put a few drops of oil on a clean medium-grit India stone. A good oil to use is a 1:1 mixture of cheap (but unused) automotive oil and kerosene. Work the stone in a pattern of small circles along the edge. Reverse the blade several times. Wipe clean and add fresh oil occasionally. The previously made file marks, which have a shiny appearance, gradually fade into a dull, grey color. Use less pressure with successive passes. When the entire edge is uniformly worked, wipe off the excess oil and grit.

Repeat the process with a finer abrasive (often the reverse side of man-made stones, or with an Arkansas stone). Finally, along the edge, make a few light circular passes, holding the stone about 5 degrees into the bevel. Reverse the blade several times to eliminate the wire edge.

Well-worn or chipped axes may be reshaped with an electric grinding wheel or a hand-turned grinder. A hand-turned sandstone wheel should pass under a spigot of dripping water or through a water trough. Water troughs should be emptied when not in use, as water softens the sandstone wheel. With an electric wheel, be *very* careful not to overheat the metal, causing it to lose temper (indicated by a blue tinge). When the metal warms up, stop and cool the axe in a water bucket. Take care not to grind away too much metal.

For woodshed axes, carefully grind a fan-shaped pattern starting ½ inch above the edge and arching up to 2 inches at midpoint. Leave reinforcement points at the corners. Then roll off a slightly convex bevel along the bottom ½ inch to the edge. Do not overgrind! Concave- or straight-ground edges have insufficient strength and are liable to chip during use.

Hewing axes and hatchets are shaped with a much finer knife edge running from corner to corner with a perfectly flat bevel on one or both sides.

POINTING FENCE POSTS

Here in southern Appalachia farmers have a way with fence posts that seems to be unknown in many parts of the country. Postholes are seldom dug. Postholes are made by repeatedly ramming a straight, heavy crowbar into the earth at one spot. After each thrust the bar is rotated a few times to widen the hole, which may go down 2 feet. The system is fast, avoids digging, and makes a well-packed orifice, far better than can be filled in with the conventional method. (The bar used can be bought. But crowbars are generally homemade by forging and tempering one end of an old car or truck driveshaft into a point, peen, or chisel shape.)

Posts are split from black locust. Cedar, cypress, post oak, and chestnut oak could also be used. Posts for this deep, narrow hole have a long, fine point, like a sharpened pencil. Hewing these sharp points is excellent practice of basic axemanship.

The split-out post, 6 to 7½ feet long, is supported with the left hand, while balanced vertically on a low chopping stump. The axe is generally a lightweight double-bit, 2½ to 3 pounds, with a rather short handle that can be deployed one-handed. One edge is ground to a very acute angle, then whetted to near razor sharpness.

Pointing a fence post with a 2½-pound double-bit axe.

The trick in making a long, sharp point is to hew off only a thin strip at a time. Start at the narrow end of the post, chopping at a very shallow angle. (Beginners often make short, stubby points.) As you work, rotate the post. Gradually hew further up the post, always working at the same shallow angle. By the time chopping reaches 1½ to 2 feet from the tip, you will have made the desired shape. In addition, posts can be chamfered around the larger head end. This prevents mushrooming later on.

Sinking a fence post is done by first ramming it down the hole made by the crowbar. Then drive the post tightly in place. A sledge or go-devil may be used on hardwood posts. A large wooden maul should be used for sinking posts made from softwoods. (Refer to Chapter 7: Clubs, Mauls, and Mallets.)

A shaving or drawing horse.
Used by permission of the Doris Ulmann Foundation and Berea College.

PART II
THE WORKSHOP

Sawbuck.

CHAPTER 5
SAWBUCK

BEFORE HAULING WOOD to the shop (or wood rick), one generally has to saw the stuff into lengths of suitable size. A device of some kind to hold branches and saplings in place for crosscutting is often needed. To this end, various sawbucks, props, and "brakes" have been invented. Common sawbucks are made of two sets of notched X-posts nailed to four 1-inch-thick boards which act as trestles and bracing. William Coperthwaite has experimented with lightweight designs for a folding sawbuck made from oak laths strengthened with wire triangulation. The traditional Japanese sawbuck is simply two pointed poles, diagonally driven into the ground crossing each other and then lashed together. Perfect for working in a permanent location!

The sawbuck that we use derives from a traditional style illustrated in *Ancient Carpenter's Tools* by Henry Mercer. This geometry results in a sturdy sawbuck with no obstructive cross bracing. And it makes an excellent practice piece for basic joinery techniques.

Materials. The sawbuck can be made from a single 12-foot length of rough (full dimension) oak 2 x 4. For the Xs, a 3 x 4 (a resawn 4 x 4) would be even better.

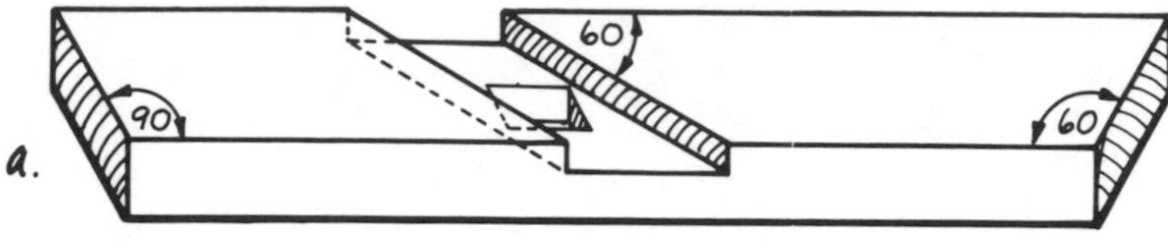

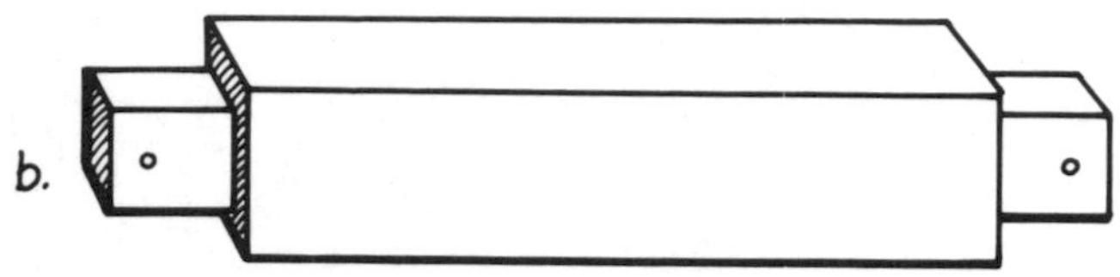

Isometric projection of sawbuck components. The mortise and half-lapped legs (a) are made in pairs that cross at 60 degrees, forming an equilateral triangle at the base. The trestle (b) is pinned through the outside legs after a test assembly.

Construction. The design is based on 60-degree angles forming equilateral triangles at the legs and arms. The X-members are half-lapped together with a rectangular mortise passing through the junction. This mortise accommodates the tenon of the single horizontal trestle. The points are pinned fast with ½-inch hardwood dowels.

The first step is laying out the four X-members. Our sawbuck has 30-inch legs resulting in a rather compact size. These are sawn at 60 degrees for the lower legs and 90 degrees for the arms. The trestle is 24 inches long. The upper edge of half-lap is laid out 7 inches from the arm corner, angling down at 60 degrees to approximately 9¼ inches. The exact point is determined by the width of the 2 x 4 used. Use a protractor to set a sliding T bevel for laying out these diagonals. The lower edge of the half-lap is also determined by the width of the lumber. Perpendicular lines are then penciled on the sides of the 2 x 4 where the diagonals meet the edges. The depth of each half-lap is approximately one-third of the 2 x 4 thickness; ⅝ inch is close enough.

When marking out these members, designate left and right pieces of each pair, matching parts of X-members for individual fit. This will help in avoiding confusion and allow for discrepancies in the rough timber or joinery technique.

The half-lap joints are made by sawing down to the guide lines (⅝-inch depth) along the inside of the marks on the face of each member. Three or four extra interior cuts are also sawn. Waste wood is removed with a stout chisel and mallet. This is followed by paring to a flat surface. Use the chisel two-handed, bevel down.

Marking out the mortises on the matched half-lapped X-members is somewhat tricky due to the angles and rough timber used. I made these mortises 1 ⅛ inches wide and 2 ⅜ inches high. This left enough wood for adequate strength around the diagonally located mortises.

Locate and mark the vertical axis and horizontal axis with the half-laps in place. Measure off half the width and height of the mortise and mark lines parallel to these axes extending to the 2 x 4 edges. Disassemble the half-laps and extend the lines perpendicularly across the edges of the 2 x 4s. (Refer to Appendix I: Mortise and Tenon Joinery.)

In this case the tenons are made to match the paired, half-lapped mortises. Extending the tenon stubs ½ inch beyond the mortise will eliminate some chance of wobble in an imperfectly fitted joint.

The ½-inch dowels are located along the horizontal axes midway between the half-lap and the face of the outside X-member. Drill through the assembled X with the *trestle removed.* Then insert trestle and with a pencil locate hole centers from both sides. Disassemble and relocate new centers 3⁄16 inch inward: toward the tenon shoulders. Bore a ½-inch hole until the auger pilot begins to emerge. Stop. Finish drilling from the other side of the tenon.

Reassemble the sawbuck. Cut ½-inch dowels about 6 inches long and chamfer one end. (To make your own dowels refer to Chapter 13: Hay Rakes.) Use a mallet to knock the dowel in place. The off-center hole in the tenon will force the joint to pull tightly into place as the dowel comes through. Saw off the excess dowel.

The finished sawbuck will be sturdy and should last for many years of service if kept "in the dry" and not thrown about too roughly. One or two coats of creosote will provide protection from weather and insect damage.

Swiss-style shaving horse.

CHAPTER 6
SHAVING HORSES

ALTHOUGH ONCE COMMONLY used by many woodworkers, shaving horses almost passed from existence after workbenches with screw vises came into general use. The principle of the shaving horse is simple, yet unique. It is not really a tool, such as the different edge and striking implements, but rather a device used for holding work to be tooled.

The worker sits on a bench and presses a foot-operated lever. At the upper end of the lever, above the fulcrum, is the shaving horse *head* with its *jaw* across the front. When the treadle is pressed, the head swings downward and the jaw tightly grips anything caught between it and a slanted *ledge* built above the bench. Because the length of the lower end exceeds the upper part at a ratio of perhaps 5:1, tremendous leverage is created with little effort. Both of the craftsman's hands are free for work. Lift the foot, and the object being held is immediately released for repositioning. In contrast, screw clamps and vises are based on a different principle, that of the wedge.

The invention is an old one. A stone relief from Gaul (Rheims, France), dated second century A.D., de-

Three-legged shaving horse with hewn bench.

picts a shaving horse similar to ones in use today.[1] An ancient form that utilized a leather loop that passed over the work and was held by one's feet was recorded by Viires in modern Estonia.

Among those craftsmen who traditionally used shaving horses were coopers, shingle makers, chair makers, basket weavers, and various tool makers. In addition, country folk used shaving horses for shaping fence pickets, making tool handles, sharpening axe heads, holding wood to be sawn, and many other jobs that required a holding device. Workbenches with screw vises were unknown or too costly. A shaving horse could be homemade, and with no cash outlay.

Over a period of centuries, European, then American craftsmen made their own shaving horses of different designs, depending on the maker's craft and local tradition. The first shaving horse that I saw (and used) was in the workshop of Herr Kohler, a Swiss cooper to whom I apprenticed. A summer's work on an old *Zug Stuhl* (literally pull bench) converted me into a true shaving-horse addict. The Swiss are great perfectionists, and to this day I prefer working on a Swiss-style shaving horse.

One may go about making a shaving horse in many ways, and over the last few years I have made several. Experiments included an English-style head (designed along entirely different lines—two swinging arms are used, bridged at the top by the clamp, and below by the foot treadle); two Appalachian versions (both three-legged for stability and hewn from logs); and another

1. Viires, *Woodworking in Estonia,* pp. 108-117.

made from commercially milled lumber [2] (designed for those who don't have access to a woodlot, or who want to get on with other projects.)

Since each worker will have to decide on style preference, dimensions, and materials, I have decided to forego a set of specific instructions in favor of a series of notes and guidelines that will be appropriate to any approach. Borrow from the different drawings and photos to design your own shaving horse. I recommend making a set of plans with dimensions before collecting materials and beginning construction.

The most important element in a shaving horse is the swinging head. It should be made of hardwood, preferably carved from a single log. (But I have built a satisfactory head from an oak 2 x 8 using nuts and bolts to attach the jaw "cheeks.")

The key is a large ratio between the length of the lower section of the lever and the length of the upper section. This gives the leverage that makes the shaving horse such an effective device. A typical head may measure 30 inches, but the top 6 to 8 inches is simply bulk, giving the overhanging jaw its strength. Again, the important ratio is between the length from the treadle to the fulcrum and from the fulcrum to the lower jaw edge. Make this as great as possible.

Another consideration is that the lower jaw edge must be shaped so that when clamped down, its surface comes flat against the work piece, making maximum contact. (A high-friction area.) The surface, actually

2. William Hylton, ed., *Build It Better Yourself* (Emmaus, Penna.; Rodale Press, 1977), pp. 865-870.

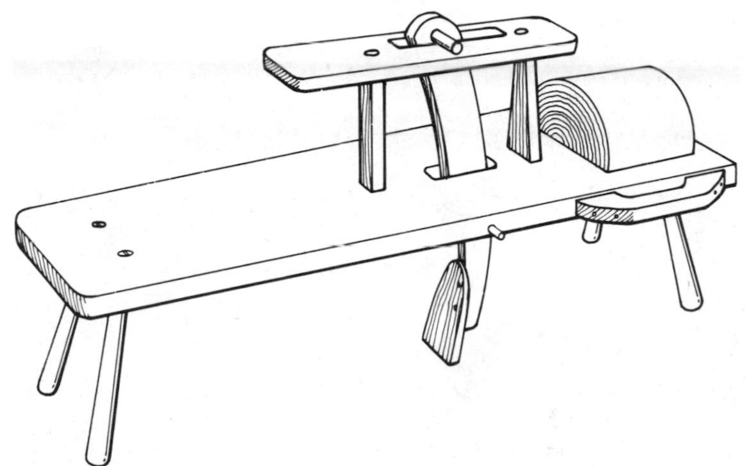

Cooper's shaving horse from Estonia. Jig at far end is for hoop bending. The fulcrum should be located much closer to the clamping rod.

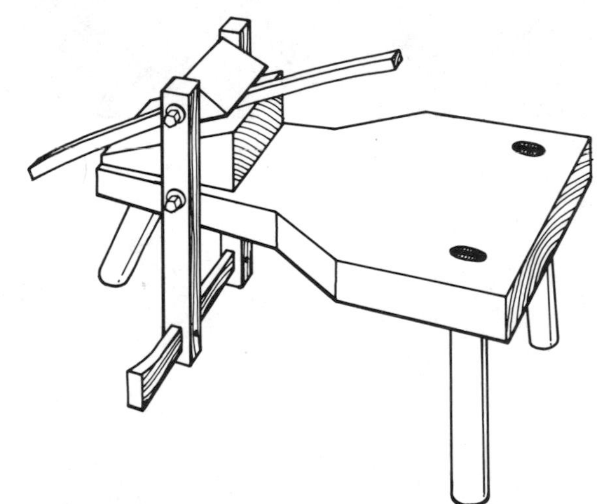

A wee, three-legged shaving horse from Britain.

Shaving horse made from standard lumber.

slightly curved to meet different thicknesses of work, is difficult to calculate but can easily be formed once the head is made and installed.

The pivot holes (a series so that different jaw depths can be set) should be drilled close to the near edge of the head. This will help to balance the unit, throwing as much weight as possible backward. If the holes are centered, the head will be off-balance, causing it to lean forward and automatically close when the work is removed. Then it must be reopened, or pulled back with a sapling spring and string—a picturesque device, but one that is unnecessary and sometimes in the way.

The overall shape is often curved. This gives maximum jaw grip and helps move the treadle toward the operator. Exact proportions are not critical.

For wood I have used apple and oak. Ash or beech would be excellent. Try to select a log having the approximate curve of the finished piece. This will make carving easier, as you will then be working with the grain.

The hard part is envisioning the finished head in that bulky log. Work right through the center. However, if the log is more than 15 inches in diameter, it should first be sawn or split in half. This would be best as the pith, which is often rotted or twisted, can be avoided. A halved log is also less likely to crack during seasoning. Locate the end view of the head so that the annual rings cross the jaw, as in quartersawn lumber.

The easiest method of carving begins when you sketch out the finished piece, as projected from side and top planes. But sketch it a good inch oversize to allow for error and final detailing. A chalk line is handy, as is the use of colored chalk for other marking on the rough wood.

Shaping can be done by making a series of saw cuts, spaced about three inches apart, down to the chalk lines, then removing the waste with a broad hatchet or a large chisel and mallet. Secure the piece on a sawbuck, using a chain with a small load binder. Or tie it with a rope and secure with a wedge (Japanese style). This rough process is repeated once again so that the approximate shape is arrived at.

Finish work is done with a large chisel and possibly a spokeshave. If necessary, thin down the sides with a well-sharpened ripsaw. A large, sturdy vise is the easiest way to hold the work in the final stages.

The final step in making the head is drilling the pivot holes. It's a good idea to wait until the bench and ledge are finished. It will then be easier to determine exactly where the holes should be. As mentioned, these holes are located as close to the near edge of the jaw as possible. Nine-sixteenth-inch holes drilled ½ inch on center from the edge are about right. The actual pivot can be a ½-inch steel rod, or a long ½-inch bolt with the threaded section cut off. When all else is done, you may want to drill one or two holes in the top of the head, perhaps 3 inches deep, for holding small tools like a knife or awl.

The treadle can be made several ways. Easiest is a stout dowel inserted perpendicularly through the lower end. This works fine, but confines one to staying close

Carving a shaving-horse head.

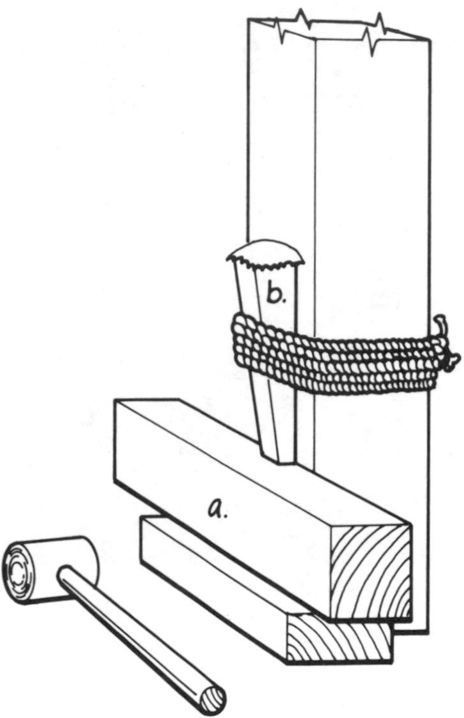

Traditional Japanese carpenter's vise. The piece being worked (a) is held firmly in place by driven wedge (b).

Low angle showing attachment of treadle with small tapered key.

up to the work, which could be awkward, or impossible with large pieces. Better is an elongated treadle, attached to the lower clamp end by a mortise and tenon with a wedged key. (This fastening technique is explained in Chapter 12: A Spring-Pole Lathe.)

Set the treadle at a slightly oblique angle so that it will be easily pushed with a foot. The treadle may be fairly long allowing the worker to sit far back. It's important to project the swinging angle of the treadle before sawing out the tenon; otherwise the treadle might run into the floor in mid-swing at the lower jaw setting. One way to avoid this is to shape the treadle in an arc so that it swings equidistance from the pivot point. A partial solution is to taper the treadle toward the leading edge.

The bench itself may be a 2-inch plank 8 to 10

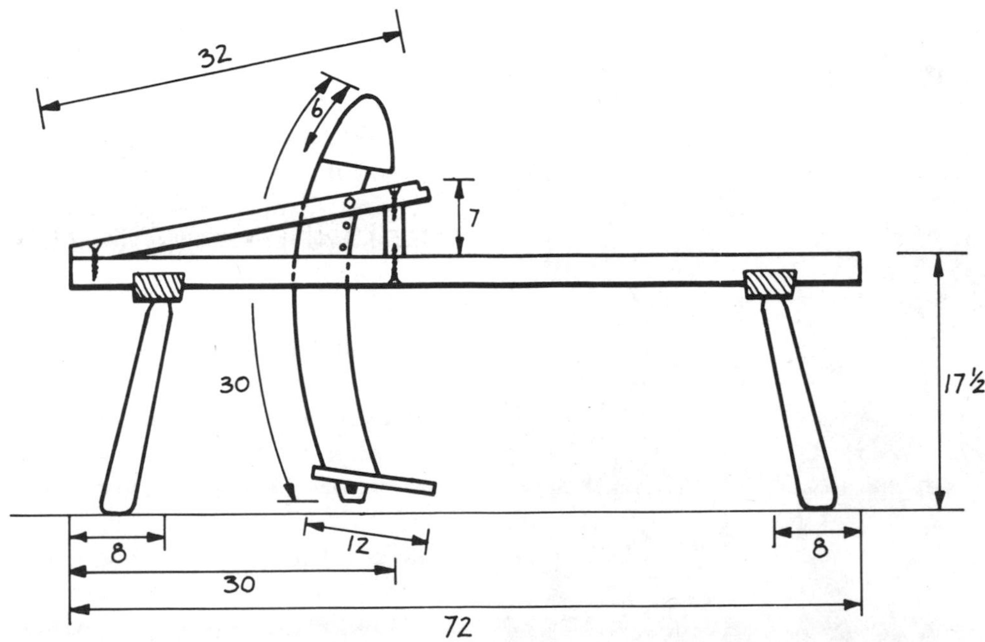

Dimensions of Swiss shaving horse. Legs are splayed 12 degrees lengthwise and to the sides. Jaw overhang is 2 inches.

Using a breast bib.

inches wide, or a hewn log, such as pine. Softwoods are fine. A typical Swiss bench is 6 feet long. Some English versions are less than 4 feet overall, handy in cramped quarters, but limited to working small projects. An advantage of a long plank bench is that it's often handy for clamping work onto for sawing or drilling work. (See Chapter 14: Pitchforks.)

A good bench height is 18 inches. The legs should be sturdy, and set angled outwards and sideways about 12 degrees to prevent tipping and jumping around the floor during vigorous work. Angled legs are a bit difficult to set into a plank bench, easy in a hewn log, but certainly worth the effort as the angle strengthens the whole unit.

On the Swiss shaving horse the round legs are fitted into 2 x 4 cross rails, foxtail-wedged (see Appendix I: Mortise and Tenon Joinery) tight from above, then dovetailed into routed-out tapered slots along the bench bottom.

The work ledge, the board that supports the work piece under the jaw, can be made from most any 6-inch board. A nice touch is to carve a step across the front edge and a 1-inch notch through the step. These details allow an extra use of the shaving horse—the ability to hold work between the ledge and a "breast bib" hanging from the craftsman's neck. This is useful when pieces must be shaved along the whole length, or in cases where grain angle causes clamping difficulties.

Once assembled, the shaving horse should be treated with two coats of varnish, or a mixture of two parts linseed oil to one part gum turpentine.

Drawknives. To use a shaving horse one needs two rather special tools: a drawknife and a spokeshave. Both are manufactured in a variety of sizes and styles.

My most-used drawknife is an American Greenlee. It has a straight blade, 8 inches long, and two nice-sized, comfortable handles set 12 inches apart. I also have a variety of other drawknives, for general use and special needs (such as convex-bladed for hollowing bucket staves or quickly reducing the thickness of a cleft plank.) Among these are a few drawknives that refuse to work properly—even after a good sharpening. Two drawknives hardly penetrate the wood, and another cuts in too deep and fast. The problem is simple, and I do not understand why manufacturers produce tools that cannot be used. Efficiency is related primarily to the cutting bevel; weight and subtle variations in shape are secondary considerations.

After measuring the bevels of various drawknives I found that the ones I use were ground at approximately 33 degrees. Two drawknives with a 40-degree bevel are just about unusable. Another, ground to 22 degrees, digs into the wood with no control at all. I have tested these tools in various circumstances—working hard- and softwoods, green and seasoned, and for rough debarking—and have continually come back to the tools ground at 33 degrees.

Use of a drawknife is simple in theory, somewhat awkward at first, then easy with practice. Unlike a plane or spokeshave, there is no built-in adjustment for the amount of wood removed, which can vary from paper-thin shavings to more than a quarter-inch thickness dur-

Drawknife, 15 inches (blade 10 inches).

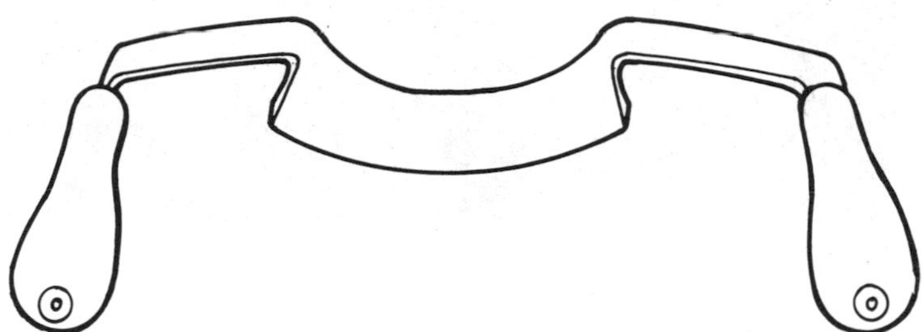

Swiss cooper's hollowing drawknife (bevel on back side), 12 inches.

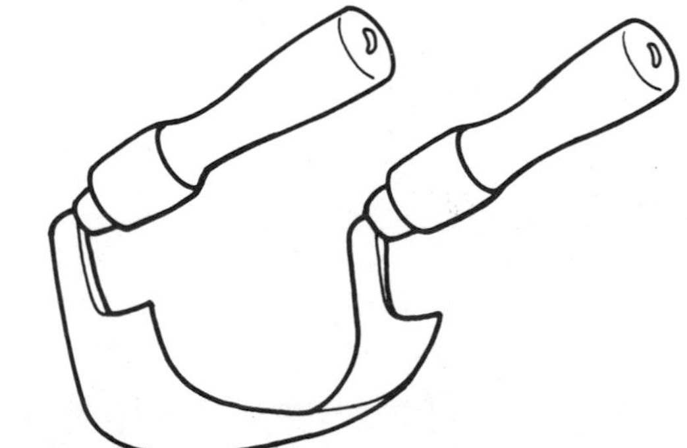

Inshave, 5½ inches.

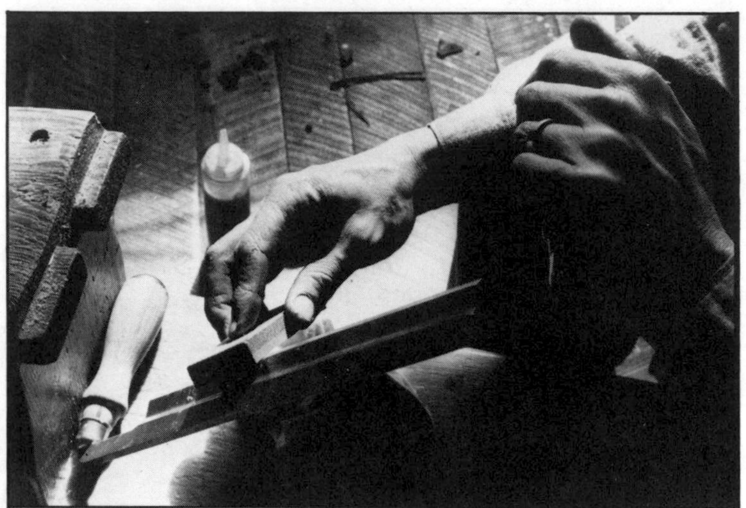

Sharpening a drawknife.

ing one stroke. Practice makes perfect and after a while, drawknife work goes very, very quickly. And builds muscles, too.

To start out, put a piece of pine or other softwood under the shaving horse jaw (or in a vise—but this is clumsy and slower going). Clamp down with a moderate foot pressure. Hold the drawknife extended in front of your chest, with the *bevel facing downward.* (It looks upside down.) Pull. To remove large hunks of wood, attack the piece at an angle (i.e., against a corner edge of the stock.) You don't have to worry about pulling the knife into yourself. But be careful not to place a thumb on the corner of the blade. Also, if the wood slips loose, it could punch you in the belly. This might happen if the jaw edge doesn't come down with good contact on the work, or if one is debarking green wood and the cambium is very wet and slippery. In such cases, slip a small block of wood, wrapped with coarse belt-sander paper, between the jaw and the work. This should hold.

For shaping a long, thin strip (basket splits or a bucket hoop) sandwich an extension stick, such as a 2-foot-long 1 x 2 between the ledge and the work piece. This will support the piece and allow work right along the edges.

Special circumstances require the use of a breast bib—for bodily holding the piece against the notch or step on the ledge.

Sharpening the long drawknife blade is somewhat different than smaller edge tools. If the blade is very dull, or nicked, it can first be ground on a hand-turned sandstone wheel running through a water trough. Face the bevel into the direction that the stone is turned to minimize formation of a wire edge. Be sure to maintain the 33-degree angle—or regrind to 33 degrees with improperly shaped blades.

Finish by whetting on two grades of hand stones, first a fine India stone, then on an Arkansas stone. There are two methods for whetting drawknives. In the first the stones tend to wear unevenly, so this stone should be reserved for whetting drawknives and carving tools that do not require a perfectly flat sharpening surface. With the bevel facing upward, hold one handle in your left hand and set the other handle against a cleat. (The corner of the bench and upright support for the ledge on a shaving horse is convenient.) Put a few drops of thin oil (use a mixture 1:1 of new automotive oil and kerosene) on the stone, which must be kept clean at all times. Hold the stone in your right hand, setting it *flat* against the bevel. Be sure to maintain the original cutting angle, so that the bevel doesn't become rounded. Work the stone in a circular motion along the beveled edge. Wipe the blade clean when grit and oil collect along the edge. Turn the drawknife over and reoil the stone. Place the stone *flat* against the back of the blade and make a few light circular passes until you can feel that the stone is making contact all the way across the blade. This removes the wire edge formed in whetting the beveled side.

Next use a finer stone. Be sure that the blade is clean before changing over. The Arkansas stone is used

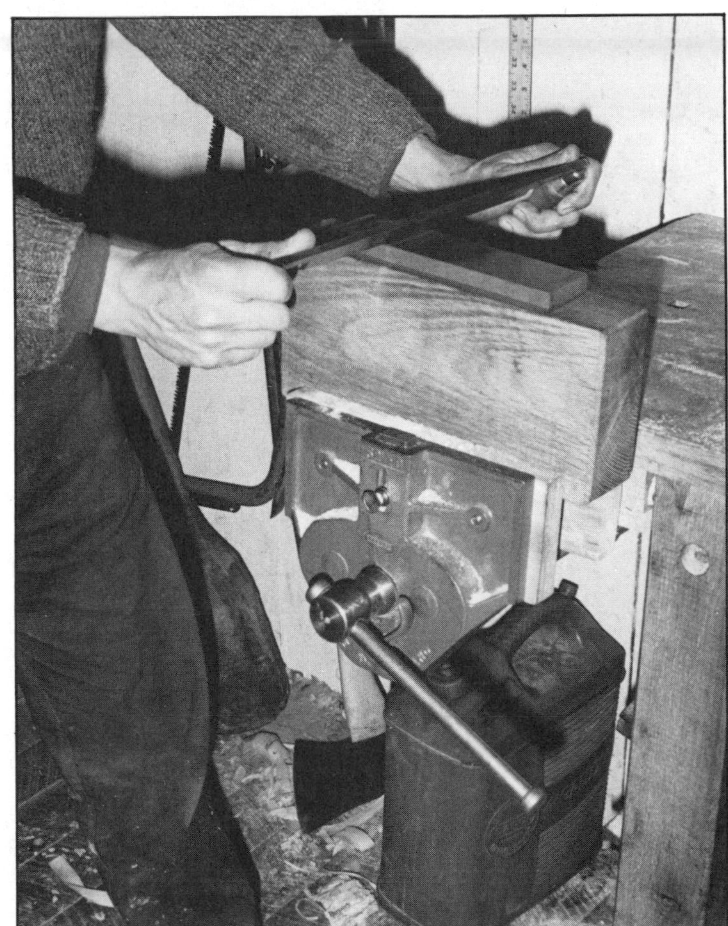

Sharpening a drawknife.

Spokeshave (with adjustable thumb screws), 10 inches.

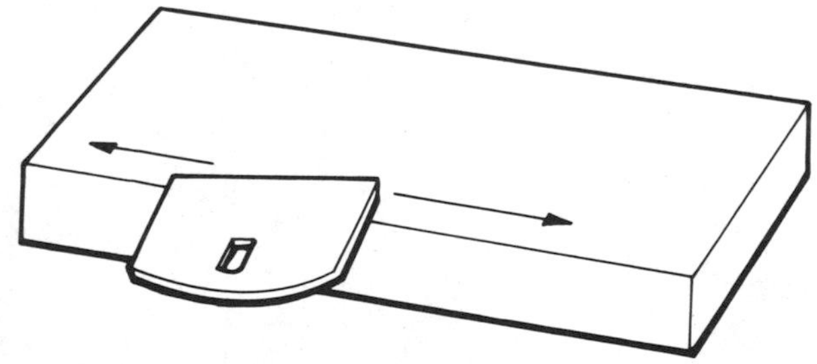

To maintain the correct bevel angle on a spokeshave, hold the blade at an acute angle to the length of the stone and rub sideways, left and right. This technique is also very effective for sharpening chisels.

like the "man-made" India stone. Be careful not to cut yourself during those circular motions. Whet the bevel side, then the back.

The second sharpening technique utilizes a bench vise to hold a routed-out wood block, 5 inches thick, containing the stones used. The block thickness is to allow the drawknife handles to be angled downward while the blade is drawn over the stone. A standard oilstone box cannot be used. Oil the stone. Place one end of the drawknife, bevel down, flat against the stone. Pull diagonally across the stone so that the pass ends at the other end of the blade. Repeat several times. To remove the wire edge, turn the drawknife over and repeat, with back of the blade flat against the stone. As with the first method, begin with a fine India and finish with the Arkansas. This technique maintains a flat stone, which can also be used for whetting chisels and plane blades.

Finally, you may polish the blade against a leather strop or the palm of your hand. Stropping is always done away from the edge.

Spokeshaves are sometimes tricky little things to use. Sharpness and proper adjustment are the keys to success. The best all-purpose spokeshave currently available is the Stanley No. 151. This is a rather large spokeshave—the weight helps eliminate chatter and the generous, flat sole gives extra control. The main feature of this model is that the blade is easily adjustable by two convenient thumbscrews. For most work adjust the blade for a very fine shaving.

Some woodworkers always push the spokeshave away from themselves. Others always pull. Either way works, and it is useful to master both techniques. After a while you will be using a spokeshave for all kinds of jobs that were difficult, if not impossible, with draw-knives, planes, or chisels.

To sharpen a spokeshave, first remove the blade from the cast-iron body. Set a fine-grit India stone in a hollowed block secured by a bench vise or against a cleat of some kind. Add a few drops of oil. Hold the blade bevel against the stone at the exact angle that it was originally ground. Work the blade back and forth on the stone, always maintaining the correct angle, so that the stone will wear even and flat. After a few minutes turn the blade over. Lay it flat against the stone and gently work off the wire edge. Wipe the blade with a clean rag.

Next use an Arkansas stone to achieve a critical sharp edge. Follow the same procedures. A few strokes across a strop gives that final touch.

Homemade clubs and mauls.

CHAPTER 7
CLUBS, MAULS, AND MALLETS

TOOL COLLECTORS LOVE to linger over planes, axes, and saws (especially molding planes, broadaxes, and pit saws). The most basic tools, striking implements like mauls and mallets, and simple edge tools such as carving knives, are left to archeologists and whittlers. For instance, one historian's book devotes seventy pages to planes, one paragraph to mallets, one paragraph to hammers, and two paragraphs to knives of all types.

Striking tools are obviously an extension of hitting with one's fist, and so go back to very early human experience. Use of a rock could provide added weight, a hard hitting surface, and protection for the hand. A stick had potential power due to its length. Lashing a rock to a stick combined the mechanical advantage of leverage to the physical property of weight. Such discoveries led to hammers and axes.

Mallets and mauls, however, are all wood. The most primitive versions are undoubtedly among our earliest tools. For certain work, such as beating on a gouge or a froe to split shingles, a mallet or club is still the best tool to use.

In the interest of clarity, clubs may be defined as

rough striking tools, carved from a single limb or sapling. Cudgels are big clubs. The term "maul" refers to any heavy striking implement. Mallets are small wooden mauls. Beetles are large wooden mauls. Commanders are the family giants, weighing up to forty pounds.

A wide variety of woods are suitable for making striking tools. The most famous material, *lignum vitae* (called ironwood) is imported from the tropics for use in sculptor's mallets. Other woods, while not as dense, make useful mauls for most purposes. Hornbeam (also called blue beech and ironwood), dogwood, American beech, and boxwood (an evergreen) are good choices. Hickory, rock elm, and apple are also commonly used. Most oaks split too easily for hard service, as does ash. But canyon live oak (*Quercus chrysolepis*—sometimes called maulwood) and eastern live oak (*Quercus virginiana*) are excellent. Swamp white oak (*Quercus bicolor*) is also tough. Persimmon, mulberry, and mesquite are other possibilities.

Cracks and checking. Striking tools are easy to make. But there is one basic complication to contend with. The problem is checking. As a rule, the denser woods tend to check, crack, and warp during seasoning. This is especially true for wood brought indoors where it is generally too warm and dry for ideal seasoning. Striking tools are often made from green wood as these materials become increasingly hard to work with aging. Cracks may develop shortly after a club or maul is finished.

There are several ways to contend with this. The best approach is to use seasoned wood, choosing pieces free from imperfections. Often only the ends of a piece check. If so, the first few inches may be discarded, exposing sound material within. For this reason, woodworkers tend to collect bits and pieces of different woods whenever they can, storing such treasures for years, even decades, in a shaded area with good air circulation. For mallets, well-encased knots and burls are not avoided, but desirable. They tend to be tough and resistant to cracking.

While green wood is seasoning, the end grain should be sealed with melted paraffin, aluminum paint, or polyurethane varnish. Very green wood is first painted with latex.[1] This helps to retard end evaporation, allowing the wood to slowly adjust to a lower moisture level with less chance of checking. Another method (not traditional, but certainly useful) is to wrap the piece in an airtight plastic bag. Expose the piece to open air five or six hours, then reseal. During exposure, surface moisture quickly evaporates. When resealed, inner moisture is wicked outward to the drier wood. Over a period of exposures, the moisture level is gradually brought down and checking is avoided. (This technique is borrowed from working with heavy ceramics where there are similar problems of cracking material in the green state.)

If nothing else, the end grain of green pieces should be saturated with oil to help retard drying. Keep unseasoned wood out of warm, dry rooms.

---

1. R. Bruce Hoadley, "Drying Wood," *Fine Woodworking*, vol. 1, no. 5.

Some English wheelwrights used to submerge green oak felloes (the outer rim of the wheel) under water.[2] The theory is that the water would displace the sap and then evaporate without cracking the wood when it's removed for drying. I've tried one experiment with dogwood—notorious for checking—keeping a chunk under water for about five months. The piece is now drying out and appears to be free of checks.

A club can be made from a thin sapling or a limb with a well-encased knot or burl, or from the root section of a dogwood or hickory sapling. In either case, the limb or sapling should be straight, as the handle and the striking head are one piece.

A nice-sized club, for use with a froe, splitting wedge, or billhook, is made from a green hickory or hornbeam limb, 3½ inches in diameter, 24 inches long. The beauty of this club is that it is quickly made, and quite disposable. This is advantageous for cleaving work where the maul is inevitably, gradually, sorrowfully destroyed through pounding the back edges of iron froes and wedges.

First strip the bark. Then mark off the head, 10 inches from the larger end. The handle can be started with a hatchet, although I use a drawknife and shaving horse for most work like this. Form the base of the handle with a gradual curve. Carefully controlled strokes with the drawknife, bevel facing downward, result in a graceful, concave profile. (Beginners often make this curve too abrupt, weakening the club.) Shape a hefty handle, 1½ inches in diameter. When finished, seal the ends with melted paraffin or polyurethane varnish, then leave outside, in a sheltered area, to season. In a few weeks, saw 2 inches off each end. Chamfer the edges of the head and handle with a spokeshave. Then treat the club with linseed oil. If possible, refrain from using it for at least one month, as even hickory is soft when green.

A cudgel is the right tool for driving wooden gluts. This tool must be stout (virtually unbreakable) and fairly heavy (maybe ten pounds) to be effective.

A good way to start is with the butt of a sapling, incorporating the section connecting the roots to the base of the trunk. Dogwood and hickory are favored because they are dense woods, and have many roots growing from an intricately composed nodule. Choose a sapling about 5 inches in diameter, with a straight trunk. Fell about 5 feet above the ground. This leaves a good handle to help lever the stump out of the ground. To grub the stump, work with a sharpened mattock-hoe, and possibly an old hatchet. (But not a *good* old hatchet.) Remove dirt to expose roots and hack away. It's sometimes possible to catch hold with a logger's hookaroon, peavey, or crowbar, then lever or pry the roots out. Some stumps may have to be cut loose all the way around.

Take this prize home, debark it, and scrub it well to remove embedded dirt and grit. Shape the head (starting out with the old hatchet). Work for a symmetrical contour. If the cudgel is lopsided, it will be hard to use.

2. George Sturt, *The Wheelwright's Shop*. Cambridge University Press, 1923.

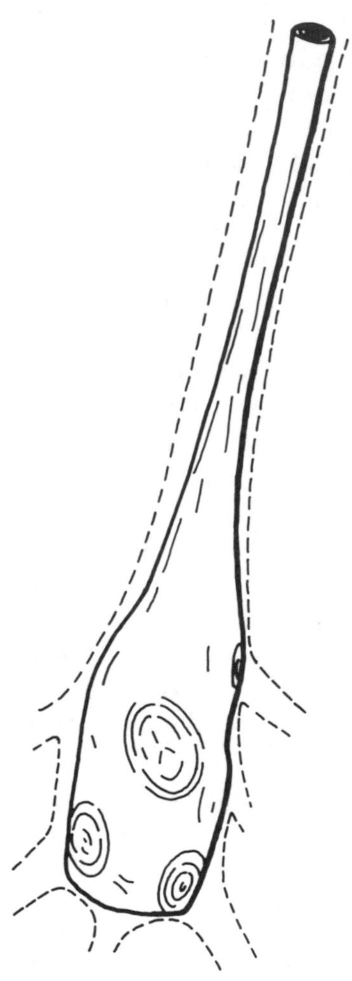

Cudgel. Carved from root and butt of a dogwood or hickory sapling. Length 28 to 36 inches, approximately 10 pounds.

For the handle, first saw off the tip to a total of 4 feet. To reduce the diameter of the handle, remove the outer wood with an axe or hatchet. Or, saw a series of 1-inch-deep rings around the butt, then remove the wood with a hatchet or a chisel and mallet. Repeat until down to a 2-inch diameter. The final diameter, 1½ inches, is best shaped with a drawknife. Drench the cudgel with linseed oil thinned 2:1 with turpentine. Season the cudgel at least two months before using. Then trim the handle to the desired length, about 3 feet.

Mallets. A more complex striking tool is a mallet made of two pieces. The advantages are: (1) the head and handle can be different woods chosen for density and toughness; (2) the pieces can be split out of a quartered section of wood, avoiding the central pith that often checks, is twisty, knotted, or possibly rotten; (3) the parts are seasoned before assembly, avoiding checks and cracking in the final tool.

Mallets can be made with round-faced strikers (like clubs) or flat heads (like hammers). With round-faced strikers, a full band can be worn down before the tool is discarded. Finely crafted round-faced mallets (usually turned on a lathe) are the preferred tool of wood sculptors for gouge and chisel work. The advantages of a flat-head mallet are that impact is carried by the end grain and that the handle has the mechanical advantage of some spring. With normal use mallets will last for many years.

In either case short billets, 3 to 8 inches in diameter, are selected. Handle holes are drilled with a brace and 1-inch (or larger) bit. In making these sockets drill only part way through, then reverse the wood and complete from the other side. This corrects for error in alignment (possibly with a little rasp work), and avoids the likelihood of wood fibers ripping when the auger bit emerges.

For a round-faced striker, handle boring should precede seasoning as large auger bits cut very poorly into the end grain of aged hardwoods. If necessary, start with a small hole (5/16-inch), then continually rebore in 1/8-inch increments to the desired size.

Handles made of ash or hickory (in England, beech; in Scandinavia, maple or birch) may be carved or shaped with a drawknife and spokeshave, or turned on a lathe. Handles made of green wood, especially hickory, will shrink a great deal in seasoning. Green handles are made oversized, then properly fitted in about a month later. At the tip of the handle, saw a slit for a wooden wedge. (Refer to Chapter 10: Wedges.) When the wood is seasoned, fit the handle and head together and wedge tight. (Further details on handles are in Chapter 9: Tool Handles.)

The carpenter's mallet has a flat-sided head, with striking surfaces inclined slightly along imaginary lines joining at the user's elbow. (Turned mallets are also made with a tapered profile.) Traditionally the shape bulges across the front, adding some weight along the center line, and also enlarging the handle socket. The edges are generally chamfered slightly to avoid chipping in use. These mallets may be carved from a small billet, or made from a 2- to 3-inch plank. Beech is the favored wood.

One-piece mallet carved from hardwood limb. (Apple, hornbeam, etc.)

Two-piece mallet. The handle is less likely to check if carved from split-out quarter-grain wood.

A slightly tapered mortise passes through the head. The handle is shaped to mate with this taper so that it continually tightens with use (as with adze and pickax handles). A variation of this mallet, easier to make, uses the same head contour, but substitutes a conventional eye and nontapered round handle, held fast with a little glue and a wedge knocked into a slot sawn across the end grain.

These mallets are suitable for cabinetmaking and general carpentry, such as beating out mortises and other chisel work.

The heads of all mauls and mallets should be oil-impregnated before use. Treatment will stabilize the moisture content and help prevent checking. In addition, it will add several ounces of valuable weight. Linseed oil should be used. You can: (1) Soak the entire head in oil overnight; (2) brush all end-grain surfaces, including the handle socket, with oil every hour so that it continually soaks in rather than drying as a surface film; (3) plug one end of the socket with glazier's putty, then fill the cavity with oil until it exudes from end-grain striking surfaces.

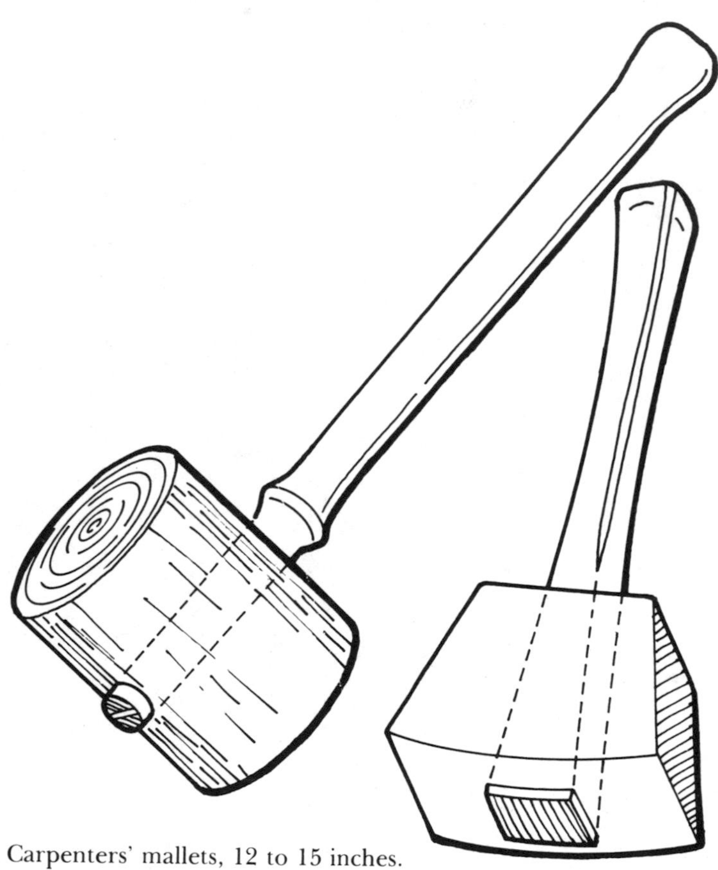
Carpenters' mallets, 12 to 15 inches.

Beetles are used for heavy work, such as fitting mortise and tenon joints in timber frame construction and driving wooden fence posts. The traditional wood in England was apple. But most any hardwood can be used. The head is often ringed with iron bands to prevent splitting under impact. These bands are generally fitted red-hot; they shrink tight in place as they cool. In use, the frayed edges of the head tend to hold the bands in place.

Clubs, Mauls, and Mallets

Clubs, mauls, and mallets make great projects for kids. A wide variety of common woods can be used, and only a few tools are needed in making them.

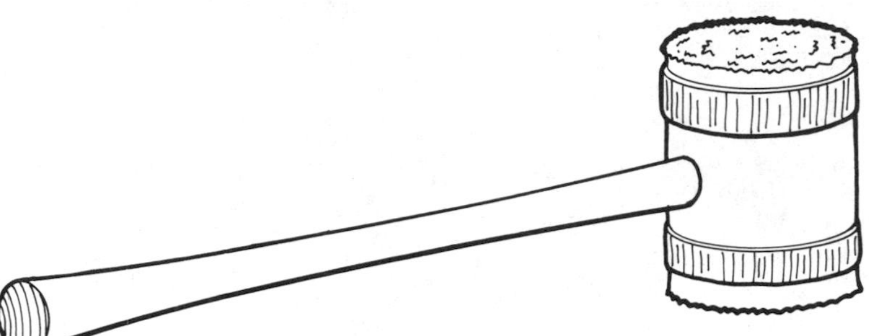

Beetle. Traditionally with beech handle and apple head, 5 to 10 pounds.

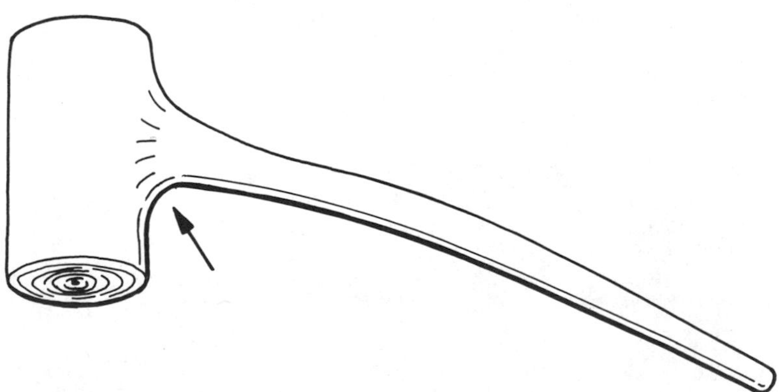

English maul used to drive tall fence posts. Arrow indicates striking surface. Ash is the traditional wood, but others such as hickory, post oak, dogwood, apple, or hornbeam would be suitable.

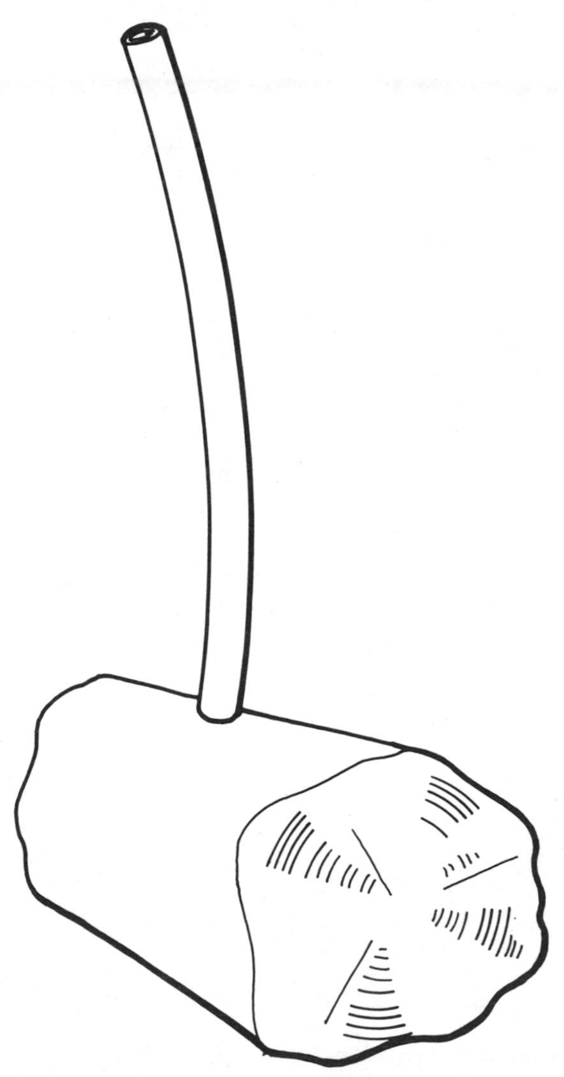

Commander. Hornbeam head with a hickory handle, 10 to 30 pounds.

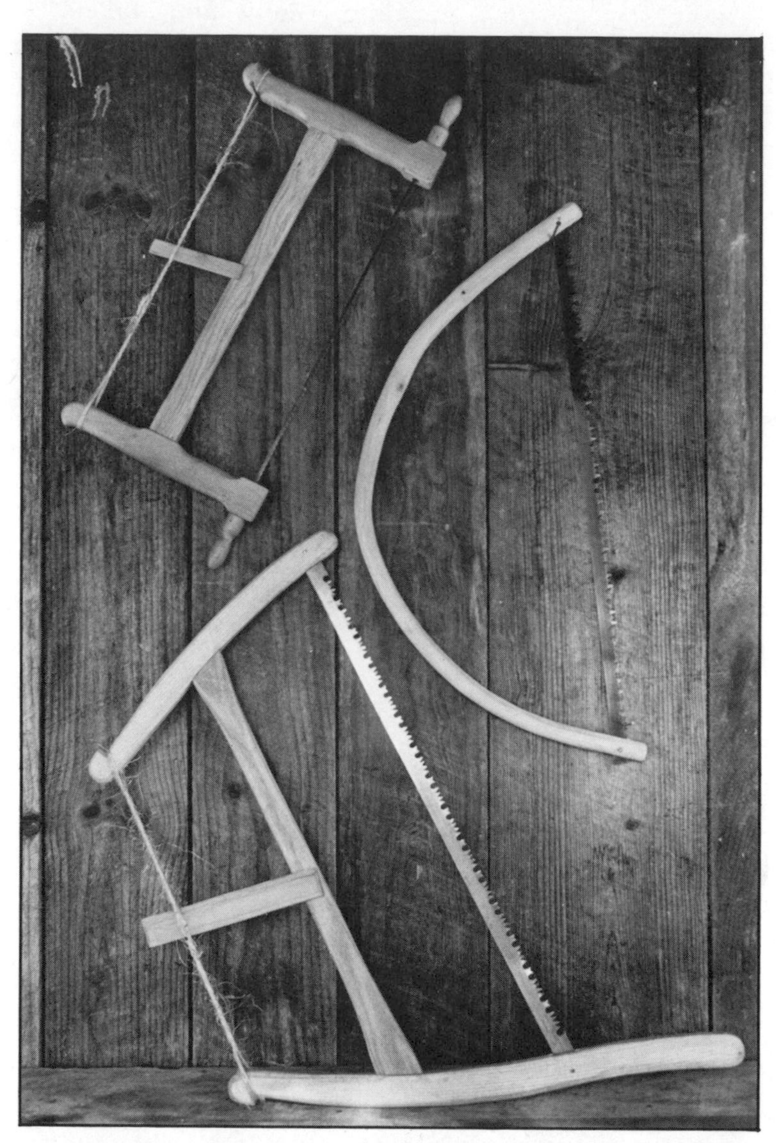

Homemade saws: (top left) turning or fret saw, (center right) bow saw, (bottom left) bucksaw.

CHAPTER 8
BOW SAWS

SAWN LUMBER—for paneling, doors, shutters, furniture, and flooring—was a scarce commodity among farmers and laborers until fairly recent times. Saws, however, have a long ancestry. Fragments of sharpened flint set into wood have been found in Stone Age excavations, but these were probably used for cutting meat.[1] Wood saws have been traced to Bronze Age Egypt.[2] But the few professional carpenters who had saws worked for the aristocracy. Remnants of ancient saws seem crude, having uneven teeth and no set. But from surviving relics, we can see that many ancient woodworkers were superlative craftsmen.

Saws of the modern style—a wide, panel-type blade and enclosed handle, working on a push stroke—were first made in eighteenth century England and Holland. These early handcrafted saws were limited in use to town and estate carpenters working for the well-to-do. In the nineteenth century, commercial saw makers began factory production of high-carbon cast steel. Henry Disston, an ex-employee of Spear and Jackson,

1. Percy W. Blanford, *Country Craft Tools* (London: David & Charles, 1974), p. 83.
2. W. L. Goodman, *The History of Woodworking Tools* (London: G. Bell & Sons Ltd., 1962), p. 110.

Sheffield, England, set up the first furnace for crucible-cast steel in America in 1855.

All ancient saws worked on a pull stroke. There was no set to the teeth and early metals lacked resiliency. On a push stroke the blade would have buckled. Nowadays most handsaws made in this country and England are of the panel type, working efficiently on a push stroke. But many European carpenters still use frame-type pull saws. The larger-toothed crosscut saws, used for bucking timber and rough carpentry, saw equally well in either direction.

Traditional Japanese panel saws are made to work on a pull stroke. These saws have very thin blades and no set, making them easy to control for precise work with (or without) guide blocks.

Saws for scrollwork, which require an extremely narrow blade, generally cut on the pull stroke and are therefore fitted to some type of frame. Coping saws are a modern example (often set backward inadvertently—for a push stroke).

There are several types of framed saws. The simplest consists of a wooden sapling or limb bent into a "bow" that holds a blade in tension. A modern version, made of tubular steel, is one of the most versatile tools of a woodlands craftsman.

The traditional farmer's bucksaw and the furniture maker's turning saw also fit in this group. These saws are fine examples of compression and tension working in balance. The central stretcher is held in compression by two arms, while the blade and straining cord are in tension. A toggle stick (Spanish windlass) winds the

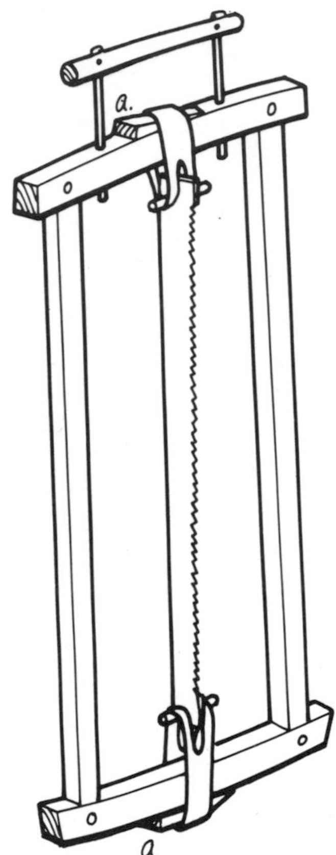

Frame saw with wedges (a,a) to tighten the blade in tension. This is a two-man version used to rip boards in a cabinet shop.

straining cord, and this transforms the saw into a rigid, integrated structure. Some versions substitute a threaded rod and wing nut for the cord and toggle.

Turning (or scroll) saws are lightweight tools, often carefully crafted. The most prominent feature is a provision for rotating the blade for scrollwork. (Very handy in blocking out spoons, hatchet handles, etc.) Bucksaws are made on the same principle, but are generally stouter.

Frame saws, sometimes called sash saws, also work on a compression-tension basis. They are, in effect, bow saws turned inside out. In frame saws, the blade is strained between two outer compression members. Wide frame saws are made for cutting curves, such as chair bottoms and wagon felloes. Long, strong frame saws were once used for ripping out lumber from sawlogs.

Bow saw. Because of its stark simplicity, the simple bow saw has a primitive appeal rivaled by few other tools. There are only two elements: a stout, springy limb or sapling, and the blade (secured by two pins, in our case cut-off nails).

For this saw, use a blade manufactured for a steel bow saw—available in 24- and 30-inch lengths at most hardware stores. The limb or sapling should be straight, or only slightly curved. It should be free of knots, and about 1 inch in diameter. A 30-inch saw requires a 44-inch bow. A good plan is to originally cut the piece 6 inches longer than the final length. The extra inches are to house two temporary pins for bending the bow.

After choosing a limb or sapling of a suitable

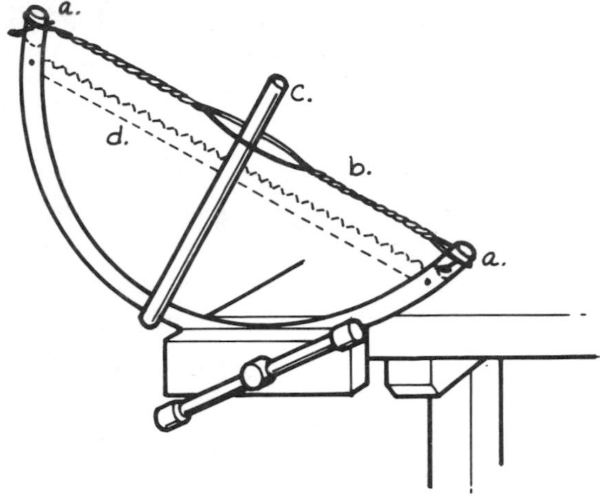

Bending a sapling for a bow saw. Temporary pins (a) hold looped cord (b), which is twisted tight with toggle (c). Permanent blade location is indicated by (d).

variety (such as locust, sassafras, hornbeam, hickory, ash, mulberry, or oak), cut to 50 inches for a 30-inch saw, or 38 inches for a 24-inch saw. Work while the wood is green, preferably right after felling. Strip the bark. Determine the most natural plane that the bend will take. One inch from each end drill a $\frac{5}{32}$-inch hole through the wood, perpendicular to the curved plane. The bow is made by heating the wood with boiling water, then tightening with a straining cord and toggle. (This boiling water technique is described in Chapter 14: Pitchforks.) While the wood is hot, tap a tenpenny common nail through each hole. Bend the wood slightly. Then wrap a good length of hemp twine (nylon would stretch) round and round the two nails, making perhaps five continuous loops. Tie. Place a thin stick, about a foot long, through the looped twine, and begin to twist. It's helpful to hold the piece in a vise so that both hands are free for twisting. Have the blade on hand to test the degree of arc. Stop bending about 3 inches before blade length is reached. The proper curvature is a compromise between maximum sawing clearance and strength of the sprung bow. As the arc increases, the tips come closer to being parallel and the spring weakens. The place to stop differs from one piece of wood to another, but it is better not to overbend. (You will want to flex the bow some more for fitting the blade.) Remember that the twine and toggle are not pinned at the permanent location for the blade; each end is 3 inches longer than the finished size.

When bending is finished, set the wood aside to season. In ten or fifteen days cut the twine. The bent frame will spring open a little bit. Lay the frame on a flat surface and determine the points for the permanent pin holes. Saw off the extra 3 inches from one end. Drill a new $\frac{3}{32}$-inch hole 1 inch from the end. Saw a slot through the end in line with the curve of the bow.

Place one end of the blade through the slot, and pin with a tenpenny common nail. Trim the nail flush. Bend the frame at maximum curvature to determine the location of the second pin. Mark. Saw off the excess wood leaving 1 inch below the pin. Drill a $\frac{3}{32}$-inch hole and saw the blade slot. Bend the frame. Insert the blade and pin it in place. Sand and oil for a good finish.

I have found this saw to be somewhat inferior to a commercial bow saw. (Mine is made from a hickory sapling.) These blades are made to cut on push and pull strokes, but the wood frame flexes just slightly on a push stroke. Learn to saw on pull strokes only. To maximize the spring, leave the blade loose when not using the saw. For light work, such as cutting small limbs for firewood, this type of saw works fine. The bow saw is a great project for kids.

The wooden bucksaw was both handmade on the farm, and a commercial production item in the mid-1900s. This saw corrects the flexing defect of the bent-wood bow saw with a frame that can be tightened to a remarkable degree of rigidity—equal to a tubular steel bow saw. The only disadvantages in comparison to the steel bow saw are the bulk of the bucksaw, and the relatively high cost of commercial production. But a fine bucksaw can be homemade using a wide range of materials and a standard replacement blade for a commercial bow saw.

Modern bow saw blades are extremely sharp when new, and they tend to bounce and skip at the beginning of a saw cut. Many a hand has come home with a row of ragged cuts due to a moment of carelessness with these saws. When starting to saw, guide the saw with the edge of the left thumb resting above the blade. This reduces chatter, eases the start, and eliminates the possibility of the blade bouncing across one's knuckles. These blades are highly tempered and are not meant to be refiled. If rocks, nails, and rust are avoided, they last a fair while. But they should be replaced when dull. (An alternative, more permanent blade, 27 inches long, can be bought from woodworking supply houses.)

The central piece of a bucksaw is the *stretcher,* sometimes called a brace. At each end is a shouldered tenon matched to mortises chiseled in the two *arms.* Traditionally, one arm extends below the saw blade forming a handle. Oftentimes the saw is held with one hand just above the blade. For extra power, or certain work angles, put one hand on the handle (below the blade) and the other hand above the stretcher. The *straining cord* may be plain hemp, wound around the arms several times, then tied with a square knot. The *toggle* is a flat, hardwood stick.

In making this saw, plan the size according to the length of the blade and the angle of the mortise-and-tenon-jointed stretcher and arms. My saw has arms split along the natural curvature of an ash log. The stretcher and toggle are cleft oak. All of these parts could be sawn

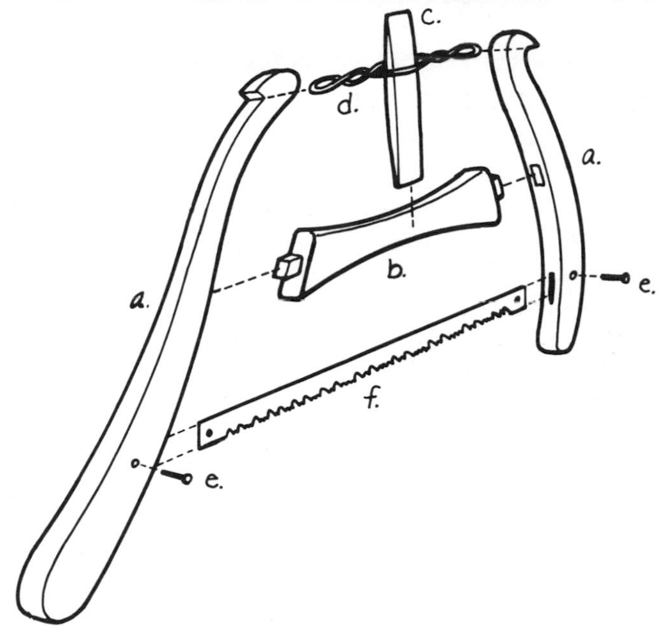

Bucksaw. (a) arms; (b) stretcher; (c) toggle; (d) looped cord; (e,e) pins; (f) blade.

from a 1-inch board. Oak, ash, hard maple, and beech are appropriate woods.

The sides and edges of the finished pieces are shaped and chamfered to reduce weight, for balance, and for feel. But it is a good idea to work with square cross-section stock until the pieces fit properly together. This is a project where eye work, personal judgment, and trial and error are utilized as fairly complex curves and angles come into play.

First lay out the two arms. On a typical saw, the extended arm is 25 inches. The far arm measures 18 inches. Saw or shape the outline with a drawknife and spokeshave. Saw out the stretcher. The arm angles result in a 24-inch stretcher for a standard 30-inch blade. Place the arms, stretcher, and blade in position on a flat surface. This will give the angle of the shouldered tenons on the ends of the stretcher. The tenons needn't be very large, just big enough to hold the arms in place. Three-quarter-inch depth is adequate. To make the tenons, saw the shoulders, then the sides. Finish with a sharp chisel.

Locate the mortises on the insides of the arms. Scribe the outline. Begin by drilling a row of shallow holes within the outline. These are blind mortises, only ¾-inch deep. Finish with a chisel. (Refer to Appendix I: Mortise and Tenon Joinery.) Fit the arms to the stretcher. The fit must be flush and snug.

With the frame members assembled, locate the pins for the blade. Drill the pin holes with a 5/32-inch bit to fit a tenpenny common nail. Outline narrow mortises for the blade slots. In addition to drilling, use a knife and a very narrow chisel to make these slots.

When the blade fits and can be pinned in place, make up a straining cord and the toggle. Wind tight and check that the parts fit properly, and in a flat plane.

Take the saw apart for final shaping and chamfering. This is a matter of taste, but in general, work for light weight and graceful proportions. Work with a drawknife and spokeshave, or a very sharp carving knife. The stretcher can be shaved amazingly thin. The handle should be comfortable. Aim for minimum cross section on the toggle.

Sand the pieces and finish with an oil mixture or varnish.

Turning saw. The main advantage of a turning saw is its ability to cut curves. This is made possible by the narrow blade, which can be rotated to any angle.

Special turning saw blades are sold through various woodworking supply houses. I use a closely toothed band saw blade, cut to length, then drilled with a 1/16-inch hole at each end.

Making a turning saw is essentially like making the bucksaw, except that the arms are perpendicular to the stretcher and are therefore somewhat simpler. The provision for holding and rotating the narrow blade calls for two extra pieces. Extending from each arm is a knob-like cylinder that is often mistaken for a handle. These are used for retaining and rotating the blade. These knobs extend into holes in the arms and can be removed. The saw blade passes into the same hole, through a slot in the knob, and is pinned outside the arm at a wide point on the knob. These pieces are generally turned on a lathe, but can be carved just as well. Symmetry is traditional but not necessary.

The turning saw illustrated was made with applewood arms and an oak straining piece (from a cargo pallet).. The saw works very well for most kinds of scrollwork and is only limited in depth of cut by the location of the straining piece. Saw on a push *or* pull stroke depending on which arm is used for a handle. When not in use the toggle is relaxed one turn.

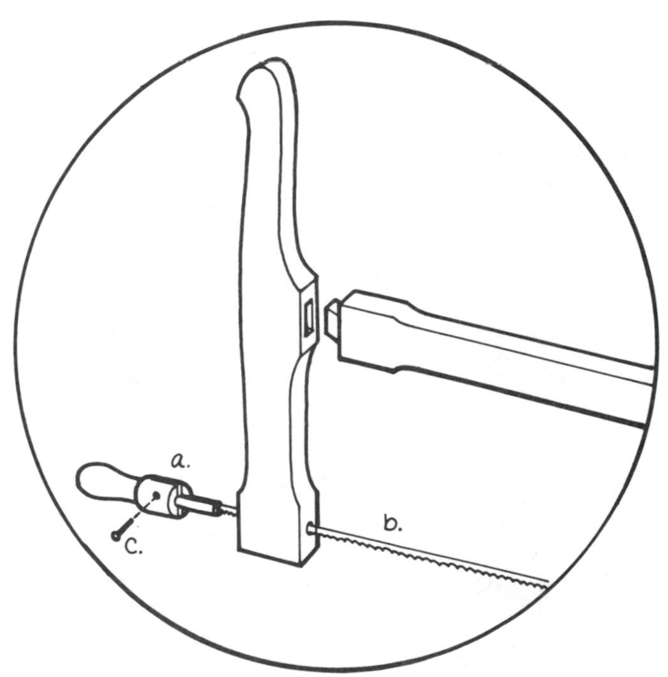

Turning saw mechanism. (a) knob; (b) blade; (c) pin.

Sawing a spoon blank.

Handmade handles.

CHAPTER 9
TOOL HANDLES

AT FIRST THOUGHT tool handles (sometimes called shafts and hafts) seem to be almost inconsequential things. Attention is generally drawn to the steel or iron part of most tools. But an old saying that "the bull is half of the herd" could be applied to tools and tool handles.

I have bought new tools that seemed useless—until I corrected a fault in the handle. An axe head without a handle is little improvement over a hand-held piece of stone. There are also a lot of good, old tools lying around barns and storerooms needing only handles. Some chisel and gouge irons are sold without handles. This saves money and gives the craftsman an opportunity to make handles exactly suited to personal needs. The ultimate "handle" might be a wooden plane.

Tool handles can be divided into two categories: impact handles that absorb shock (as for axes and hammers), and others which mainly provide something convenient to hold (such as chisel or saw handles).

The preferred wood for shock-absorbing tool handles is hickory. USDA Handbook No. 101, *Wood: Color and Kinds,* states: "Some woods are stronger than hickory and others are harder, but the combination of strength, toughness, hardness, and stiffness possessed by hickory has not been found to the same degree in any other commercial wood."

Hickory handles are generally made from green wood. Only clear, straight-grained wood should be used. If a section of the handle is heartwood, it may season at a different coefficient causing the handle to warp. Green hickory handles should be made oversized as they shrink a great deal in thickness; but hardly at all in length. It might take a green hickory handle six to eight weeks of seasoning before it is given final shape and "helved" (fitted) to an axe or hammerhead.

Ash is used for quality tool handles in places where hickory is less prevalent. For tools that require bent hafts (such as scythe snaths), ash is the number one choice. Ash also weighs somewhat less than hickory, so it is preferred for long handles (mainly for garden tools like shovels, rakes, and hoes).

In some parts of Europe, hard maple is considered a fair substitute for hickory or ash axe handles. In England, beech is often used for maul and mallet handles. Scandinavian axes traditionally had birch handles. Froe, hand adze, and hatchet handles can be made from oak.

Wood for handles that don't take much shock should still be relatively hard, but also easy to carve or turn on a lathe. Appropriate woods include beech, maple, dogwood, and apple.

Axe handles. Making a handle for an axe is an elementary project for the country woodworker. After making one by hand, any woodsman will be more considerate of handles than he was previously. Directions for making axe handles cover the same steps as for hammer, adze, froe, and peavey handles. The differences are in detail, rather than technique.

The size and shape of an axe handle is determined by the weight and type of axe head, the use intended, and the craftsman's personal preferences. Single-bit axes traditionally had straight handles. An eighty-five-year-old neighbor who is one of the last old-time mountain farmers of southern Appalachia still makes and prefers to use straight handles on polled axes.

A popular story among "experts" is that curved handles were invented during the pioneer years of the American frontier. This may not be true. It's easier to make a straight shaft, but various curved handles have been found in relics from the Old World. The "dog-leg" haft is supposed to give a polled axe better balance and directional stability. I like making and using curved handles, but there is a danger of weakening if they cross the grain at too much of an angle. Historically the popularity of curved handles coincides with the machine age. To some extent entrepreneurs depended on novelty for sales, and the dog-leg shape lent itself to newly developed manufacturing techniques. Curved handles do "feel right" for certain work, especially on hatchets and axes used for shaping and hewing work. To satisfy the demand for curved axe handles, one manufacturer (Blue Grass) actually bends straight-grained hickory to the popular dog-leg shape. At any rate, one might observe that double-bit axes always have straight handles and suffer none from them.

The swelling at the heel, sometimes called a "doe's foot" or "colt's foot," definitely makes it easier to hold onto an axe, without risk of its slipping loose during use.

The cross section of an axe handle is oval, resulting in a nice, comfortable grip. Axe handles should be made as thin as comfort allows so that weight is centered toward the head. This results in a certain amount of spring or resiliency that adds to the power of a swing and also absorbs shock on impact, saving the handle, cutting edge, and woodsman from wear and tear. Hatchet handles should be somewhat thicker, with a comfortable tight grip as the primary concern.

Just behind the eye section, axe and hammer handles are swollen into a "shoulder." This helps secure the head, and it reinforces the handle at its weakest point.

There are two general approaches taken in handle making. Working green wood is fast and appropriate to making a number of handles at one time. The roughed-out handles need to season a few weeks before being used. The other approach is to shape the handle when needed from preseasoned wood. This requires having narrow split wood on hand as a round of hickory remains green for many months. Working seasoned hickory is more difficult, but the head can be fitted immediately.

Green handles. Start out by locating a hickory (or other suitable tree) wide enough at the butt to fit a handle perpendicular to the annual rings within the sapwood section. Be sure that the butt is straight and free of knots. For large axe hafts it is necessary to fell a tree at least 10 inches in diameter. Plan to make a quantity of handles while the wood is green. Extra handles, shaped quickly and somewhat oversized, can be stored indefinitely, creating the luxury of having several types of seasoned handles on hand whenever one is needed.

After felling (See Chapter 3: Felling) crosscut a bolt several inches longer than the handles that will be needed. Axe handles are generally 21 to 38 inches long. Peavey handles may be 60 inches, although 48 inches is about average.

Split the bolt in half. Quarter one half. And eighth one quarter. (Splitting techniques are detailed in Chapter 14: Pitchforks.) Don't split up all the wood at once as it might season faster than you can work it. Store bolts in a shaded area off the ground to avoid premature seasoning or damp rot.

Take an eighth-sized bolt and cleave off the heartwood. If the bolt is still wider than the planned handle, split again, but leave plenty of working width, especially for the heel of an axe handle, which should measure 1½ inches across. For getting started, a 2-inch width is about right.

Shaping. Many an axe handle has been shaped with a hewing hatchet and jackknife. This is an excellent way to make short, curved handles that cross the grain.

Long or straight handles are easiest to shape with a drawknife.

First square off the bolt, making four reasonably

Carving a hatchet handle.

flat planes to work from. Use a pattern (a flat silhouette made from cardboard or a thin wooden split) or an existing handle to sketch out the profile. Consider the piece of wood from different angles and directions, locating the pattern in the most advantageous position. Be sure that the grain forming the eye section runs parallel, not at an angle.

Handles are usually made on a shaving horse. However, a handle clamp can be made which facilitates this work. Handle clamps resemble a simple lathe, having a fixed end and a movable section that slides along a rail. (The spring-pole lathe described in Chapter 12 can double as a handle clamp.) The work is grasped by steel points pressed into the end grain making it accessible for work along the full length with a drawknife or spokeshave.

The advantage of a handle clamp is that the ends of the wood can be worked toward the center. This can't be done with a drawknife on a shaving horse. The problem for the shaving-horse user comes when the end of a piece has to be flaired outward (i.e., at the heel of an axe handle). When a handle clamp isn't used, a flaired end may be made by holding the piece in a vise. Or hand-hold and shape with a carving knife. For most handle work, the shaving horse works very well.

At first leave the top and bottom planes of the handle flat; just shape the profile. If a vise is available, the initial work can be done with a turning saw. Work a little oversized. This is a purely reductive technique. There is no way to put the chips back together. (As one observer commented, "The work is really the scraps on the floor. Your handle is what's left over.")

With a chalk line snap a center along the top of the handle. Using a caliper and another handle for reference, sketch out the width at various points. Shape with a drawknife.

Go back to the profile, correcting any small variations. Bring the top and bottom planes to exact size. Finally, round out the handle to an oval cross section.

When the handle approaches the desired shape, switch to using a spokeshave. Leave the head end oversized. If the grain reverses back and forth, the drawknife or spokeshave will tend to cut in too deeply and control is lost. Or, the handle may take on a wavy shape as it follows buckles in the grain. In such cases, a rasp can be used to level bumps or to work across troublesome grain. (I like a "shoe rasp"—a four-in-one tool, 8 or 10 inches long, flat on one side, half-round on the other, with a rasp and a bastard file section on each side.)

At this point it's a good idea to stop work. Green hickory shrinks a lot, so there is no point in helving the axe for a few weeks.

Put the handle aside to season. At first leave it in a sheltered place, but not in a dry, warm room—it may crack or warp if seasoned too fast. After a few weeks move the handle indoors, perhaps setting it several feet from a wood-burning stove. To avoid bending, the green handle should be rotated every few days, or hung from a small hook driven into the heel. During seasoning, hickory loses about one-third of its green weight to evaporation. Well seasoned, the wood is considerably harder, and it actually feels dry.

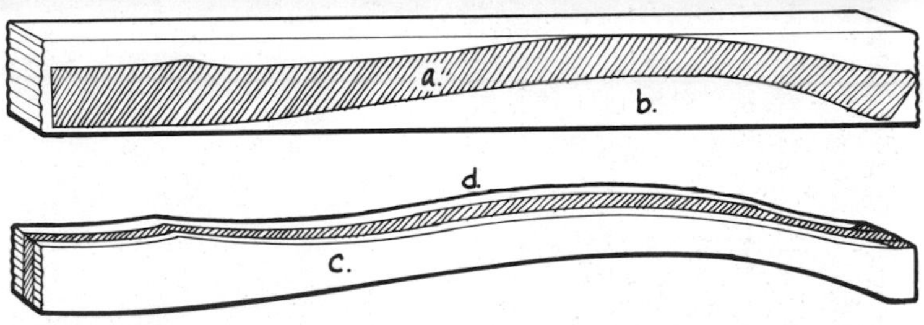

Pattern (a) is traced onto a bolt of straight-grained hickory (b). The profile (c) is sawn out or shaped with a drawknife. Lateral dimensions, indicated by shaded area, are shaped with drawknife or carving knife.

Technique for slicing across the end grain.

Sanding an axe handle.

This is the time to smooth the shaft and helve the axe. Trim to final dimensions with a spokeshave. Smoothing is done with a scraper blade or a piece of broken glass, and sandpaper. Hatchet and adze handles need not be extremely smooth as one's hands remain stationary using these tools. Axe handles, which require a sliding action in use, should be slick and glassy.

At this time the heel is sawed to correct shape, and chamfered around the edge. Use a spokeshave, carving knife, or rasp.

Helving requires care as the axe head must fit snugly along the full length of the eye. It must also have good alignment with the handle. Measure the eye for width and height. Draw vertical and horizontal lines along the axis of the end grain. Sketch out an approximation of the eye shape using measurements from the axe head.

Trim the eye section very carefully with a spokeshave or carving knife. As the fit becomes close you might switch to using a rasp, scraper blade, or piece of broken glass.

To helve an axe or hammer do not pound directly on the head. This can damage the shaft or iron head. Slide the head part way onto the handle. Hold the tool vertically, with the head hanging downward, and strike the heel with a maul. This drives the head tightly into position.

Several test fits are usually necessary. Be careful not to remove excess wood around the end while shaping toward the shoulder. Make sure that the head and handle remain in alignment. Just before the final

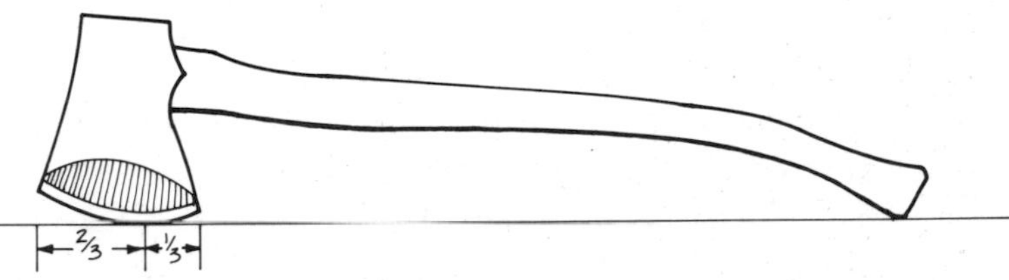

Properly hung woodsman's axe.

helving, saw a fine slot through the axis of the handle tip, 2 or 3 inches deep, to accept a wooden wedge.

Check the "hang" of a woodshed axe by placing it on a flat surface, with the cutting edge of the bit and heel making contact. On a correctly hung axe, the point of contact of the curved bit will be two-thirds behind the leading corner. This rule does not apply to axes and hatchets used for shaping or hewing work.

Drive the head up snug to the shoulder. Make a wooden wedge the full width of the slot, but somewhat longer. (See Chapter 10: Wedges.) Apply a bit of white glue to the sides of the wedge. Tap in place with a small mallet. If the head is at all loose it can be tightened by driving a small iron wedge (made in axe and hammer sizes) across the wooden wedge.

Finish axe handles with three or four coats of linseed oil or varnish. Between each application of varnish, sand lightly to give "tooth" to the succeeding coat. (Refer to Appendix II: Wood Finishes.)

Seasoned handles. The sequence for making seasoned handles differs from working green wood in that the head is test-fitted early in the shaping process—immediately after basic roughing out. With head in place it's easier to align the shaft and check for balance and feel as work progresses. The shaping technique is the same as in making green handles.

Peavey Handles. In woodcraft jargon axes and hammers are "helved", whereas peaveys are "stocked." Regardless, fitting a handle to the tapered ferrule of a peavey iron is a different operation than fitting eye-headed tools.

The procedure for making a peavey handle is basically the same as in shaping an axe handle. (However, this is a handle that is perfectly round, so it can be turned on a lathe.) The wood used should be hickory or ash, and it should be green when the work is done. Because of excessive shrinkage, the diameter must be kept oversized, as much as ½ inch at the widest section

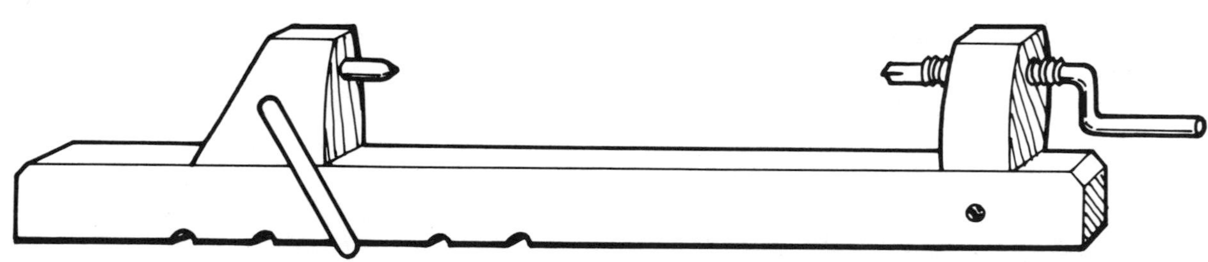

Handle maker's clamp. May be secured in bench vise.

of the ferrule. (It can easily be trimmed down after seasoning.) The spike hole should be drilled while the wood is green. Auger bits can be used even though they are not well adapted for boring into the end grain of seasoned hardwoods. To match the tapering shank it is necessary to bore a series of holes, beginning with the smallest diameter.

After seasoning (perhaps 6 weeks) take the handle and iron parts to a blacksmith's forge. Remove the hook from the ferrule. Heat the ferrule red-hot and drive into place on the handle. Immediately quench it in water to prevent charring the handle. Place the cold spike in the hole and pound it into place using a hollow drift (such as a small piece of cast-iron pipe).

If the hook is dull, heat red-hot and draw out a new point. Then retemper. Forge-shaping is preferable to grinding. A better shape can be made, and with almost no loss of material. If only a grinding wheel or file is available, reshape the inside of the hook. Do not grind the outside as this impairs the grabbing angle of the hook.

Chisel and gouge handles can be carved or turned on a lathe. Handles for small carving tools are traditionally octagonal in cross section. This shape is easy to make and gives a good grip. Carving tools with octagonal handles will not roll around when placed on a table.

Octagonal handles may be carved from any fine-grained hardwood such as beech, dogwood, holly, or fruit wood. Split out straight-grained blanks from seasoned wood. Saw to length. Drill a slightly undersized hole as deep as the tang is long. Taper the hole with a reamer or by redrilling it with a tapered bit or with a series of gradually larger bits. (See *Round Handles* below.) Drive on the blank to within ½ inch of the hilt. Rough out the handle with the iron in place. This assures straight alignment. Mark the face and the iron for alignment, then remove the iron.

Fill the handle hole with water to soften the wood. With a cold chisel, nick the corners of the tang toward the tip making small barbs.

A shock-absorbing leather disk is then cut to fit over the tang. It should be made of sole leather, with a hole punched through the center, and dampened before fitting.

Finish shaping the handle to an octagonal cross section with a comfortable, rounded pommel. Drive into place. Sand smooth. Soak the entire handle, including leather, in linseed oil overnight.

Round handles for firmer and mortise chisels and stout gouges are often turned on a lathe. These should be reinforced at the tang and heel to avoid splitting from pounding with mallets. Commercial handles are made with brass or steel rings that are tightly fitted against shoulders at both ends. An alternative is to wind stout cord around the tang and striking sections. Braided nylon fishing line sealed with epoxy works nicely. (Not traditional; but a craftsman should be open to new ideas.) Regardless of the method of reinforcement, shape the shoulders like commercial handles. A further refinement is the placement of a shock-absorbing leather disk between the tang and handle.

Boring the tang holes is somewhat tricky. The problem is to drill a parallel hole so that the iron fits in proper alignment. Without a specially set up drill press, this becomes something of a chancy operation. The best that one can do is to hold the handle vertically in a vise, then drill very cautiously, continually checking alignment from two perpendicular angles.

You can use tapered drills made for countersinking wood screws. These come in seven screw sizes ranging from number 5 to 12. For a good, snug fit, drill tang holes undersized. Slip the iron loosely in place and rotate to the point of best alignment. Then tap the striking end of the handle with a mallet or against a work table to drive the tang home.

A gob of epoxy will secure tangs in oversized holes.

File handles are easy to make. But often they are not fitted, which results in numerous injuries to palms and fingers. First a guard made of brass, copper, or heavy leather should be slipped over the tang. This will protect fingers from becoming meat if the file slips while sharpening edge tools. Handles may be carved or turned. A workable expedient is simply jamming a dry corncob on the tang.

Saw handles. One seldom must make a new saw handle. But saw handles occasionally break. And some new saws are sold with uncomfortable or especially unattractive plywood, plastic, or metal handles that cry for replacement. Anyway, I like making saw handles. Here's a chance to experiment with different shapes, such as the fanciful designs used by cabinetmakers of the past.

Panel saws, such as carpenter's, keyholes, and one-man crosscuts, use handles cut and shaped from milled lumber. Maple and beech are most commonly used. The wood must be flat and well seasoned. Planed thickness varies between ¾ and ⅞ inch.

Pencil the outline on an appropriate blank with the handle facing in line with the grain. The pattern may be taken from a favorite saw or improvised. Use the saw to mark the depth of the blade slot. In most cases, the slot will be sawn with a crosscut or tenon saw as a 4½-point ripsaw would make too wide a kerf. Experiment on a test block with different saws, choosing a kerf that holds the blade snug.

It is imperative that the slot is sawn parallel with the handle. Set a marking gauge for half the wood thickness minus half the kerf of one slot. Scribe the slot on the blank. Saw carefully, being sure to work exactly along the waste edge of the scribed line. First saw the leading edge. Saw part way down one side. Reverse the blank and saw down the other side. (Refer to the diagram for sawing tenons illustrated in Appendix I: Mortise and Tenon Joinery.) Fit the blade in place to check the depth of the slot and its alignment.

The handle blank is next sawed out with a turning saw (described in Chapter 8: Bow Saws). Saw on pull *or* push stroke, with saw teeth cutting into the work. When rotating spindles, be sure that the blade remains flat. A parabolic twist in the blade makes the saw uncontrollable. Saw curves gradually. Tight corners are made by sawing "in place," gradually rotating the frame. Saw the handle slightly oversized. With practice one will develop a knack with the turning saw and suddenly intricate shapes are made quite easily.

Bore a ½-inch hole within the outlined handhold. Relax tension from the turning saw and remove one keeper pin. Slip blade through hole. Pin the blade and rewind the windlass. Saw out the handhold.

Continue shaping with a half-round rasp or file or a 4-in-1 shoe rasp. Deep curves are shaped with a rat-tail rasp and finished with a round file. Work on push strokes only. Scrubbing back and forth roughens the wood and dulls tools. Most saw handles are shaped with a curved bevel around the handhold, top, bottom, and back sides, with flat bevels along the leading edge joining the saw blade.

Drill screw holes in appropriate places.

Sand and finish with two or three coats of varnish, or rub in several coats of oil, allowing at least one day between applications.

Wedges, left to right: The two large wedges are gluts, used in splitting logs. The flat wedges are tapered keys, for securing mortise and tenon joinery. The wedge with the dotted line shows how small handle wedges are taken from a lath. The two large, narrow wedges are used in felling work, to avoid pinching the saw, and to help control the direction of fall.

CHAPTER 10
WEDGES

THE TRADITIONAL WOODWORKER has many uses for wedges of different sizes and shapes. Small, flat wedges secure hammer and axe heads and "fox-tailed" mortise and tenon joints. Keys and tusk tenons are wedges set perpendicularly through tapered slots in tenon stubs that protrude through larger mortises. These joints are tightened by pounding down the key, or quickly taken apart by removing the key, then slipping the tenon from its mortise. (The spring-pole lathe described in Chapter 12 incorporates several keyed mortise and tenon joints.) Gluts are large wooden wedges, used for splitting logs. Timber wedges are used to open the kerf of a felling cut during tree harvesting.

The trick in making wedges is holding onto the material in order to do the shaping work, which in itself is very easy. Because of the tapered shape and direction of the grain, wedges are awkward things to hold. The solution is to make wedges from extra long stock, then saw them to size after shaping work is finished.

The degree of taper is the most important factor determining how well a wedge will work. Wedges, keys, and gluts will tend to work loose, or suddenly pop

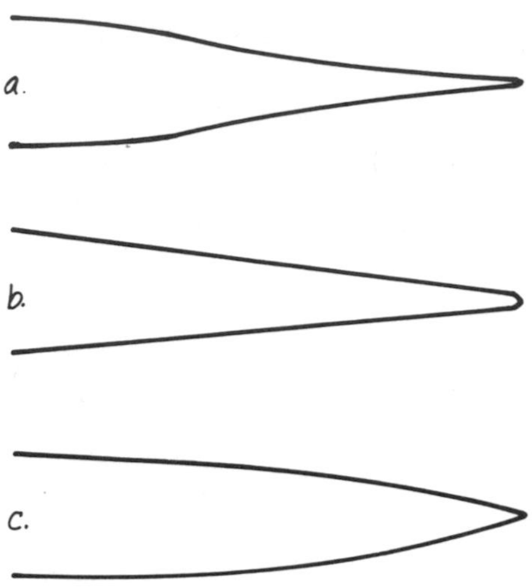

Wedge and glut profiles. Concave shape of (a) tends to pop loose. Straight sides with a blunted tip (b) make good contact and stay in place. Convex shape (c) only makes contact on leading half and often works loose.

out if they bulge or are shaped too obtusely. The general rule is to make the beveled angle as slight as is practically possible.

The beveled sides of a wedge must be flat. If the profile bows outward, only the mid-section makes contact; the back part of the wedge is loose and useless. A concave profile tends to drive in part way, then pop loose where the curve begins to widen.

With any type of wooden wedge, the leading edge should be given a very blunt, obtuse angle in order to avoid splintering when being driven in place.

Small wedges and keys can be made of any convenient, straight-grained hardwood. For gluts, use the toughest wood available.

Small wedges for handles and furniture work are made from long, thin strips of wood kept specially for the purpose. Wedges should be made as wide as possible. The wood must be thoroughly seasoned, or the driven wedge will shrink and be useless for holding tools or joints together. Shape wedges off one end of the stock as needed. This way, there is plenty of material to hold onto under the shaving-horse jaw.

Work the stock (which might be 1 x ¼ inch in cross section) with a drawknife to the approximate wedge shape. The material might flex or wobble in the shaving horse. If so, place a narrow stick, such as a 1 x 2, about 2 feet long, between the work ledge and wedge material. Let the stick extend well in front of the jaw. This extension provides a tight hold and plenty of room for drawknife maneuvering.

After roughing out, the bevels are flattened. This is

quick work with a rasp, used first rough side, then smooth. Be sure that the rasp is worked *flat* across the entire side. Leave the edge blunt.

To finish up, cut off the wedge with a fine-tooth saw and put an obtuse bevel across the leading edge.

Wedges may also be carved from overlength stock with a sharp jackknife. Again, be careful to make flat sides, perhaps using a rasp to finish up.

To place a wedge, first saw a slot into the handle or tenon. A narrow-bladed saw, such as a small backsaw, works best. Apply a bit of white glue to the sides. Then carefully drive the wedge into place with a small mallet. A hammer might split or tear the wedge apart.

Keys are made from straight-grained hardwood boards resawn to size. Carefully rip to the thickness of the tapered mortise. A curved drawknife or scrub plane can also be used. The bevel of the tapered slot should be minimal, perhaps ¼ inch for every 2 inches of length. Be sure to make the bevel flat, or it won't hold properly. After sawing to length, the outside corner of the large end should be slightly rounded or chamfered to avoid splintering when the key is driven into place.

Make gluts in pairs, back to back. This leaves a wide center section for holding in the shaving-horse jaws. A typical glut is 2½ to 3 inches in diameter, and 12 to 15 inches long. Off-setting the tapers of the back-to-back gluts 90 degrees to one another results in adequate space to grip along the side of the rear glut.

Use straight lengths of saplings or limbs from hornbeam, hickory, dogwood, beech, or other tough hardwood. Cut the sections about 6 inches longer than the

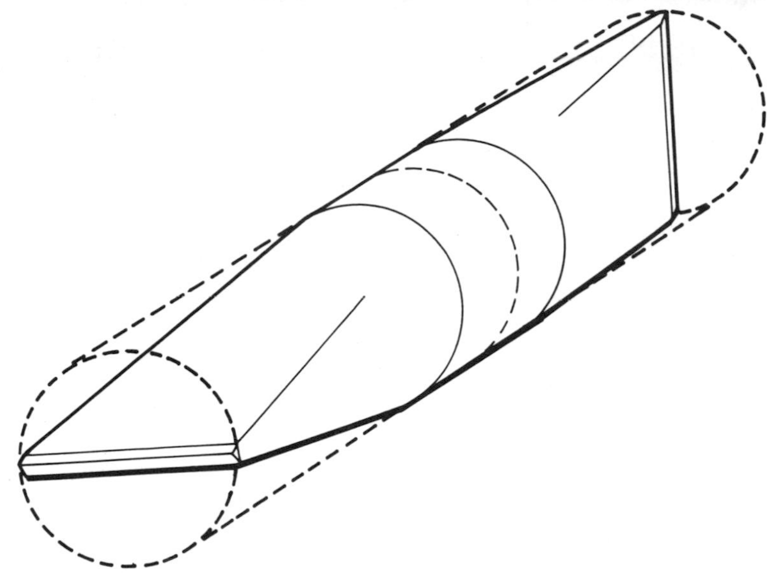

Two gluts can be carved back to back from a hardwood sapling. The perpendicular twist results in parallel sides for holding in a shaving horse or bench vise. Another method is to shape gluts from an overlength pole, sawing each glut loose as finished.

final pair of gluts (30 inches for two 12-inch gluts) and set aside to season a few months. Checks generally develop along the end grain of heavy woods. These are sawed off before making up the gluts.

To start, sketch a center line across the end grain as a guide. Shaping is done with a drawknife, smoothing with a spokeshave.

After both gluts are shaped (one angled perpendicular to the other), saw the two apart. Chamfer the heads all the way around to avoid splintering in use. Put a blunt bevel across the leading edge.

Gluts should be thoroughly seasoned so that they are really hard and tough before using. (Of course, many gluts have been cobbled up right in the woods; but these usually splinter rather quickly.) Don't oil the beveled sides of gluts. They won't hold as well, and may even pop out.

An all-purpose workbench.

CHAPTER 11
THE WORKBENCH

EVEN A SHAVING HORSE NUT, such as myself, will readily admit that a workbench has advantages unexcelled for certain types of work. In the best of worlds, shaving horse and workbench are complementary. The shaving horse is suitable for drawknife work, and can be built easily without using commercial materials or hardware. The workbench is a more sophisticated device, demanding considerable care and planning in construction and, usually, an investment for timber and hardware, including one or two (expensive) vises. The lumber used is generally selected-grade hardwood, properly seasoned. There is nothing like a flat, solid surface, at just the right height, for such work as planing, chiseling, precise sawing, or layout and assembly work. These requirements result in a very special piece of shop furniture.

By "workbench" I refer to the traditional joiner's bench; a long, narrow table, waist high, very heavily constructed, and made to exacting specifications. Commercially manufactured benches may be purchased complete with front and end vises, recessed tool tray, and built-in drawers. Prices range from about $250 to over

$500. However, I think it's fun, and appropriate, for a craftsman to build his own workbench. It may be difficult to obtain beech, the preferred wood of continental bench makers. But a variety of other timbers are suitable, such as oak (preferably white oak because the pores are naturally filled making it impervious to moisture) or maple. Southern yellow pine would also make a good workbench. The built-in end vise featured on imported benches would be hard to fabricate. However, a good conventional vise with a built-in extendable "dog" may be mounted as a suitable tail vise. One should be able to build a fine workbench, possibly not as elaborate as

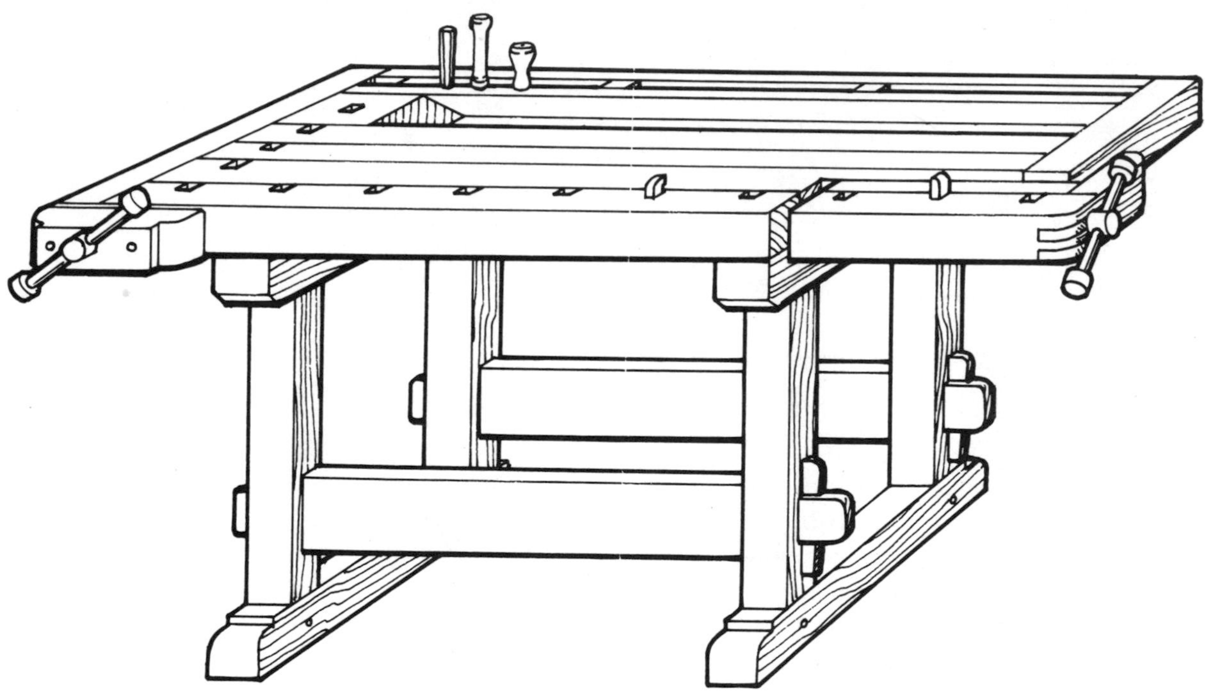

Workbench with built-in front and tail vises. Typically made of 3- to 4-inch-thick beech. The rear section includes a recessed tool tray and a narrow slot for chisels, saws, etc.

the manufactured ones, but just as useful, using only hand tools and care in construction. A good bit of money will be saved, even after buying select lumber and the hardware, including a pair of quality vises.

The old peasant workbench was, in fact, just a bench. It was nothing but a plank supported by three or four legs. Three legs won't wobble on an uneven floor. However, a three-legged bench tips over easier than one with four legs. Generally the bench was straddled, with work secured in front of the craftsman by pegs or wedges. Often special jigs were built into the bench. An elaborate type evolved into the shaving horse. (One interim arrangement was a cooper's bench using a loop of twine, worked by foot action, that held the work fast to a rounded form set on the bench top.) Some rural craftsmen never used a bench, but simply worked on the end grain of a stump, either naturally rooted in place, dug in, or well balanced. Homemade jigs were often driven into the ground, or attached to living trees. Carvers could sit anywhere.

The work benches that we have nowadays are a development of urban joiners and so came to country craftspeople at a rather late date. The joiner, who used planes as far back as ancient Rome, needed a flat surface upon which to secure his work. The German word for workbench is *hoblebank,* literally plane bench. When I studied with Herr Kohler, the *Meister* would often show how certain steps were accomplished on the shaving horse, before the rural coopers had modern benches.

Popularization of the workbench followed the industrial development and subsequent marketing of

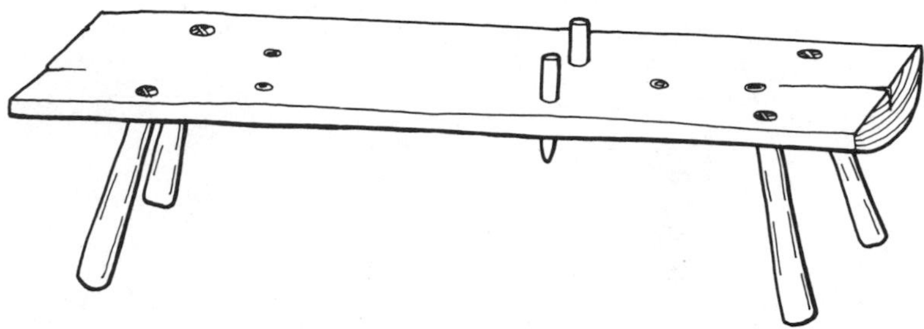

A simple workbench.

An unusual, but useful bench. (From the North Carolina mountains.)

steel-screw vises. Previously, vises had massive wooden screws. Making these screws was a special skill, one that few craftsmen were prepared to undertake.

Over the last few years, I've made two workbenches, and I am presently building a third. All of these benches are dimensioned similarly: waist-high, long and narrow for placement against a shop wall. The differences lie in methods of construction and weight of materials. Any one of these workbenches would serve the needs of most woodworkers. Dimensions range in width from 20 to 25 inches, and in length from 60 to 85 inches. The height is 33 to 35 inches. I'm 5 feet 8 inches, so a taller worker might want a higher bench. Legs can always be shortened.

Each bench has a long, narrow tool tray recessed along the rear edge. My second and third benches have a series of square holes arranged in line with the two vises. These hold "dogs" for securing long material across the bench top. (Mainly for planing or chisel work.) Another feature is a long, narrow slot running along the back. This is used to hold saws, chisels, and screwdrivers.

In building a workbench, use materials that are as heavy as practicality and budget allow. There is an amazing difference when chiseling or pounding on a heavy bench. A light bench may be sturdy, but it will always vibrate and move around during vigorous work. It's not necessary to bolt a heavy workbench to the floor. It should stay in place, unless one purposely moves it, which is sometimes necessary when assembling large panels, or for clamping along the back edge.

Bench tops may be up to 3½ inches thick. One and one-half inches is minimal. Legs are generally dressed 4 x 4s. Lumber should be carefully selected for clear, straight grain and few, if any, knots (which must be small and well encased). If possible use quartersawn lumber. Slash-grain wood is more likely to warp and isn't as strong as edge-grain material. Green lumber should be seasoned in a well-ventilated shed, with stickers, pieces of 1 x 1, between the flat stacked boards for air circulation. This may take as long as one year per inch of thickness. Before construction, the wood should be brought indoors for a few months for final moisture stabilization.

Half-lap workbench. My version of this bench was Douglas fir. Not ideal, but adequate for general carpentry. The rails are attached to the legs by bolts. Each rail and leg is half-lapped at the joint. This makes a very sturdy framework. The tabletop boards are bolted up through the frame rails with hex-headed lag bolts.

The 4 x 4 legs are chamfered on the edges and across the feet. This gives a lighter appearance, and helps to protect the legs when the bench is relocated or if heavy objects are moved around the bench. Bolt holes are countersunk so that no protruding hardware can catch clothing or get in the way.

Butt joint workbench. The second bench is made of oak, with a "slicker" although by no means superior joinery technique. The rail ends butt flat against the legs, and are held tightly in place by bolts and nuts in tension passing through the members. A ⅜-inch dowel

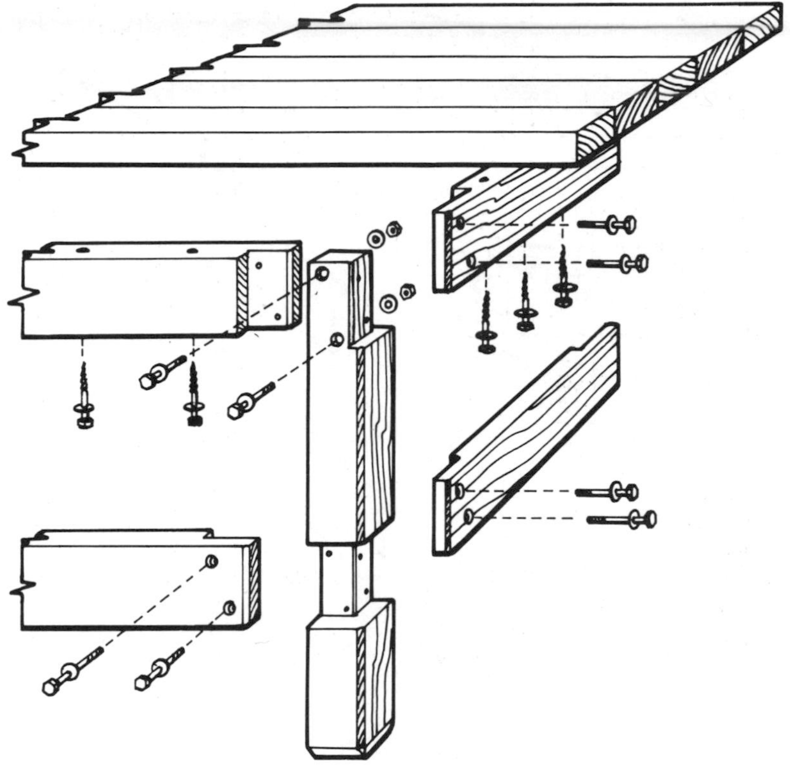

Detail of half-lap framed workbench. The upper front rail is bolted inboard from the post, providing an overhang useful for clamping.

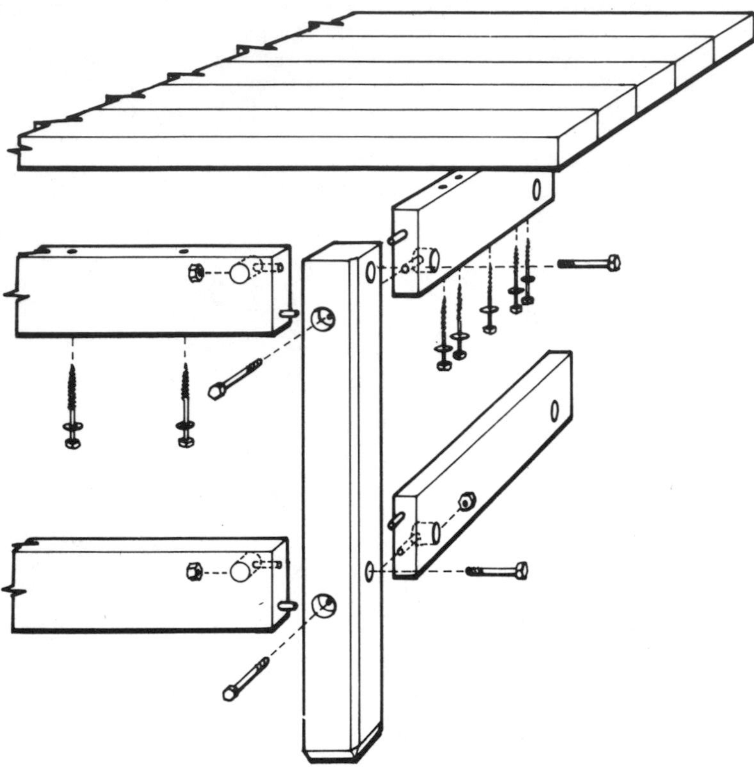

Detail of butt-joint framed workbench. Small dowels (⅜″ x 3″) help to locate each rail in correct alignment.

keeps each rail "joint" in alignment.

In building this bench (or any other piece of furniture using hand tools and techniques), number or label all of the parts as they are fabricated so that they will fit together properly during assembly. It is only when parts are made using machine tools that they are truly interchangeable. When drilling the bolt holes with brace and bit, use an auger 1/16-inch larger than the bolts to be used. Use a square to check alignment at right angles as soon as the drill begins to self-feed. With auger bits, it's possible to correct alignment angle during the first inch of boring. Dowel centers can be used to help match rail holes to leg holes.

These joints, which must be cut accurately square, create a frame free from any wobble. But the engineering suffers in the strength of the rails as load-supporting members. This fault may be alleviated by eliminating the upper front and rear rails and using a very heavy, laminated tabletop, at least 2½ inches thick. The top is then bolted to the upper end rails only. This is the approach taken by most commercial bench makers. A further advantage is that the lack of upper lengthwise rails results in more space for edge clamping. It's also easy to hang a drawer from the bench undersides.

Keyed mortise and tenon workbench. My new bench will use the modified layout of the second bench (no lengthwise top rails) and a heavy 3½-inch laminated work surface. The other difference is that the joinery requires no commercial hardware as each element is secured by mortise and tenon work, with keyed wedges and pegs. Joinery details are identical with the system followed in making the spring-pole lathe (Chapter 12).

Workbench construction. First make a set of measured drawings and a list of needed materials. If wood is purchased green, it should be seasoned before planing or making up the different elements. The tabletop should be built from several pieces, even if this means ripping wood that was purchased in impressive widths, then planing the edges of the new pieces and gluing them back together.

The work must be done precisely. A workbench is a large, cumbersome object, but the flatness of the table and the squareness of dimensions will be reflected in projects for years to come.

A laminated tabletop is not necessary. But it is somewhat stronger and is much nicer to work on. There are no little cracks for screws or brads to get caught in, and it's far easier to keep clean. Before gluing up the boards, plane the edges until they fit quite perfectly. If regluing ripped planking, alter the end grain angles so that the original pattern isn't duplicated. This helps to eliminate the possibility of warping. Number the matching edges because hand planing will generally be slightly uneven. Before assembly, notch the dog mortises along the board edges, and hollow out the tool tray. (Or fabricate from lighter stock.) It's a good idea to insert dowels between each board. This simplifies gluing. Be careful. Lack of accuracy causes more problems than the dowels solve. These pegs can be slightly barrel-shaped, so that they fit tightly at the board junctions, but are slightly undersized within their sockets. This accommodates slight errors in drilling the dowel holes; a dif-

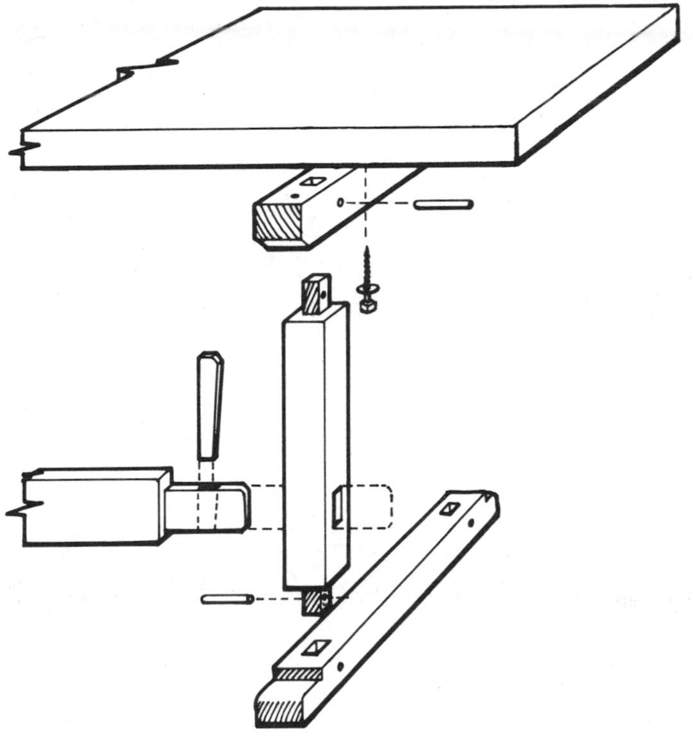

Detail of mortise and tenon construction. An offset dowel is driven through each leg tenon to tighten the fit. Keyed wedges secure the tenoned trestle. The bench top is held with lag bolts.

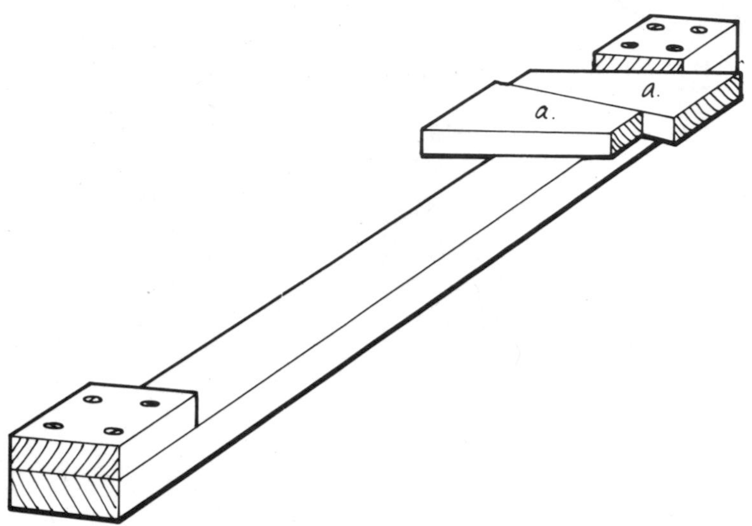

Homemade bar clamp using two wedges (a,a) driven against each other.

ficult thing to do perfectly by hand and eye.

When it comes to gluing, have everything ready and neatly organized. Remove debris and stuff that might get in the way. Work in a clean, sawdust-free environment. This operation takes advance planning and efficiency. Otherwise things get messed up.

Use a slow-drying, waterproof glue, such as plastic resin glue. Have lots of long clamps on hand, at least six. Bar clamps that fit on threaded pipes work fine.

It's also easy to make long clamps. Nail two small blocks of wood to a 2 x 4. Make the distance between them about 3 inches greater than the width of the tabletop. Saw out a pair of long, thin wedges. The "clamp" is set across the boards, then the pair of wedges is driven into the space at one end, with the wedge points crossing so as to form an adjustable plane parallel to the bench. This old method works just as well as manufactured clamps.

(In another system each board is identically drilled with four to six holes through the width. Rods which are threaded at each end are run through the boards, tightened up with nuts, and left permanently in place. Glue should also be used.)

The major difficulty in gluing up a tabletop is avoiding warping or buckling while tightening the clamps. Use a straight edge to check for flatness as the clamps are tightened. Thick boards stay aligned better than thin boards. Warping is partially avoided by using clamps on both sides of the tabletop, so that each set counteracts the other. (Gluing procedure is discussed in Chapter 28: A Farmhouse Table.)

After the bench is assembled there are scraping, sanding, and other touches to look after. A tough finish, such as three or four coats of urethane varnish can be applied. Or simply oil. Finally, the vises are bolted on. Be sure that the jaws are squarely lined up, as poorly installed vises don't grip as well as they're meant to.

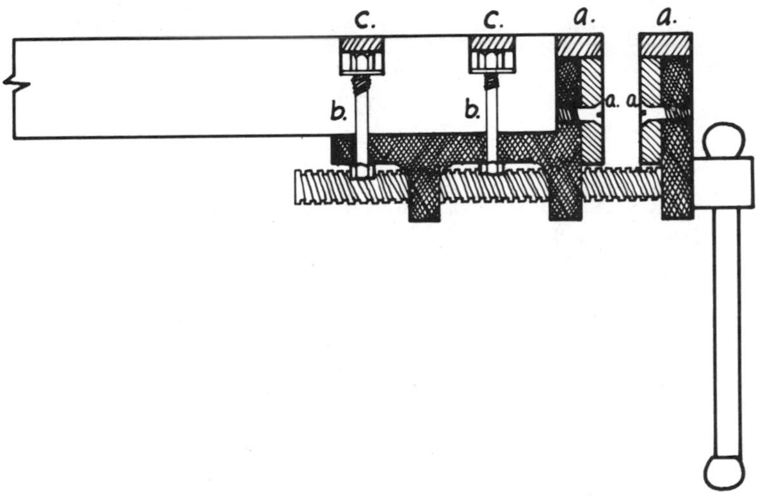

Correct mounting for wood vises. (a,a,a,a) indicate two-piece inner jaws. Bolts (b,b) are countersunk and capped with wood plugs (c,c).

BEFORE VISES

Before the popularization of screw vises (which were apparently invented in the seventeenth century), craftsmen used a variety of holding devices to secure their material. Many country craftsworkers have never adopted modern vises. The woodland craftsmen had their "brakes," "monkeys," and "horses," many of peculiar design and all of local make. The old village craftsmen also had a variety of devices for securing work for planing, chiseling, and sawing.

Most old workbenches have a variety of peg holes, often square shaped, which were used in various ways. One or two pegs, set very low, were used to hold a board for planing. Another pair of pegs could be located at right angles to keep the work from side-slipping. The front peg (a) called a "dog," might have an iron top plate with teeth cut in it to hold the work better.

A simple rig used to hold wood for sawing is a "bench rest" (b). This consists of a pair of boards with cleats at each end, but on opposite sides. These are set against the front edge of the workbench. The piece of lumber to be sawn is placed across the bench rest, against the rear cleats. The wood is then held firmly in place with one's left hand during sawing.

A "hold down" (c) is used to secure wood on

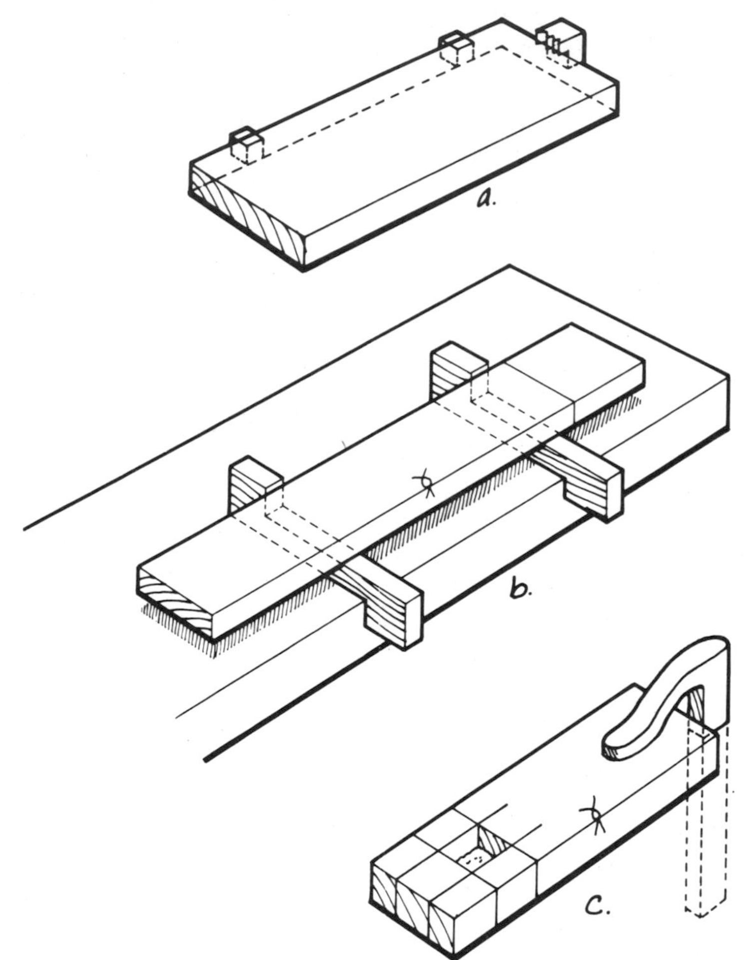

(a) dogs; (b) bench rest; (c) holdfast.

a benchtop for chiseling or mortise work. This device, made by a blacksmith, resembles an upside-down, L-shaped piece of iron. The stem is jammed into a hole with the extension pressing hard against the workpiece.

A good way to hold material for gouge work, especially large, awkward objects like dough troughs, is to set the piece onto a partially filled sandbag. The outside can often be worked by placing the stock against two pegs protruding from the benchtop.

Furniture and cabinetmakers have different types of miters used for sawing boards at precise angles. A simple miter (d) for sawing square and 45-degree angles can be made by screwing a small

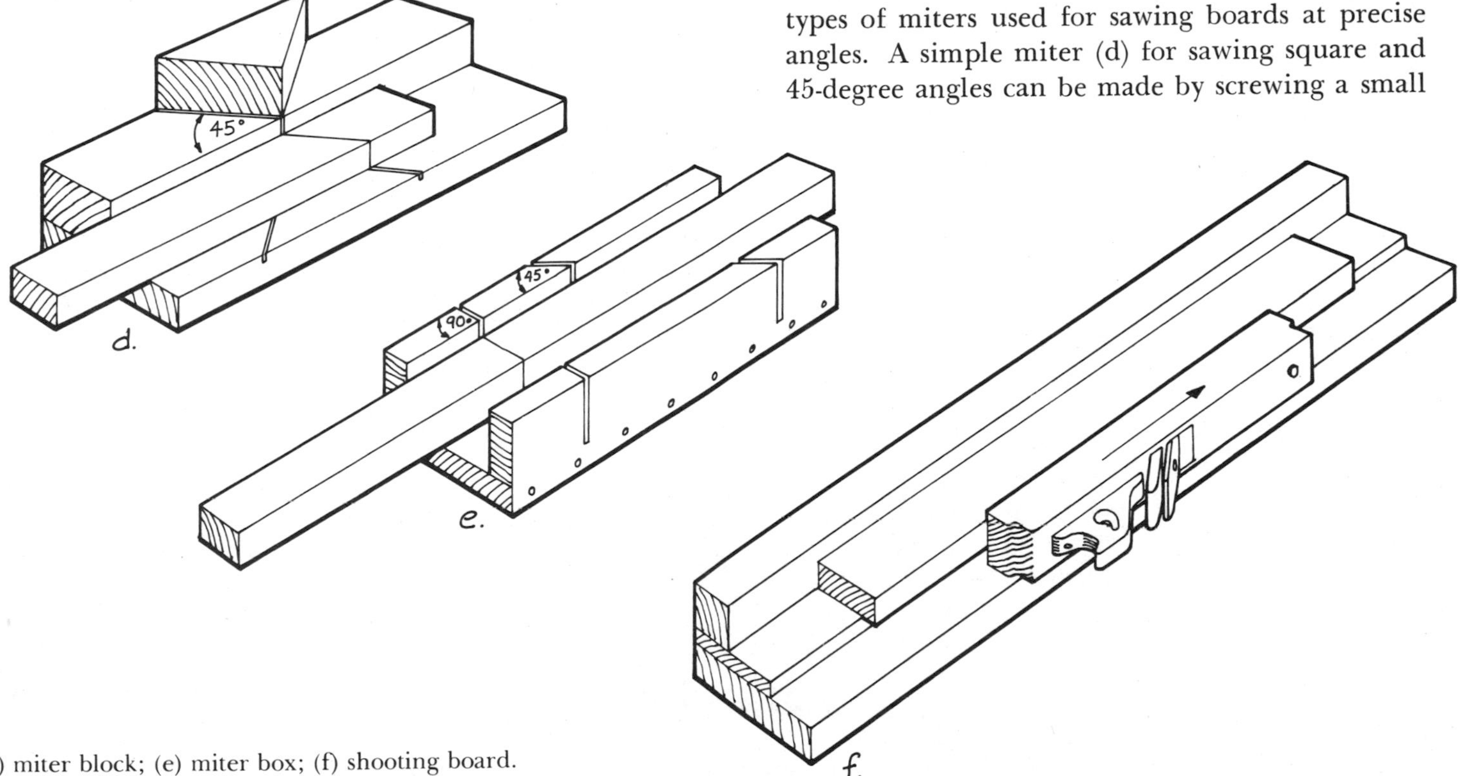

(d) miter block; (e) miter box; (f) shooting board.

block, cut at the precise angle needed, onto two stepped boards. A variation is the well-known miter box (e). Three straight boards are glued or screwed to make a U-channel. Then, very carefully sawn cuts at 90- and 45-degree angles (or any other angle that might be needed), are made through the box sides straight down and slightly into the base board. An aid in making these cuts perpendicular to the sides is to tack a small piece of square stock on top of the channel to act as a saw guide. Both forms of miters are used by holding the work against the backboards, then sawing down along the slotted guides.

The task of planing panel edges to an exact right angle may be simplified with a "shooting board" (f). This is a long, straight plank, with a narrow and thinner board glued on top. The piece to be planed is clamped on top of the upper board, or there is an additional narrow strip attached in back to act as a stop. A long plane is placed on its side, then automatically guided at a precise right angle by the bottom board. Shooting boards are nice to use where flat edges are joined together (tabletops, bucket bottoms, etcetera).

BENCH VISES

The invention and gradual adoption of the woodworker's vise is quite recent when compared to other hand tools. Development depended on the screw, which required precise thread making. Few craftsmen could carve them. Others used a die, similar to the kinds used for threading pipe, only much larger, and with a wooden body. Expert turners could make a screw on a lathe. A round dowel was first turned. The pitch was marked out at four points with a ruler or divider, and penciled in spiraling around the dowel. A shallow saw cut was next made following the penciled lines. The piece was set in the lathe and a diamond-point chisel used to cut the threads, following the saw cut. And I once heard a story about an Appalachian woodworker who turned large screws used for cider mills. This man set a small log between two spindles, wound a rope around the log, then commanded his mule to pull the rope as he worked on the rotating log. Eventually, steel screws could be bought from urban manufacturers.

In addition to the screw it is necessary to secure the jaw so that the vise remains more or less parallel to the bench face. An old solution utilized two screws, both loosely set through the front jaw so that first one may be tightened a little, then the other.

Homemade leg vise.

Another design, basically a variation of a blacksmith's vise, has the jaw extended into a leg which rests on the floor where it is pinned to another board acting as a guide. As the vise is opened, the guide board must be adjusted by relocating a second pin passing through a bench leg. The advantage of this vise is that the jaw can carry a great load, such as that of heavy pounding, without the screw being damaged or the vise being ripped off the workbench. With this design the screw is fitted somewhat loosely, which is advantageous for clamping irregular workstuff.

The "leg vise" is easy to build and handy to have around a farm shop. Screws may be purchased from several sources, or parts may be salvaged from an old vise or piece of machinery. The wooden parts are usually sawmill lumber.

Modern bench vises use a central screw flanked by two spindles that serve as guides for the jaw and a support for the work load. Older vises of this pattern were all wood. The screw might be 3 inches in diameter, with two 2-inch square guides. On newer vises, the jaw is sometimes wood, but usually it's a machined iron casting with wooden liners. The ultimate models feature a special ratchet thread that can be instantly released for quick repositioning. The solid steel spindles on large vises are a full inch in diameter. Some vises also have a built-in sliding "dog" that can be used in conjunction with another dog fitted into one of the several mortises on the bench top. These large vises are expensive, but they are made to provide long, hard service. Less dear vises can be had; however, cheap materials and poor machining often result in a purchase that can be more frustrating than useful. For instance, the jaw depth of cheap vises is limited to 2 to 2½ inches. Deep jaws are needed to support heavy or long materials. If the jaws are not parallel, they will not grip well. Quality vises are marked by massive screws and spindles and generous iron castings.

An interesting variation of the bench vise is found on some workbenches made in Denmark. The design is really quite old: Estonian woodworkers were using similar vises toward the end of the nineteenth century. Conceptually, the conven-

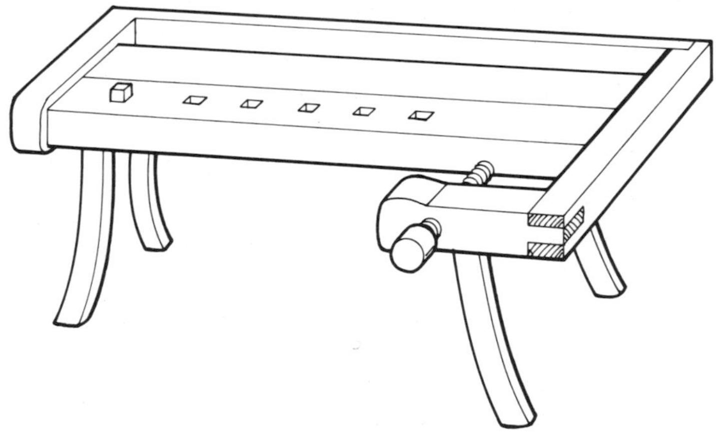

Estonian joiner's bench. (Probably late nineteenth century.)

tional vise is turned inside out: An elbow extends from one end of the bench. The screw and spindles pass through this piece. On the inside a pressure plate and on the outside an end plate maintain alignment. The advantage of this elaborate design is that the screw and spindles in no way obstruct the jaw. This results in greater holding power for large vertical pieces and for certain kinds of carving and furniture work. On the other hand, it's impossible to hold large material horizontally with these vises, especially for sawing. The design is excellent for certain woodworkers, very limiting to others.

Some traditional craftsmen (such as wheelrights) prefer a machinist's vise rather than the so-called wood vise. The machinist's vise holds the piece well above the benchtop in small but powerful jaws. This makes it much easier to do certain kinds of shaping work with a drawknife, spokeshave, or chisel and mallet. The work is at a better height; one needn't hunker down so much. And knuckles don't bump into the bench top as often happens using a drawknife with a wood vise. A further advantage is that the machinist's vise is mounted on top of the workbench, often directly over one of the legs. This makes it suitable for very heavy work. As part of the installation, the standard knurled steel liners are replaced with similarly shaped hardwood blocks.

Spring-pole lathe.

CHAPTER 12
A SPRING-POLE LATHE

THE USE OF TURNING LATHES originates somewhere in the back corners of unwritten history. The concept is simple: a stick is rotated between two spindles while a cutting tool is applied, thus producing a perfectly symmetrical object. Commonly turned woodenware includes bowls, chair and table legs, and various parts of spinning wheels. Mallets and some tool handles are also turned. Modern lathes that work on an eccentric principle can shape complicated ovular shapes such as rifle stocks.

Early lathes may have been inspired by potter's wheels. In some areas turning might have originated with the metal arts. Bronze can be turned at relatively low spindle speeds.

The technological history of turnery divides into two sections, based on the type of rotation utilized. All known early lathes worked on a reciprocating basis—e.g., the work was rotated back and forth between stationary spindles. Power was applied by wrapping a cord around the stock, then pulling back and forth by various means. Speed was limited and cutting could only take place on turns toward the cutting tool.

Reciprocating lathes were often operated by a bowed stick attached to a string wrapped around the work stock. An assistant bowed back and forth as the master applied his tool. Some craftsmen managed the whole job themselves, even bringing their feet into the act.[1]

In a Chinese arrangement, two foot pedals were located beneath the lathe, each pedal activating one end of the cord. Another solution was the use of an apprentice who pulled the cord ends back and forth.[2]

The spring-pole lathe is a refinement utilizing a wraparound cord and foot power to turn the piece in one direction and an overhead spring pole to return the stock to its starting position. This arrangement leaves both hands free for the actual turning work. Bow and spring-pole reciprocating lathes are still in use in scattered "underdeveloped" areas.

The invention of various means for continuous rotation meant that high-speed lathes could be developed utilizing momentum—a basic force that was distinctly worked against in reciprocating lathes. A continuous-action lathe was proposed by Leonardo da Vinci and some were in use by the sixteenth century. Power was usually applied by an apprentice who hand-turned a large, external wheel connected to a mandrel on the lathe by a wide belt. Others were powered by small rooftop windmills, waterwheels, and later, flywheel-

1. Christopher Williams, *Craftsmen of Necessity* (New York: Vintage Books, 1974), p. 170.
2. Rudolf P. Hommel, *China at Work* (Cambridge, Mass.: The M.I.T. Press, 1969), pp. 252-254.

treadle arrangements, usually located beneath the lathe bed. These could be worked by a single craftsman.[3]

In deciding to build a lathe I chose the reciprocating model. I figured that while continuous action made turning easier, construction of the later type would be much more complicated. On the other hand, I had an apprehension that using a reciprocating lathe would be difficult and too slow to be practical. Several books asserted that in use, the chisel had to be moved in and out of action in synchronization with the reciprocating rhythm. (Foot down, chisel in; foot up, chisel out.) It seemed that this would be a difficult (and distracting) skill to develop. However, I had also read about craftsmen who turned quality work on reciprocating spring-pole lathes.[4] If they did it, I could certainly try.

Old photographs and drawings depict spring-pole lathes made many different ways.[5] The simplest design consisted of two massive posts, sunk into the earth, with a pair of cross rails spiked between them forming the lathe bed. The head stock was often a spindle stuck in one upright. The puppet (or tail stock) was a smaller timber hewn so that its lower end fitted between the bed rails. It was generally held in place by a tapered mortise and key. There was also a tool rest, which often consisted of a stick attached to the head and tail stocks.

3. Viires, *Woodworking in Estonia,* pp. 194-210.
4. Jenkins, *Traditional Country Craftsmen,* pp. 11-17, 53-59; Edlin, *Woodland Crafts in Britain,* pp. 32-36; Viires, *Woodworking in Estonia,* pp. 194-210.
5. Blandford, *Country Craft Tools,* pp. 159-167; Henry C. Mercer, *Ancient Carpenter's Tools* (New York: Horizon Press, 1975), pp. 214-219.

A Spring-Pole Lathe

Many variations of this basic pattern were built. English chair bodgers, who worked in the woods in temporary locations, needed a portable setup and lightweight gear. Lathes for indoor work were generally of a smaller scale, often built to more exacting specifications. The Welsh craftsmen who turned a nest of four or five bowls, one within the other, required a lathe built to fairly close tolerances.

The design of my spring-pole lathe went through several stages of development before actual construction got underway. The lathe had to be freestanding and sturdy. I also wished to avoid store-bought hardware. I planned to use the lathe for a variety of projects: for "spindle turning," such as making mallets or spinning-wheel parts, and "face-plate turnery," bowl making. I felt that the lathe should be aesthetically pleasing, complementing other furnishings of the wood shop (workbench, shaving horse, tool cabinet). Finally, I did not want the lathe to be too complicated. In choosing the reciprocating lathe, I was opting for a solution in a simple tool, not a technically complex machine.

The design is based on mortise and tenon construction throughout. The materials used are oak bridge timbers and oak 2 x 6s. The large timbers were originally 3 inches thick, and were subsequently milled to 2½ inches. Other hardwoods could be used, or if not available, Douglas fir or yellow pine would work.

The framework consists of two *feet* (made from 2½- x 5½-inch stock); two *legs*—one of which includes the headstock (from 2½- x 9½-inch material); and two *bed rails* (2 x 6s actually measuring 1½ x 5½ inches). The

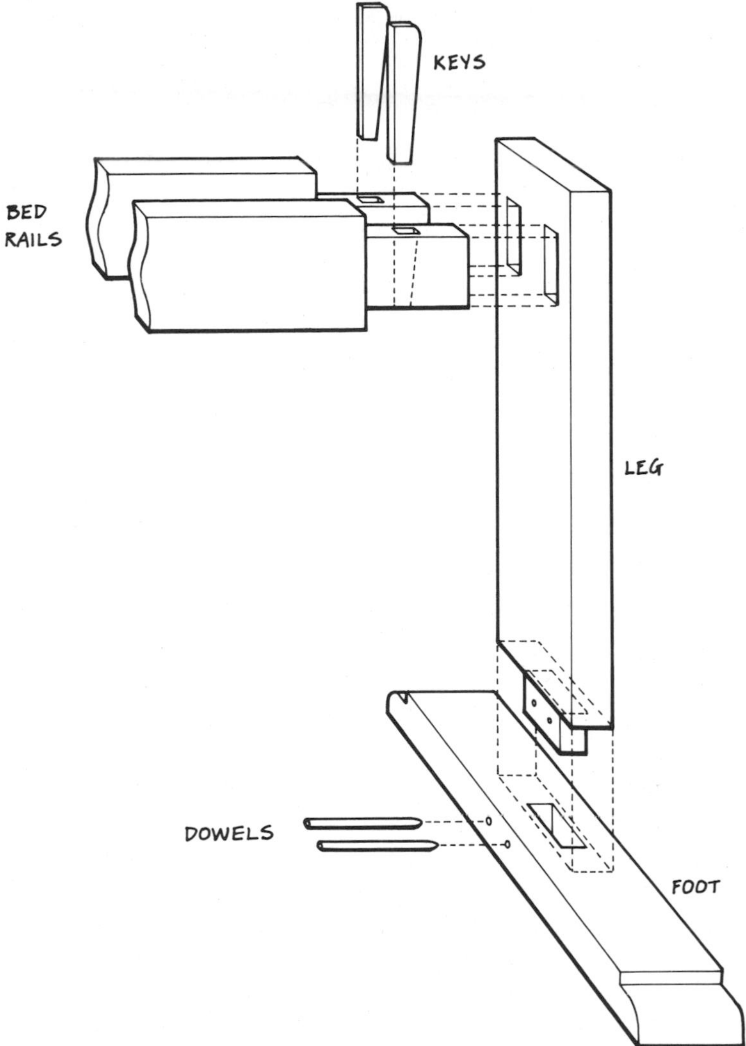

Mortise and tenon details. The bed rails are secured with keys running through tapered slots in the matched tenons. The foot and leg joint is fastened with a pair of dowels.

puppet is also made from 2½ x 5½ inch stock. The *tool rest* is based on 2 x 6 stock resawn and planed to various dimensions.

The legs are tenoned and doweled into the mortised feet. The rails are tenoned and keyed to mortises through the legs. The resulting frame is sturdy and vibration free. The headstock and puppet were made rather tall so that two turning systems could be used on the same unit. For spindle turning there is a pair of spindles 4½ inches above the bed. For bowl work, the puppet is positioned close to the headstock and a mandrel is run through both at 8 inches above the bed. A face plate can be attached to the mandrel outside of the puppet. This arrangement allows for turning a bowl or plate up to 10 inches in diameter. The tool rest is designed for easy adjustment in height and distance from the work piece anywhere along the bed rails.

Construction details. In building this lathe, be sure to use material milled at square angles. Dimensions may be improvised; however, I would not make the front of the left foot any larger (as it is somewhat bothersome as is). Be sure that the square used is accurate. (Don't use an adjustable combination square; choose a larger, fixed instrument.) Stick with one measuring rule, or carefully check one against another.

Begin by sawing the frame members to length. Designate left and right, top and bottom, and front and back of each piece. Although standardized dimensions are used for the joints, individual adjustments will probably have to be made along the way.

Lay out the leg tenons with shoulders having 1¼-inch ends and ½-inch sides. Saw out the shoulders (along the waste side of the lines) all the way around. Then rip down the cheeks. Measure and if necessary lightly dress the tenons using a chisel and spokeshave.

Remeasure the tenons before laying out the mortises. Make adjustments as necessary. Important: do not dowel joints or chamfer edges at this stage. (For further details refer to Appendix I: Mortise and Tenon Joinery.)

The tenons at the ends of the bed rails extend 4 inches beyond the legs (6½ inches overall). These are 3 inches high and 1¼ inches wide to accommodate the angled slots and keys.

Make the leg mortises 4½ inches apart to fit specific bed tenons. Permanently code each joint for identification when units are assembled, torn apart, and later reassembled. A simple method is to punch a series of coded holes in each joint (. / .; . . / . .; etc.).

Lay out the angled slots which accept the wedge-shaped keys. The inside, vertical edge is ⅛ inch within the outside edge of the legs. The outer, tapered angle is set at 5 degrees from vertical. The width is ½ inch throughout. Be careful when drilling the pilot holes for these deep, narrow mortises.

Rip out ½-inch-wide keys, 8 inches long. Plane smooth. Round off the upper outside corner of each key to protect the end grain when it's knocked in place.

Make the feet with through mortises to fit the tenons on the bottom of the legs. An optional approach would be to use only one foot, on the right leg, allowing the left leg to contact the floor.

The frame should now fit together and be quite sturdy. (The feet are not yet doweled—this will add considerable rigidity.)

Like the other components, the puppet is first laid out along square planes. The dimensions are 2½ x 5½ x 22½ inches. A two-sided tenon (flat-faced), 11½ inches long, is sawed 4 inches wide to fit between the rails. A 3-inch angled slot is beat through the tenon, ⅛ inch within the rail bottoms. A wedge 10 inches long secures the puppet rigidly in place in any position along the bed.

The tool rest went through several developmental stages, but I think I've got it right now! The vertical *armature*, 12 inches long, is made something like the puppet, with a tapered slot that accepts a large *keyed wedge* holding the tool rest in position. The armature rests on a hollowed-out, adjustable *slide*. The *support* for the tool rest is bolted between the actual tool *rest* and the slide. The top edge of the rest should be just slightly higher than the spindle centers. Refer to the drawing for proper tool rest cross section.

A square cavity is chiseled from the inside of the block, allowing it to slide over the top of the armature. A corresponding notch is cut out of the upper corner of the armature so that the unit may slide quite close to the spindle for turning short pieces.

Fore and aft adjustments and positions along the bed are made by loosening the large key, then positioning the rest as required. For face-plate turning, the small support is replaced with a similar, but taller support and correspondingly longer bolts.

The spring pole is made from a fairly straight

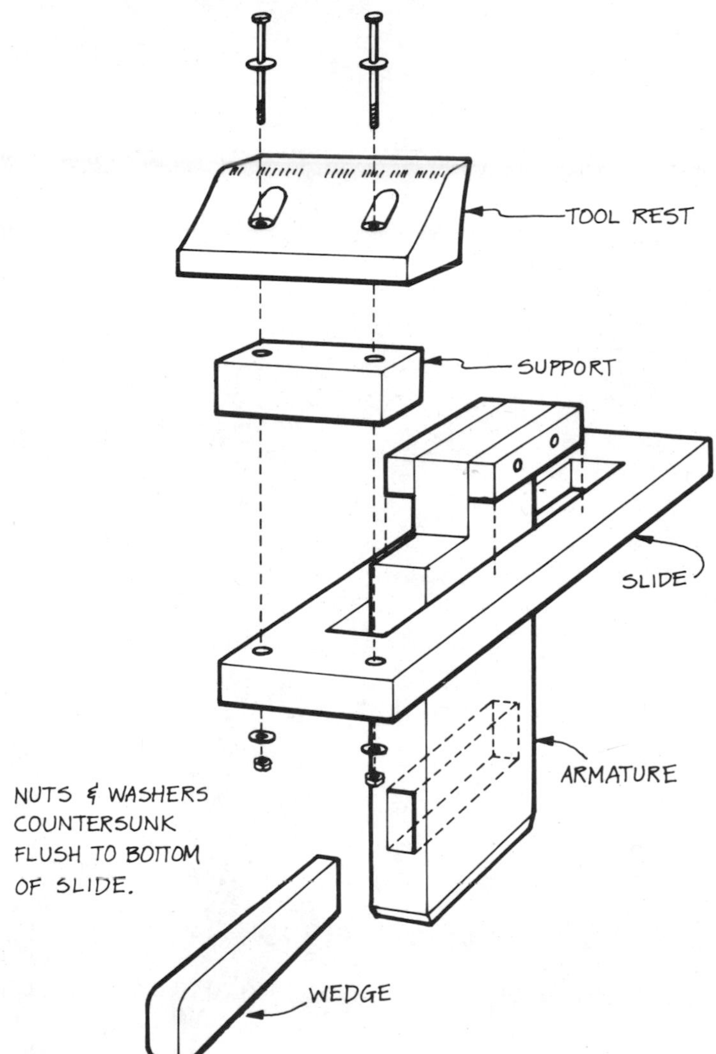

Adjustable tool rest. In use, small blocks laminated to the head of the armature rest on the slide. Height is adjusted by shims or substituting different-sized support. Unit is adjusted for horizontal and lateral placement by loosening the wedge, which fits tightly against the bottom of the bed rails.

The spring pole.

sapling, about 3 inches in diameter at the butt, and approximately 15 feet long. English turners preferred ash, larch, or alder poles. Sassafras, locust, hickory, and hornbeam saplings will also work. Traditionally, the butt of the pole was lashed onto a stake driven into the ground, or to a convenient stump. I substituted a roughly made mortise and tenon joint pinned with a wooden dowel for the lashing. Any wobble at this point decreases efficiency of the pole. The pole extends from the stake and forward to a point several feet above the lathe bed. It is propped in position by a stationary crosspiece some 4 feet from the tip. The best location will have to be determined with each installation. For my lathe a sassafras sapling was used, supported by a crossmember nailed just outside the shop window. Another type of spring might be a piece of inner tube suspended from above. This would require a rather high ceiling.

The cord that I'm using is a strip of ⅜-inch rawhide. Other suitable materials are deerskin, or any soft leather strip that's not stretchy, or very pliable rope. One end of the cord is tied to the pole tip. It passes in front of the work, then around back, up, and again down past the front (through the rails) to the treadle.

The treadle may be a stirrup, a board, or a triangle of thin sticks lashed, bolted, or mortised together. The stirrup is awkward and the least efficient. With a board or triangle, the cord can be attached to the far end somewhat higher than the turner's foot placement. In this setup, foot depression results in a pull on the cord longer than the distance of leg movement. A plain board works quite well, but tends to wander somewhat. With the triangle, two stick ends contact the floor, resulting in a stable base. Other, more elaborate treadles have also been devised.

The final components are the center spindles, mandrel, and face plate. For the stationary center I used a ⅝-inch lag bolt, with the tip ground to a 45-degree point. The adjustable puppet spindle was made from the screw of a broken 4-inch C clamp. A hole 1⁄16-inch smaller than the thread diameter was drilled through the puppet. I then filed four shallow V-grooves within the hole and rubbed paraffin across the screw threads to help relieve friction during the first fitting. The screw tip was ground to match the stationary spindle.

For face-plate turning, use a short length of standard ½-inch pipe, with a cast-iron flange threaded to one end. For an accurate, long-lasting fit, the pipe should pass through bushings set into the headstock and puppet.

The last steps before use involve shaping the feet, headstock, and puppet, chamfering the headstock and leg edges, and doweling the feet to the legs. The notched and rounded shape of the feet and headstock are made by first sawing out rectangular blocks, then shaping with a chisel and spokeshave. The chamfering is done with a spokeshave or plane, except for a few blind corners or areas where the grain reverses. Then use a chisel. The mortise and tenon joints connecting the feet and legs are each secured with two ½-inch dowels. These should be hand-carved, slightly oversized, from well-seasoned hardwood. (For dowel-making

Treadle lathe set-up for turning a dogwood maul.

techniques refer to Chapter 14: Pitchforks.) Drill through the foot with the leg removed. Fit the leg in place and insert the auger, giving just a slight twist to mark the centerpoint. Remove the leg. With an awl, punch another center 3/16 inch above the original mark. Drill through at this second point. Replace the leg and drive the dowel through the foot and offset leg hole. This will help to pull the joint tightly in place.

Using the lathe. A wide variety of woods have been used for turnery. Beech, turned green, was the bodgers favored material for making Windsor chair legs. Seasoned elm is reputed to be best for bowl turning. It was also the first choice among wheelwrights for wagon hubs. Other common turning woods include sycamore, birch, maple, poplar (seasoned), cherry, apple, dogwood, spruce, and yew.

Tools for spindle turning on a spring-pole lathe need not be of the long and strong type. The shorter lathe tools, properly ground and sharpened, work well enough. A good selection for general work includes ¼-inch and ½-inch gouges, and ½-inch round and diamond-point parting tool.

The lathe works better (or easier) than I expected. To begin, mark center holes in the work stock. Apply a dab of tallow for lubrication. Fit between the spindles, turning the adjustable puppet spindle until it begins to tighten when the wood is revolved, then back off a bit. Wrap the cord around the piece, first passing down the front side. Tie the end to the treadle. Locate the tool rest as close to the work as possible. Place the chisel blade, bevel down, against the tool rest. Grip the blade close up with your left hand. Grasp the handle quite far back to achieve good leverage and tool control.

The best way to learn proper technique is to locate an experienced teacher working on a modern, electrically driven lathe. This way special turning skills are learned without the distraction of working the treadle. Fine points of turnery are thoroughly discussed in many books devoted to the subject.[6]

At the spring-pole lathe, the hardest step is getting the stock perfectly round, as slight bumps stop the lathe. It is important to shape the piece as round as possible with a drawknife before beginning to turn. There is sometimes a tendency for the cord to wander off the piece, bringing work to an abrupt halt. Usually some adjustments of the pole, cord, and lathe relationships will alleviate the problem. On a piece having small and large diameters, turn the small part first. Wrap the cord around this portion to gain an extra turn or so with each treadle depression. Other than these few points, using a spring-pole lathe is much like turning on a continuous rotation lathe.

It is not necessary to move the chisel in and out with each stroke. If a small enough shaving is taken, the work will just clear the chisel on each return rotation. However, one must roll the tool over into each cut, and this requires practice.

---

6. Peter Child, *The Craftsman Woodturner;* Dale L. Nish, *Creative Wood Turning.*

Sleds take the place of wagons.

Used by permission of the Doris Ulmann Foundation and Berea College.

PART III
AGRICULTURAL IMPLEMENTS

Raking leaves for mulch.

CHAPTER 13
HAY RAKES

ONE OF MY FAVORITE projects is making wooden rakes. Louise wonders why I keep making them. But every now and then I take a notion to have a go at another variation. At this point we have more hay rakes around the place than we could possibly use. My fascination is really an exploration into geometry: e.g., various ways of fastening the rake head to the handle making lightweight, strong, and efficient tools.

In this country, wooden rakes have all but disappeared. This is mainly because there is little, if any, handwork involved in making hay anymore. But, truth is that there's nothing like good loose hay. Wooden rakes work fine for windrowing and turning the small quantities of hay needed on many farmsteads. The wooden teeth won't grab, tangle, and chatter as steel teeth would. And the rake head is much lighter for its size, which may be 2 to 3 feet across on a typical haying rake.

Wooden rakes can still be purchased in a few New England hardware stores. Here in southern Appalachia the farmers apparently never used hay rakes. They "gathered in" hay with pitchforks. But there were many beautiful early American styles, some still to be found in old barns and dusty attics. In Europe these rakes are

Detail of half-lap joint held with a ¼-inch bolt and nut.

still used where small quantities of loose hay are needed by farmers.

Hay rake design is dependent on materials available, the type of land being worked, the kind of hay that is handled, desired degree of permanence in construction, and local preferences or style.[1] For instance, short hay, or hay grown on rocky ground, is best handled by rakes with short, stout tines—perhaps 2½ inches long, set close together, about 2 inches on center. Tines are less likely to break. And if one is lost it won't be missed as the others are so close together. Long, leafy hay is worked with long rake tines (4 to 5 inches) that may be set farther apart (3 inches on center). For hay cut on steep slopes, an extra-long handle (sometimes over 8 feet) is used. An especially large rake (4 to 5 feet across the rake head) with 5- to 6-inch tines is called a "bull" or "buck" rake. (Or a "drag" rake in England.) This type, which is sometimes double-handled, is used to haul large amounts of dry windrowed hay to a wagon, or in some mountain farmlands, to a sled or loosely tied net.

Many styles. The greatest variations in hay rake design are found in the method of joining and supporting the rake head to the handle. The most common method is to drill a hole through the rake, drive the handle in, then fasten with a small nail. This secures the head as such, but it would wobble, and come loose during vigorous work. To steady the head, stiff wire braces are attached from a point on the handle to the tips of the rake head, making a triangle. On a large

1. Jenkins, *Traditional Country Craftsmen*, pp. 63-71.

rake of this type, two or three sets of braces can be used for extra support.

Any type of heavy-gauge wire can be used—straightened-out coat hangers will work. Using a pointed pliers, bend the ends into small loops. Then heat the loops red-hot (a small propane torch works fine) and flatten with a hammer against an (improvised) anvil.

Another easy-to-make rake head is joined to its handle by a half-lap fastened with a ¼-inch carriage bolt. In this case the rake head may be a 1 x 1 strip of hardwood, with the half-lap cut through the handle only. Use wire braces as above. I made two quick rakes this way, and they were very serviceable.

From here we find many variations, aesthetic choices, and so-called improvements. All of these rakes give good service.

The first refinement is to make a square mortise fitted to a shouldered tenon held tight by a hardwood pin (¼-inch dowel). The advantage of the square mortise is that it tends to keep the rake from axial wobbling on the handle.

One variation substitutes two or three pairs of long, semicircular wooden dowels for the wire struts. The dowels are made of a wood that bends easily, such as white oak or ash. For adequate strength, they should be hand-formed, following the natural grain. Store-bought (turned) dowels would probably break during bending because the dowel-making machines don't follow the natural grain. This style is very attractive, but I think too fragile. It would be difficult to replace a dowel should one break. (But ours is in use and doing fine.)

Mortise and tenon secured with a ¼-inch dowel.

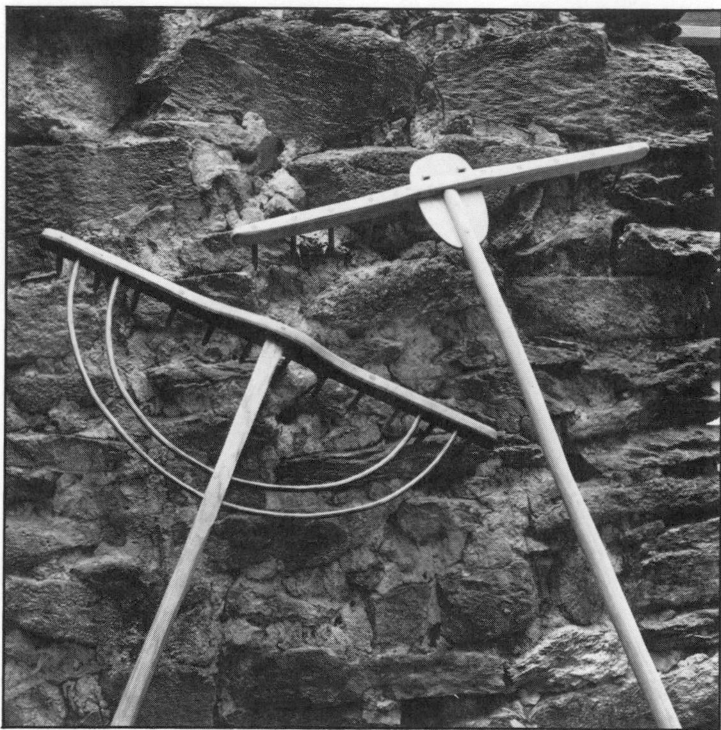

Two elegant hay rakes.

For another style, the struts and handle are of integral, one-piece construction. The rake handle (ash or oak) is made something like a wooden pitchfork, with the braces sawn out and riveted at the joint to prevent splitting, then bent apart to form a well-braced unit. (See Chapter 14: Pitchforks.) This is work, but it certainly makes a stout rake.

In an English variant, the central member is eliminated altogether. The handle is sawn down the middle and riveted or wrapped with a metal band. The struts are bent apart and held by two dowel spreaders—just like the pitchfork design. In this pattern, the joints at the struts and heads are round holes pinned with small nails.

Perhaps the most elegant hay rakes, certainly the most unusual that I've seen, are made in Finland. There are no struts or braces. The whole design is different. At the handle end there's a wide slot into which half of a wooden oval disk is inserted, then fastened by two dowels. This disk passes through a corresponding slot in the rake head, which is then held fast by two wedge-shaped keys mortised against the rake head and through the disk. An effective triangulation is formed between the two keys and the surface where the handle butts against the head. The design is elegant, works fine, and is easy to disassemble (very handy when replacing broken tines, as the long handle isn't constantly bumping into things in the workshop.)

A further variation comes from France. In this rake, used for turning windrowed hay as one walks along, the head is mounted in the same plane as the handle, but at a 45-degree angle. Only one brace is necessary, resulting in a Y-shaped configuration.

Finally, some old rustic prints and a painting by Breugal depict rakes with tines located above and below the rake head. This way one can have two types of tines.

In any case, all wooden rakes share the same basic requirements. To do the job, a rake must be strong, properly proportioned, lightweight, and comfortable to handle for many hours.

Materials can vary a great deal from one area to another. English rake makers prefer ash, then willow—both tough, springy woods. Hazel, pine, birch, and alder could also be used. I've made several rakes with maple heads and white oak handles (tough, although somewhat overweight). But I also prefer ash. My Finnish-style rake has a locust handle. I've also used a seasoned popular sapling for a handle.

Construction. Rake heads are easiest to make when sawn from a 1-inch board. Another method is cleaving, if an easily split wood, such as ash, is available. A cleaved rake head will sometimes have a graceful curve to it. However, working irregularly shaped stock does create extra problems in layout and measurement. For this reason, I generally work cleft wood into a square cross section before marking out the mortise or doing the shaping work.

Lay out a pattern having an even number of tines. This leaves a space in the center for inserting the handle. Exceptions are the Finnish design, where the center tooth is omitted to make room for the wooden disk, and the double-handled drag rake.

The socket or mortise for the handle varies from rake to rake. It is generally made perpendicular to the rake head. But in very hilly regions, the joint is angled downward as much as 45 degrees.

The easiest joint, used by the English rake makers, is a round hole and a round handle tip, pinned together with a small nail.

For rakes with a mortise, lay out the square joint before shaping the head. At this stage there are still flat surfaces and right-angle edges to measure against. Start the mortise by drilling one or two holes through the outlined area with an undersized auger bit. Finish with a sharp chisel. (Further details on mortises are in Appendix I: Mortise and Tenon Joinery.)

Shape the rake head with a drawknife and spokeshave. Do not chamfer the edges before tine holes are drilled.

Tine holes are generally drilled ⅜ inch in diameter. I used to drill blind holes—with the idea that the tines would be less likely to come loose. But this causes other problems: shallow depth, air pockets during gluing, and extra work when replacing broken tines. Now I drill straight through the rake head. The tines are set deeper. And they can be sharpened before insertion, then driven down through the rake head with a wooden mallet. The glued tines won't work loose if the fit is fairly snug. In boring these holes, drill from the top of the rake head until the auger pilot begins to emerge on the bottom. Stop, reverse the head, and finish boring from the bottom. This will prevent wood from splitting out when the auger comes through.

Tine holes should be angled just slightly toward the handle (about 5 degrees). This prevents the rake from jumping about while you are using it.

You may want to do some detail and finish work on the rake head after making the handle mortise and drilling the tine holes. This is a good time, because after the teeth and handle are installed, the rake becomes a rather clumsy thing to handle or clamp in a vise. Chamfering the upper edges of the rake head saves weight, eliminates some possibility of damaging the wood, and adds to the general appearance.

Rake tines can be store-bought dowels (3/8-inch), or homemade. Commercial dowels are inferior because the machines that make them cut across the grain, making a weak tine, especially for long-tined rakes. Moreover, commercial dowels aren't made of the toughest woods, and you want tough wood for tines. Nevertheless, commercial dowels are quick and easy to install and replace.

The best dowels are cleaved from straight-grained hardwoods such as oak, ash, beech, hickory, locust, or mulberry. The Finns traditionally use lilac.

If you're making just a few rakes, the tines can be formed with a drawknife and spokeshave. First split out blanks from a 12- to 15-inch-long bolt with a froe or narrow wedge (such as a wide-bladed axe struck with a maul). At the shaving horse, sandwich the narrow blanks between a 1 x 2 extension stick and the jaw. To size the dowels, first use a caliper set a little oversized; then work for a snug fit through a hardwood block drilled to the correct size. Saw the 12- to 15-inch dowels to correct size when shaping is finished.

If many teeth are being made, I recommend rigging up a tine former. Special dowel makers can be used on an electric lathe. But there is a traditional hand tool that will work well enough. This is a tube-shaped knife mounted on a steel plate above a hole on a workbench or horse. Short lengths of roughly shaped dowels are pounded through the tine former, emerging nicely rounded. To reduce friction, the inside of the tube is made slightly larger than the cutting diameter.

Tine formers have not been manufactured for some years. I was about to have a machinist fabricate one when I discovered that tube-type leather punches work on the same principle. These punches are made in 1/16-inch increments, and are available at a reasonable price from leather supply shops.[2] To convert into a tine former mount the punch on a steel plate with a properly sized hole drilled in the middle. Welding is the easiest way to do this. To complete the tool, drill and countersink a hole in each corner of the plate for mounting screws.

A typical rake handle is 1 inch in diameter and 6 to 7 feet long. For some mountainside rakes, 8-foot handles are used. American buck rakes often had short handles, perhaps 5 feet in length. (A variation used two parallel handles, joined with a crossbar.) Regardless, the wood should be strong, springy, and, of course, as light as possible.

Handles can be made from saplings, willow and sourwood being prime choices. But other woods such as

2. A mail-order source for leather punches is: MacPherson Bros., 730 Polk St., San Francisco, CA 94109.

alder, pine, and poplar can be used. Sapling handles are easiest to make, if you can find appropriate young stands in need of thinning. In general, saplings are not so strong as cleft handles, but should match sawn-out handles.

Making a sapling handle is fast and easy. Simply debark and trim with a drawknife. Be sure to season any handle at least one month before fitting it to the rake head or it will shrink and come loose.

The best cleft handles are made from the trunk of a straight-grained ash, although other woods such as oak or even locust can be used. (The method for splitting is discussed in Chapter 14: Pitchforks.)

The handle cross section should be round and nicely smooth. An octagonal-shaped handle, which works fine on a pitchfork, will become uncomfortable to the hand as it slides back and forth countless times during haying work.

Like tines, handles are roughly shaped with a drawknife, then detailed with a spokeshave. A refinement would be the use of a concave-bladed "half-round" or "hollow-edge" spokeshave.

For small-scale production of rake handles, English country craftsmen invented a tool called a "whichet" or "stail engine." [3] (No kidding.) This is something like a plane with a hole in the side or a giant version of those little pencil sharpeners that consist of a small plastic cube with a cone-shaped orifice and a blade set along an

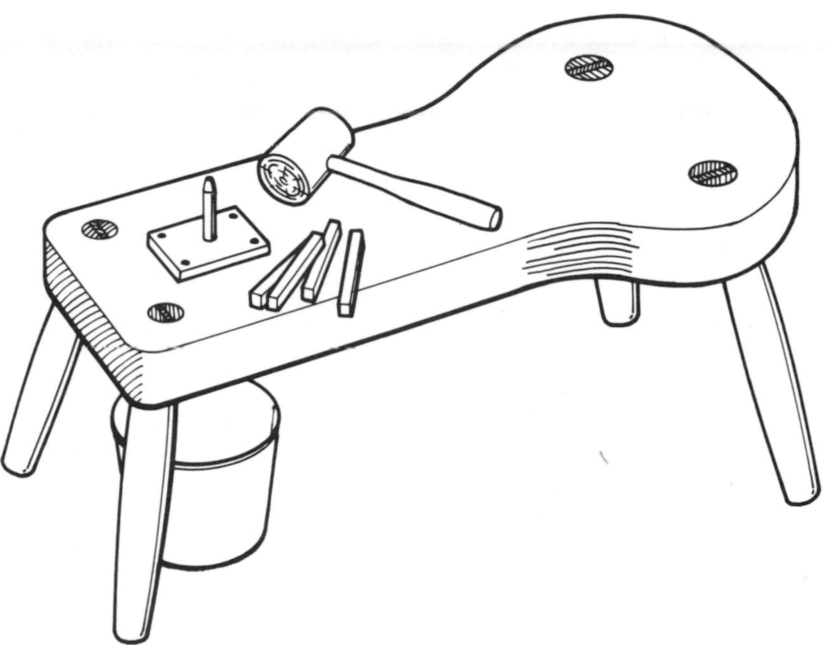

Tine former mounted on a special horse.

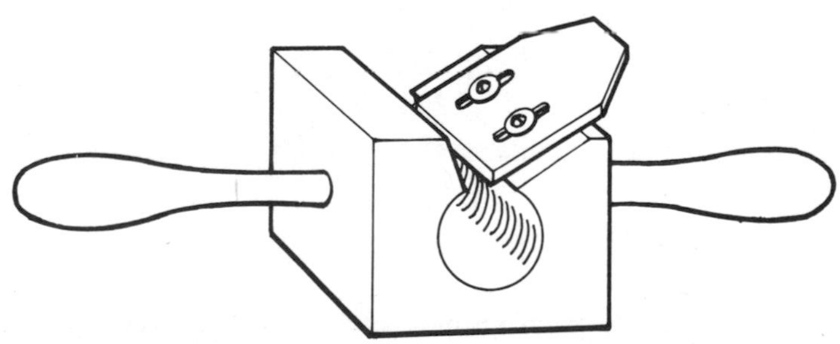

Handle former or stail engine.

3. Blandford, *Country Craft Tools,* p. 165; Jenkins, *Traditional Country Craftsmen,* pp. 63-71; Edlin, *Woodland Crafts in Britain,* p. 35.

interior slit. Like the pencil sharpener, the stail engine is set over the stick to be shaped, then turned round and round as it's worked from one end of the handle to the other. The tool was generally homemade, so there's a great deal of variation from one to another. The blade is usually an old plane iron, held in place by two screws set over small slots so that the depth of cut may be adjusted.

Handles sawn from boards can be fine if care is

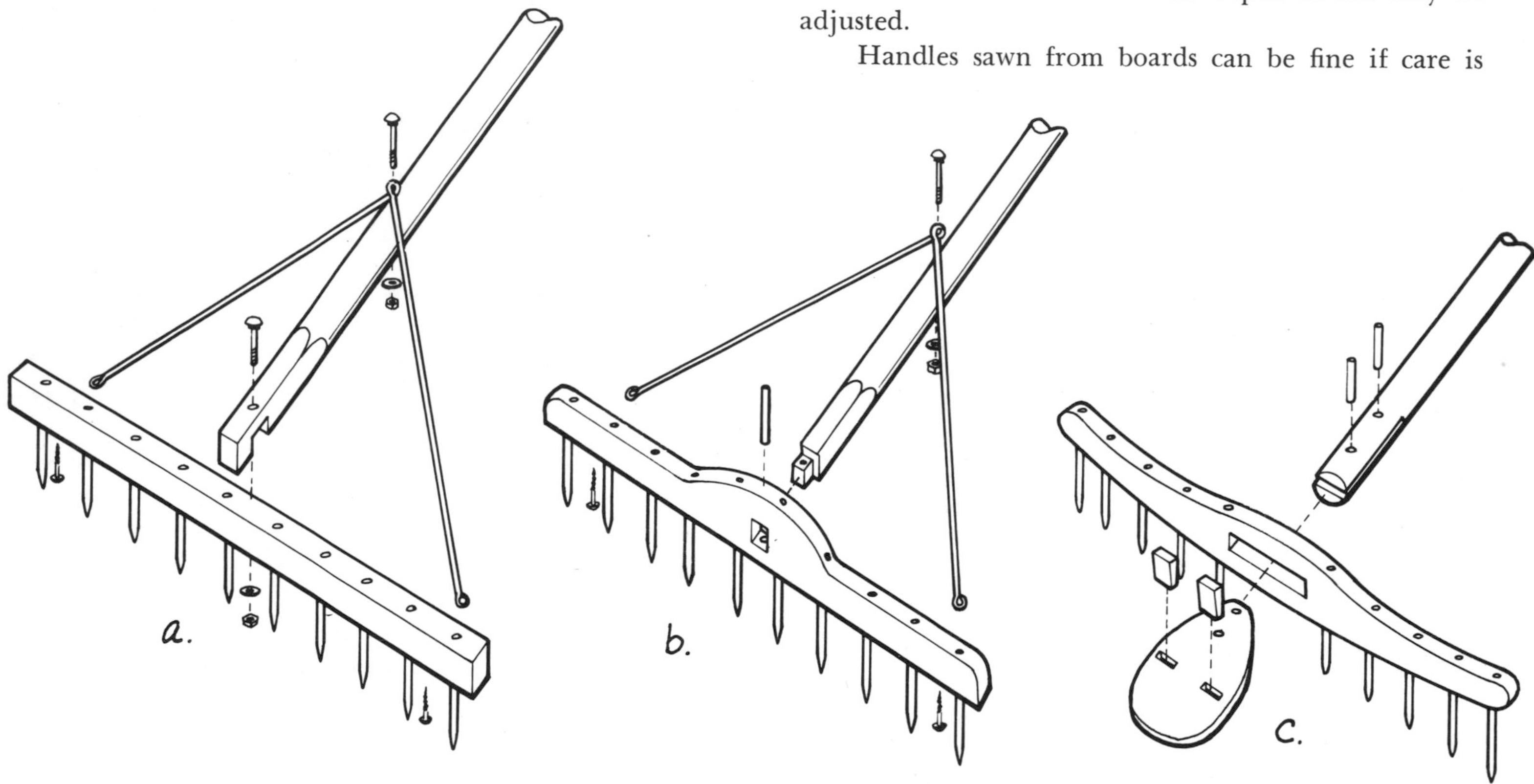

Rake head geometry and mathematics. Simplest joint (a) is a bolted half-lap secured with carriage bolt and reinforced with wire struts. Mortise and tenon (b) held with a wood dowel is somewhat sturdier, Rake from Finland (c) is held tight by two "tusk tenons" passing through mortises in the disk, which slides into slot through handle.

taken to use select lumber with very straight grain. If the original boards are milled without straight-line edges (leaving the original tree contours for an outline), then it becomes possible to saw out handles exactly following the original growth. (This is illustrated in Chapter 2: Materials.)

Some rake makers like to give their handles a slight bend, between 5 and 10 degrees, about 2 feet from the rake head. This is done by steaming or pouring boiling water over the handle, then setting it in a jig to season for a week or two. Bending the handle serves the same purpose as fitting the teeth into the head at a slight angle.

At the lower end, the handle will have to be shaped for whatever joint is being used. For the very simplest, a half-lap held by a bolt and nut, the handle end should be left in a square cross section for maximum bulk. The actual joint is made by sawing halfway through the handle, then knocking out the waste wood with a chisel. A ¼-inch carriage bolt works fine as it gives a good grip and has a nicely rounded contour on top.

For a shouldered tenon fitting a mortised head, it's best to leave the handle end slightly oversize, shaping it to a square or rectangular cross section. (Refer to Appendix I: Mortise and Tenon Joinery.)

Handles where the struts are an integral unit are made by flaring the socket end to the combined thickness of the central square tenon (1 inch), plus the two braces (½ inch each), plus an allowance for the saw kerf made in ripping out the two braces (about 1/16 inch per kerf). The total width of the handle along the length of the struts is 2⅛ inches. The cross section is rectangular, about 1 inch deep. (Ripping the struts, making the rivet, and final shaping methods may be modified from the detailed instructions in Chapter 14: Pitchforks.)

The English handle, which splits into two struts (leaving no central stem), is first shaped round from one end to another; but is enlarged to about 1¼ inch in diameter toward the socket end. The struts are then ripped. The rivet or grasp is fitted. Struts are bent and dowel spreaders inserted. Each strut is rounded at its tip to a ½-inch diameter. Holes are drilled in the rake head. The handle is inserted and secured with small nails pinned through the head and struts. (See Chapter 14: Pitchforks for details.)

A further innovation (I think French) is pointing the end of the rake handle. This looks lethal, and could cause an accident in careless use. The idea is that the rake can be stuck in the ground when not in use. Such rakes are easy to find in a field of tall hay (or weeds) when they're set aside for a rest. We have learned that tines are usually broken when a rake is stepped on.

After assembly, rakes should be cleaned up with a scraper, sanded, and finished with two coats of a mixture of 2 parts linseed oil to 1 part turpentine. Rub down with a rag to polish the handle between each coat. During use the real polishing job takes place.

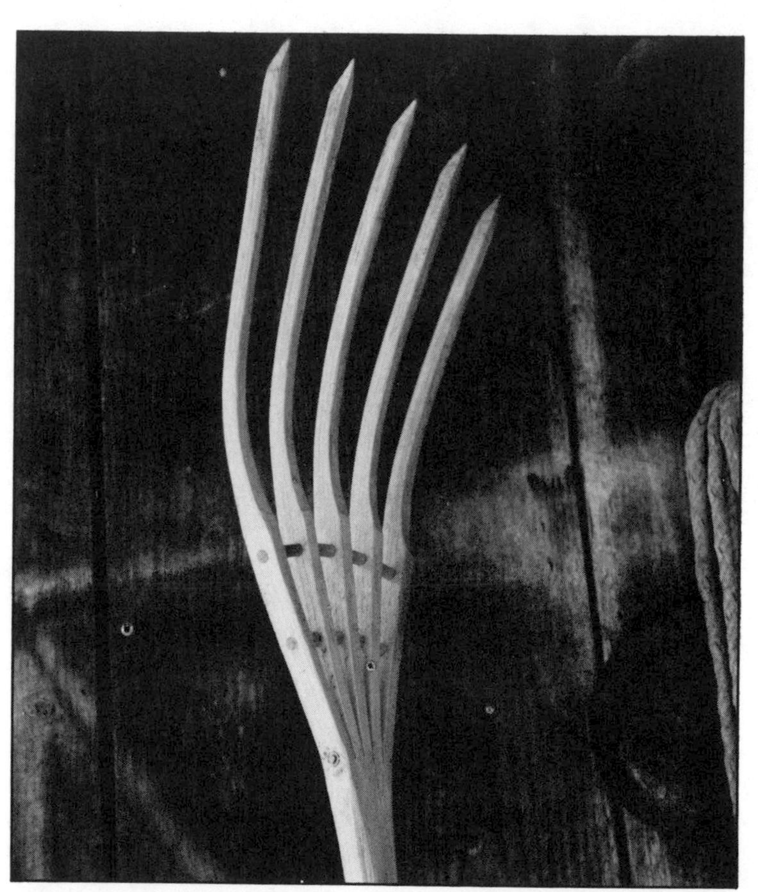

A pitchfork.

CHAPTER 14
PITCHFORKS

THE EFFECTIVENESS OF A PITCHFORK (or hayfork—they're the same thing) is determined by the shape and number of tines, length of handle, overall strength, and toughness. For gathering hay only two or three tines are needed. Tines should be nicely curved and finished smoothly to reduce friction. A long handle is useful for stacking or pitching hay up to a mow or stack. Forks for heavy work such as turning compost or barn chores need four or five tines, and must be strong enough not to break or bend at the neck.

The design of hayforks has evolved very little over the ages. Primitive forks were simply selected cuttings from saplings and limbs that naturally grew in a fork-like shape. Similar forks are still used by farmers living in some very isolated areas.[1]

Man-made wooden forks are crafted from a single piece of wood, or built up using several elements mortise-and-tenoned together.[2] The one-piece design described in this chapter derives from a commonly found Pennsyl-

1. Viires, *Woodworking in Estonia,* p. 78; Williams, *Craftsmen of Necessity,* pp. 102-5.
2. Langsner, *Handmade,* p. 163.

vania Dutch pattern. This fork has two to five tines that are sawn out of a single piece of wood which also includes the handle. The tines are held apart by two dowel spreaders. At the base of the tines there is a rivet (or "grasp") which prevents splitting down the handle. The tines are curved by heating them with boiling water, then setting them in a jig for one to two weeks to stabilize.

This fork works quite well for haying, but fails to equal the modern tempered steel-tined counterpart. The needle-like tines of a steel fork cannot be matched in wood without a severe loss of strength, which must not be sacrificed. In heavy work, the wooden fork tends to bend slightly at the neck, although I have never had one break.

The appeal of this project is not the utility of the fork. (If it's a pitchfork you need, then visit your local hardware or feed store and buy a good-quality fork, such as Blue Grass or True Temper.) I have given the wooden fork prominent attention because (1) I think it has aesthetic and historical appeal, and (2) I can think of no other project that includes so many processes and skills typical of country woodcraft. (Cooperage is more complex, but also more specialized.) The skills and tools combined in the making of a wooden fork constitute a good sampling of country woodcraft.

To present the hayfork I have gone into details that would otherwise be scattered, helter-skelter, throughout the book. Making a fork is a fun project; not too hard or too easy. I have made several hundred without becoming bored. I suggest reading through all the

steps in making a pitchfork, even if you have no intention of doing one.

Material. The best wood is white oak, though red oak and ash can be used. The wood must be worked relatively green. This means that you will probably have to select a standing tree and fell it.

The minimum size usable tree is 8 inches in diameter just above the tapered buttresses. This tree should make four hayforks. Larger trees can be used. I have made over fifty forks from a single tree by splitting blanks from concentric rings and consecutive tiers. The butt must be more or less straight and free of knots or imperfections for at least 6 feet.

Felling. This may be done any time of year. Plan on working the wood as soon as possible. If oak is harvested in summer, it is liable to be invaded by ambrosia beetles. Prompt work and removal from the forest site is the only nonchemical method of avoiding damaged wood. (For felling details refer to Chapter 3: Felling.)

Bucking. After the tree is down, it's bucked into logs and bolts for various uses. Crosscut a 6-foot section of clear wood for hayforks. (This gives 6 inches leeway; the fork measures 66 inches.)

Buck the remainder of the tree for other uses. It's often easier to cut bolts for firewood right in the woods. Logs that are skidded become imbedded with grit that quickly damages any type of saw blade. Oak and ash make premium fuel woods so effort should be made to recover all of the tree, including the smaller limbs.

Begin splitting the fork wood at the felling site.

The butt of a large oak is extremely heavy and awkward to handle. Quarter sections are much more manageable.

Tools needed include a maul or go-devil (8- to 12-pound head), three iron wedges, two wooden gluts, and a hatchet. A fan-shaped iron timber wedge is useful but not necessary. A peavey is helpful for rotating large logs (over 10 inches in diameter).

Take along all of the tools that might be needed. I usually carry a rucksack that ends up weighing thirty pounds, not including the peavey and maul that I also tote. The rucksack is useful for holding tools together on the job—plus sweaters, refreshments, etcetera. Things are easily scattered in a leaf-strewn forest.

With an iron wedge and hatchet, hammer a line across the end grain of the butt from the bark to the central pith. If the log displays a similar crack, then follow that line. Drive the fan-shaped wedge into the line until a lateral crack develops along the bark. Drive an iron wedge into the crack to within ¾ inch of the striking head. The fan-shaped wedge should drop free. (Put it in the pack.) Drive a second wedge ahead of the first one. The first wedge should loosen. Remove it from the crack and reinsert it in front of the second wedge. Continue leap-frogging to the end of the log.

Use the gluts to further open the crack (not necessary with small logs.) Gluts should be placed so that they are unlikely to run into interior cross fibers. Gluts tend to split apart if driven into tough fiber.

Oftentimes a log splits clear through but opens along one side only, leaving the back halves pinched together by cross strands connecting one side to another.

Halving a white oak log with a maul and glut.

Splitting out eighths.

In this case, roll the log over, then drive iron wedges and wooden gluts into the incipient crack. With gluts holding the split open, chop out cross fibers with the hatchet.

Continue by splitting the half sections into quarters. Use the same method as for splitting out halves. If the quarter sections are wider than 6 inches, you can split again into eighths. This last split should, however, be delayed until just before fork-making begins, as the wood will quickly begin drying out.

In splitting narrow sections, one sometimes has a problem of the wood tending to "run" to a side. This may be caused by starting the split off-center, or by twisted grain. It's sometimes possible to save both pieces by stopping work at the butt end, then beginning again from the other end. Hopefully, the two sections will meet. It may be necessary to chop across the sections with a hatchet. I have saved otherwise hopeless situations by chain-sawing the waste wood between two sections that are splitting contrary to one another.

Cleaving. The next step involves cleaving a quarter or eighth section parallel to the growth rings. Tools needed are a "brake", froe, narrow club, and a good, sharp hatchet.

With a thick, narrow section, it may be possible to fit in two forks, one out of sapwood, and another smaller fork of heartwood. In any case, place the froe near the middle of the piece. Attempts to cleave much off-center often result in the piece running toward the smaller segment. For two forks from one piece, first cleave the piece in half, and then cleave the outer half again. With a very wide piece, it might be possible to make a third fork from the inner heartwood segment. But the central pithy section is generally too gnarled and knotty for anything but stove wood or fence posts.

For cleaving, you will need a holding device called a brake. An excellent brake can be made from a limb that forks into two more or less parallel branches and two stout sticks, each about 4 feet long. Support the brake with the two sticks by running them up through the branches from either side. Working "contrary to each other" they will hold up the brake at any convenient height, depending on how you set them. The large end of the forked limb is propped upon a log lying on the ground at a right angle.

Insert the small end of the chosen section, sap side downward, through the legs of the brake. Place the froe across the end grain halfway between the apex and bark. Strike the froe with the wooden club. When full depth is reached, pull the froe handle downward to open the split. Slide the froe forward and continue to the end.

If the split begins to run toward the sapwood, turn the section over and pry down toward the pith. It is also possible to reverse the section, restarting cleaving from the smaller end until the sections meet or can be chopped apart. The final section should be 2 to 4 inches wide, and approximately 1½ inches thick.

Next, set the small end of the piece on a low stump and chop the lower two-thirds into a rough handle-like shape, about 2 inches wide. Square off the angular sides along the wider end.

Shaping. Until now we have worked out-of-doors.

Riving a blank. The holding device is called a brake.

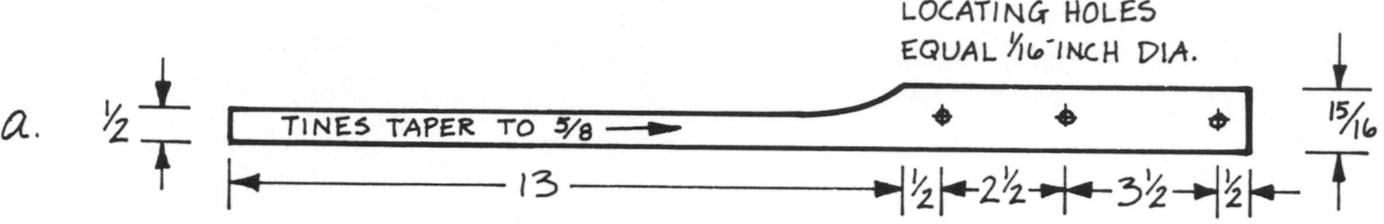

Hay fork template.

At this point I generally take my material into the shop, as it's too easy to misplace any of the small tools that are needed.

Tools used to shape the fork blank are a shaving horse, drawknife, spokeshave, hand saw, tape measure, various templates (see illustrations), chalk, and a chalk line.

Examine the end grain at the butt and small end. Remember, the initial bolt was bucked 6 inches oversized. In sawing the piece down to 66 inches, you may take waste wood from either or both ends. Look for checks and cracks at each end. Try to determine if the butt end is doaty (punky, affected with dry rot). Saw to 66 inches overall.

Place the piece in the shaving horse and remove bark and any rough wood from the sides.

With the chalk line, snap a center guideline from one end to the other. Try to make the centerline follow the linear grain of the wood. If the piece is curved, snap two half-length guidelines, one from each end, joining somewhere in the center. Fighting against the grain weakens the fork.

Using the long, narrow profile template, chalk crosslines at the point where the tines narrow, and at the large end of the template. Chalk a third crossline approximately 6 inches from the second line. (This marks the neck.)

Face gauges are used to determine the width of the fork along different sections of the tines, head, neck, and handle. Separate gauges are needed for two-, three-, four-, and five-tined forks. The widest slot indicates the width of the fork blank from the tip of the tines to the drop just before the larger dowel. The middle slot corresponds with the width at the rivet. The remaining slot (which is larger than the middle slot on the two-tined fork) indicates the width at the neck and along the entire handle. Gauges can be made from cardboard or wooden slats.

Use the gauge to determine how many tines the material will allow. Then center the gauge over the snapped guideline and chalk marks to indicate the fork width at the tine tips, tine drop-off, rivet, neck, and at

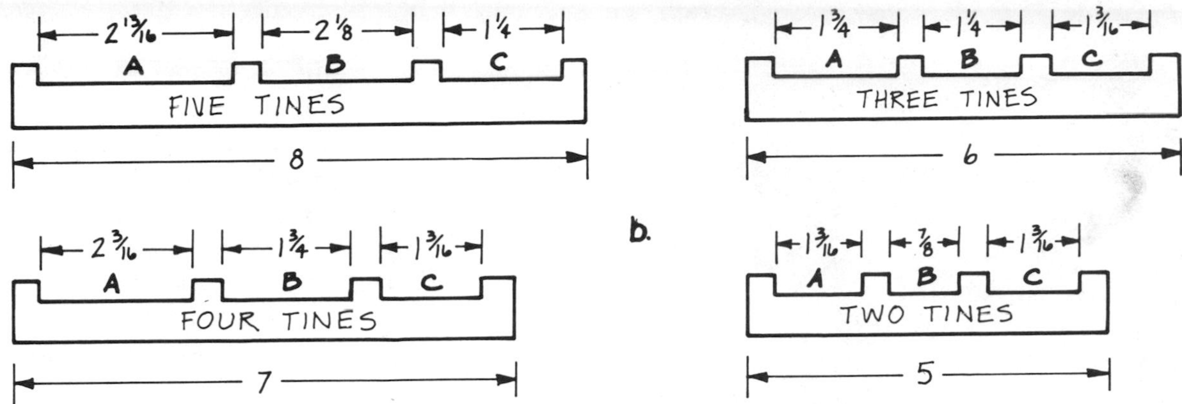

Face gauges: Spaces A, B, and C correspond to the width of the rake head as illustrated below.

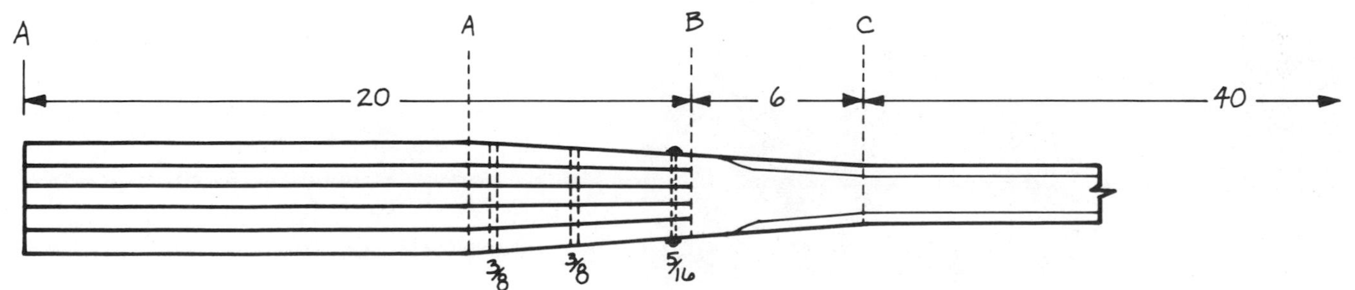

Hay fork layout.

Using a face gauge.

several places along the handle.

Back at the shaving horse, use the drawknife to rough out the width of the fork. Work with the blade bevel down.

Make chalk lines down the sides corresponding to the lines across the face. Determine the face and back of the fork based on the natural curvature of the wood. Using the profile template, shape the face and back. The handle may be left thicker slightly past the neck. Shape the thin tine profile by working in very tightly controlled downward arcs. Renew the marks across the top of the fork.

Rough out small bevels on the sides of the handle, making an octagonal cross section. Be careful not to shave too deeply. Avoid going out of control where the grain turns "foxy." Reverse the piece and shaving direction as necessary.

Finish shaping the blank with a sharp spokeshave. Spokeshaves work equally well on push and pull strokes. The Stanley No. 151, which has two adjustment screws, makes work a little easier. Holding the tool at an angle to the direction of work results in a smoother cut. The order of final shaving is sides, face, back, bevels, and finally, chamfering around the butt of the handle.

Boring. Clamp the fork to one side of the shaving horse seat. Two C-clamps are necessary. (I like aluminum C-clamps; iron clamps react to oak, leaving a purple stain.) Using the profile template, punch marks indicating dowel and rivet holes. With a straightedge, pencil lines across the back corresponding to the punch marks.

Use a 3/8-inch auger for the dowel holes. Stop boring when the auger pilot begins to emerge; drilling straight through is likely to break off wood as the cutters come through. Stopping also allows a degree of recentering from the reverse direction.

Use a 5/32-inch twist bit for the rivet hole. With a hand drill it may be necessary to bore in stages, pulling out the drill now and then to remove waste material packed in the bit fluting.

Turn the fork over and finish boring the dowel holes from the reverse side. It is possible to correct off-center holes up to 1/8 inch. Clean up rough edges with a knife or rat-tail rasp.

Sawing tines. Clamp the fork to the shaving horse seat with the back of the head facing upward. Marking out can be done with a ruler or dividers. Make reference points at tine tips, first dowel, and rivet. A 2-B pencil makes a legible line on green wood.

For two- or four-tine forks, first make a centerline. With a 4½-point ripsaw, saw exactly to the rivet line. For a four-tiner, make new lines down the center of each of the two halves.

Saw cuts for three- and five-tine forks cannot be marked with the same method of division. Use caliper dividers to mark out spacing by trial and error. Then rip the tines in any order.

In some cases, the head will curve or sway following the natural grain of the wood. A bent head is much stronger than one where an attempt is made at correction resulting in a shape going across the grain. In such cases it is necessary to add extra cross marks, making

Sawing tines with a 4½-point ripsaw.

guidelines that follow the arc or S-curve. Ripping along curves is facilitated by holding the saw at an angle very close to the plane of the fork.

Rivet. This is made from a common tenpenny nail and two size 00 flat washers. Put the nail through one washer, then drive it through the 5⁄32-inch hole. Snip or hacksaw off the nail point, leaving a 1⁄8-inch stub protruding through the fork. Set the fork, nail head down, against a striking surface (anvil, piece of railroad track, machine vise, whatever). Place the second washer over the nail stub. Use a ball-peen hammer to rivet the stub down over the washer. Loose, easy strokes pivoted from the end of the hammer handle are most effective. Peen around edges of the nail, then across the crown. (I have never known of a failure with this rivet.)

The dowels used as tine spreaders should be made in advance. They are most easily shaped from green wood, which, however, shrinks a bit in diameter during seasoning. About a week is called for. Alternately, dowels can be made from preseasoned billets and put to use immediately.

The wood used is generally heart of oak, often from the same tree that supplies the main fork wood. The grain must be straight and free of knots. Store-bought dowels will not work. Machine-made dowels are turned from weaker woods and are milled irrespective of the wood grain. Commercial dowels would weaken the fork, or break during installation. (Methods of dowel making are discussed in Chapter 13: Hay Rakes.)

The easiest method is to make a single dowel, 3⁄8 inch in diameter and 12 inches long, that will be cut into unequal segments after the tines are spread. After shaping, point the ends so that the dowel may easily be driven through the spread-out tines.

Bending. Freshly cut white oak, especially sapwood, will generally bend with no problems. But not always. A cracked fork is a wasted fork. Other woods, or white oak that has partially seasoned, require some

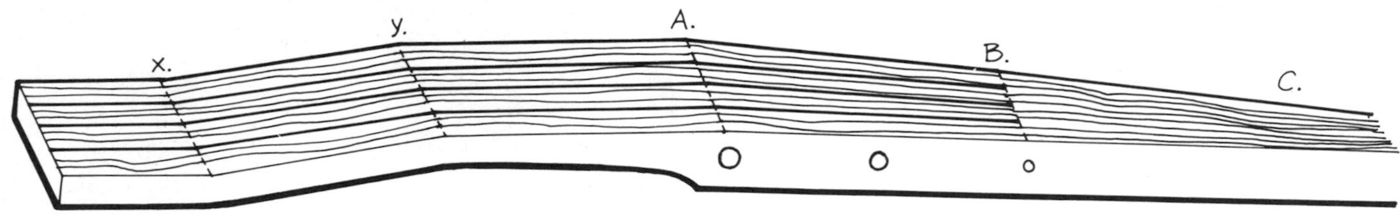

The wood used should be straight. But for maximum strength, lay out the fork head following any deviations in the material. In this (exaggerated) case, extra markings (x,y) are made for the guidelines used to saw the tines. This fork should jig up and season to the correct shape.

softening before bending. A steam box would be best; I use boiling water.

A gallon of water is brought to a boil in an old coffee pot. The fork is placed in a bucket, tines down. Boiling water is slowly poured down the face and back of the fork head. The kettle is refilled and the pouring repeated two or three times. Pour hot water over the dowel too; then while the dowel is hot, carefully bend it into a slight crescent shape.

Spreading tines. Working quickly to take best advantage of the heat, clamp the fork to the shaving horse with its head extended, face upward. Carefully bend each tine outward, then gradually upward. Simultaneously, grasp across the tine near the rivet with your left hand forcing a gradual bend.

Insert small wooden wedges between the tines and slide them toward the rivet. With a hammer and small wood block, tap each wedge inward. For four- and five-tined forks, stop when the wedges are centered between dowel holes. When making a three-tined fork, tap the wedges just past the inner dowel holes. For two-tined forks, place two wedges side-by-side, and drive them in tandem past the inner dowel holes.

Place the 12-inch dowel across the outer dowel holes. Mark and saw to length. Hammer the dowel through the holes until the end is flush. Repeat the process in fitting the remaining dowel in the inner set of holes. Saw off the protruding dowel stubs.

Release the clamps and set the fork lengthwise on the bench, face down. Place a small block of wood under the outer dowel (so that there is direct contact between

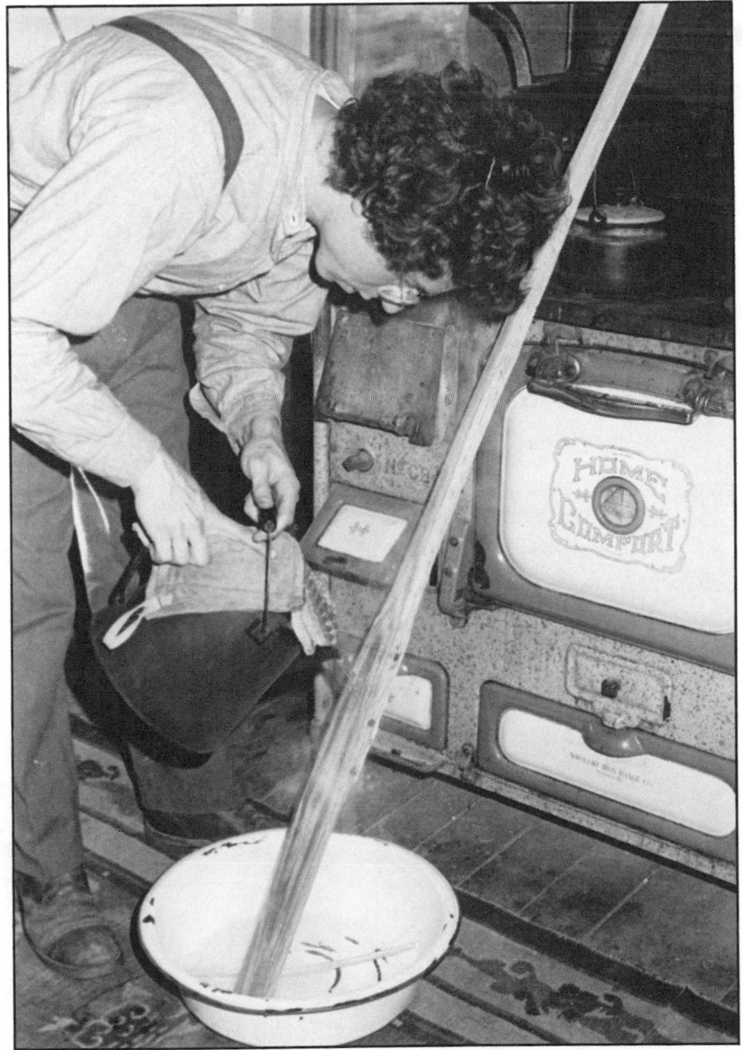

Pouring boiling water over tines just before spreading.

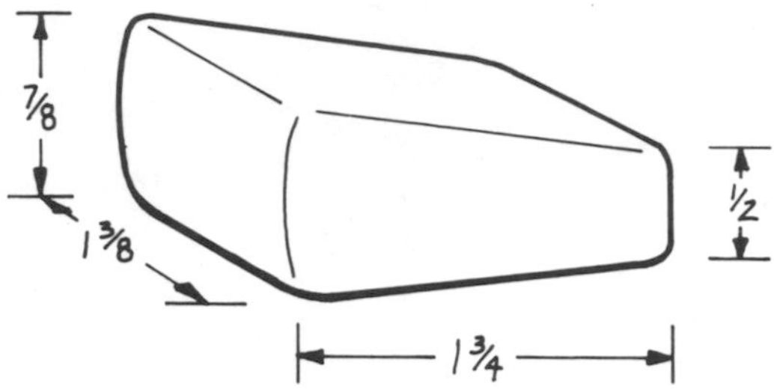

Wedge for spreading tines. A set of four is needed for a five-tined fork.

fork, block, and bench). Hammer and countersink small nails through each dowel-tine junction. Several types of nails can be used:

6/8 x 18-gauge last-makers channel nails (from cobbler-supply outlets)

7/8 fine-cut headless brads (Woodcraft Supply Corp.)

3/4 x 18-gauge brad (any hardware store)

Shaping tines. With a drawknife, bevel the top and bottom of each tine tip. Shape it so that the points have an upward sweep. Rotate the fork and bevel the side of each tine tip. Shave the tine edges to an octagonal section. Smooth the tine flats, being sure to shave with the grain.

Shaping tines with a spokeshave.

Construct a jig according to the measured drawing. Slowly pour boiling water over the fork head and neck. Set the fork through the jig, seating the tines in proper slots.

First bend. Place two 2 x 4 blocks beneath the handle end. Stand on the jig, and bend the handle upward. Insert the short dowel through the holes at the end of the jig. This will stabilize the jig. Bend the handle further, until the larger dowel can be fitted through holes beneath the handle. Remove the smaller dowel.

Second bend. Turn the jig upside down. Place 2 x 4 block under each jig sideboard at the head end (to protect tines). Put two stacked 2 x 4 blocks under the handle end. Stand on jig and bend handle upward, reversing the first curve. Insert the short dowel through the holes at end of the jig.

Allow the fork to season approximately two weeks.

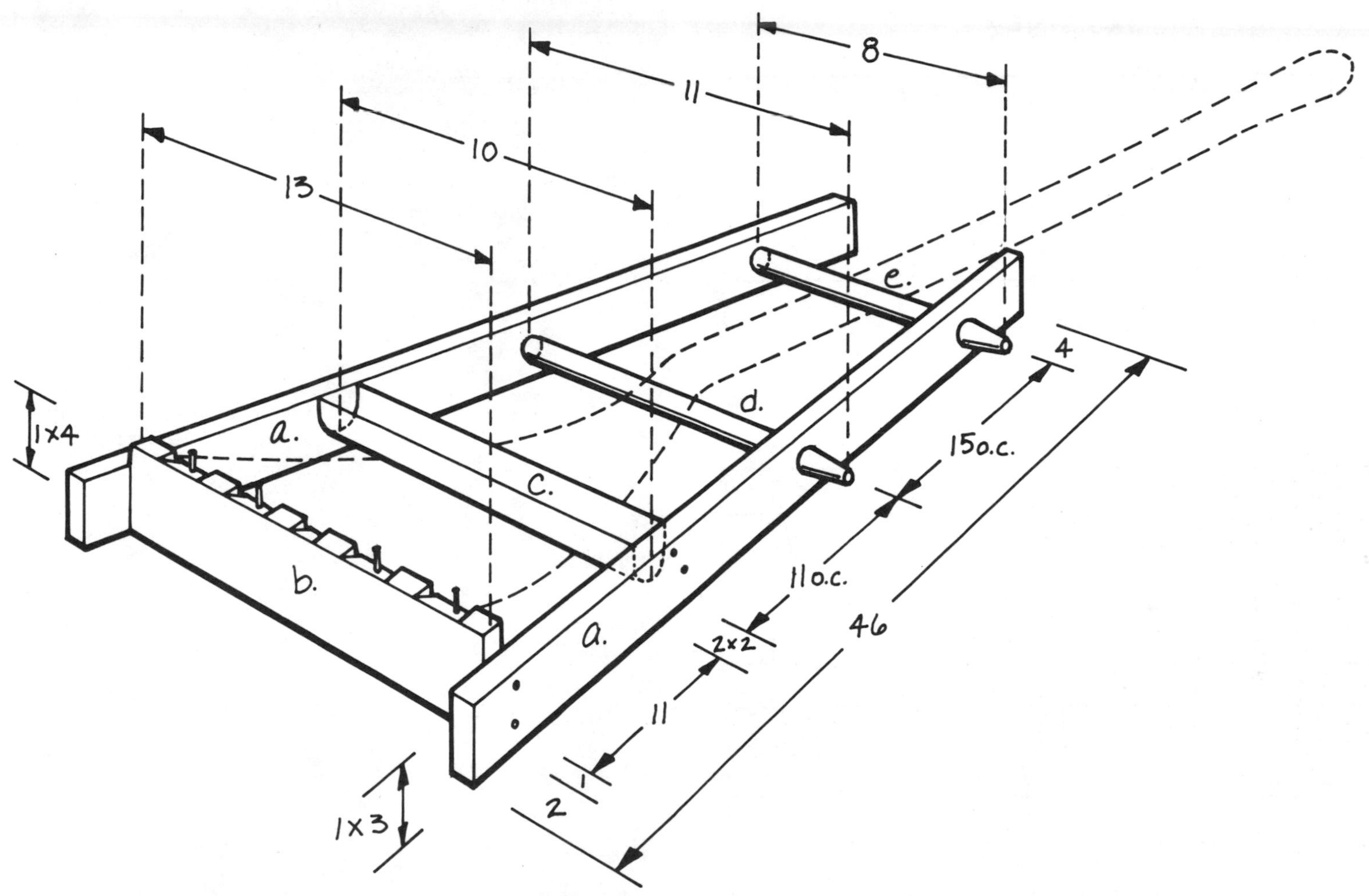

Bending jig for hay forks. Side rails (a,a) are nailed to notched spreader (b) at 82-degree angles. Similarly angled brace (c) is rounded on bottom contour and is also nailed to rails. Removable dowels (d,e) are 7/8-inch diameter and chamfered at one end to aid insertion through 1-inch dowel holes.

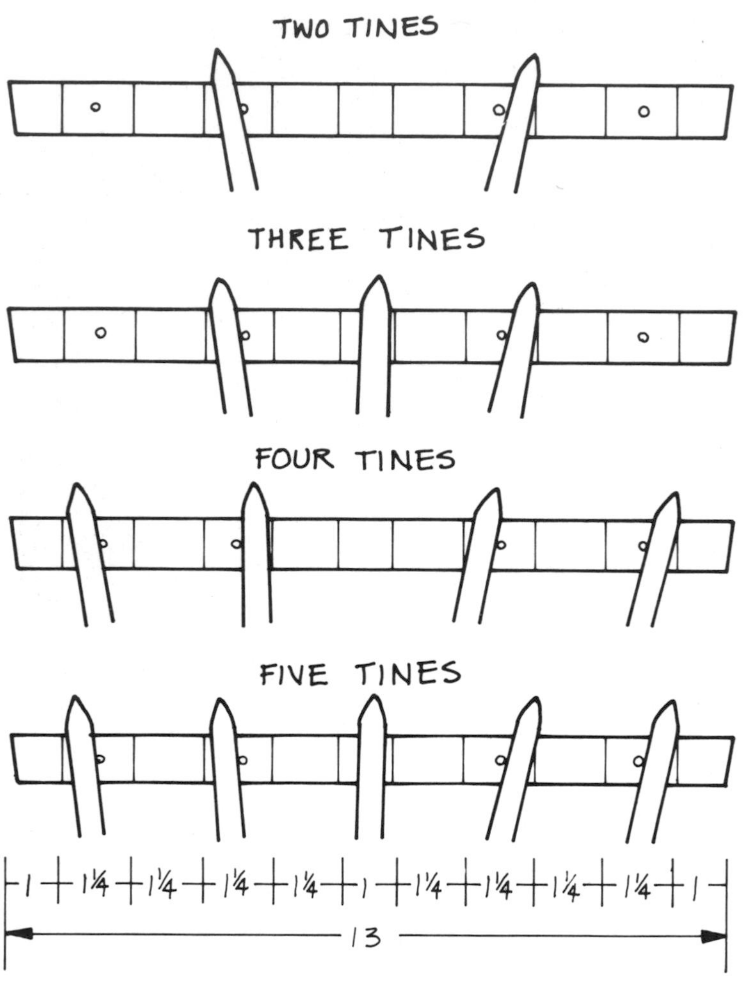

Spreading scheme for two-, three-, four-, and five-tined hay forks. The small circles within the angled slots represent ten-penny finishing nails used as dividers.

Bending a fork.

A test for seasoning is made by checking for a lack of tension against the dowels.

Finishing. Remove the fork from the jig. Rasp the dowel stub flush. Fill any cracks and countersunk nail holes with "wood dough." Sand the head with 80-grit, D-weight garnet paper. Smooth the handle with a scraper or a piece of broken glass, then used sandpaper. Finish with a mixture of two parts raw linseed oil to one part turpentine.

Note: Some hayfork makers traditionally fire hardened and coated tines with melted pine rosin. I tested forks with various tine finishes and found no difference in wear from one to another. Michael C. Contezac, of the USDA Forest Products Laboratory writes: "As far as we have been able to determine . . . so-called fire hardening . . . does not improve the hardness of wood but rather satisfies a common belief by many people that such handles are of higher quality. This practice is popular among manufacturers of handles for impact tools."

Jigged forks set in about ten days.

FROES

Froes were traditionally forged by village smiths or in local shops in small runs. The special interests of various craftsmen and particular types of wood called for different specifications.

In selecting or making a froe there are certain refinements that separate a tool that works properly from one that can cause more frustration than necessary.

A froe made for all-around use should be forged from ⅜- by 2-inch stock. Overall finished length is 12 to 15 inches. After forging, the 9- to 12-inch blade is about 2½ inches wide.

The striking surface across the top of the blade should be nicely rounded, as should the profile of the nose (blade tip). This helps to preserve the froe club as long as possible. The blade should be gradually tapered forming a fairly acute angle at the cleaving edge. In cross section, the flanks are slightly convex so that the contact point rolls across the blade as the froe is levered back and forth. In face view, the cleaving edge is also convex, but just a bit. This makes penetration easier. There is no need for a sharp knife edge—toughness is more important.

The eye can be round, oval, or cone-shaped. The loop of the eye may be joined by forge, gas,

Using a froe.

or arc welding, but it must be smooth on the inside. A cone-shaped eye accepts a handle enlarged at the end, like a pickax or adze handle. It's supposed to hold better.

Froe handles take a great deal of shock in normal use and are therefore prone to loosening. (With the cone-shaped eye there is a tendency for the iron to bounce back against the enlarged stub.)

Handles may be shaped with a drawknife or turned on a lathe. Heart of oak, hickory, and ash are among the many acceptable woods. For adequate leverage the handle of a 14-inch froe should be 18 to 20 inches long. Before stocking, saw a slot across the end. The handle should be carefully fitted to the eye and secured with a deep, acutely angled wooden wedge glued in place. (Refer to Chapter 9: Tool Handles and Chapter 10: Wedges.)

Froe clubs are quickly made from any hardwood at hand—hickory, oak, hornbeam, dogwood, apple, etcetera. Clubs should be seasoned before being put to use. (Further details are in Chapter 7: Clubs, Mauls, and Mallets.)

Homemade wheelbarrow.

CHAPTER 15
THE WHEELBARROW

THE DESIRE TO GET A LOAD OFF ONE'S BACK has been great for farmers and builders for a long time. This is a nonnewsworthy subject, commonly ignored by "experts." The story of the wheelbarrow must be put together largely through conjecture. As I see it, three streams of development led from the original "wish."

First, there are various ways of personally carrying a load; by hand or shoulder, with backpacks and tup lines, or directly on one's head.

Then come different methods of dragging. Hauling poles to a building site or camp fire would be a typical example. The *travois,* used by North American Plains Indians and other primitive cultures, consisted of two long poles with a bundle lashed onto the trailing ends. This worked well over smooth grass or snow on the American prairie.

Finally, there are methods of harnessing energy independent of our own flesh and bones: draft animals, wind and currents, and engines powered by fossil fuels.

It is the second group that concerns us here. Surely tens of thousands of years separate *travois* poles from a

Two-man barrow.

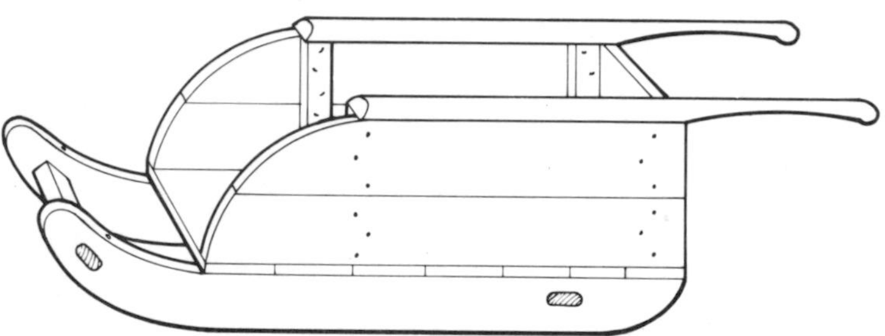

Sled barrow.

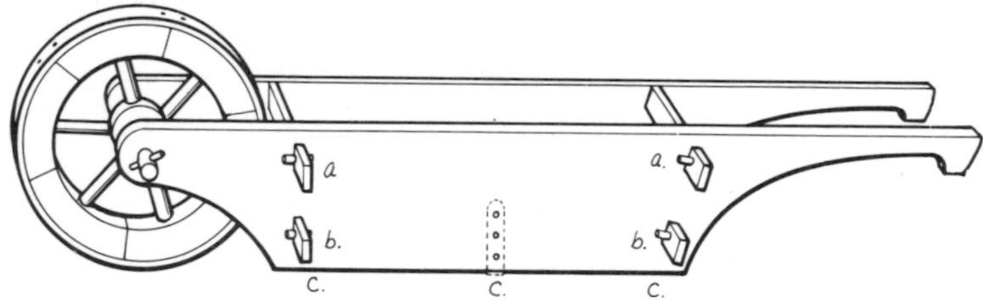

An old type of wheelbarrow. The tusk tenons (a,a,b,b) hold the sides together. The bottom is supported by a slot in the sides and end pieces. Or, tenons (b,b) are omitted and iron straps (c,c,c) are used instead.

"modern" wheelbarrow. It would be interesting to search for a variety of carriers evolving over the ages and in different areas. A good many of these preindustrial barrows can be seen in use today. And some are still very practical.

For instance, the two-man hand barrow, either flat or with a built-in box, is superior to a wheelbarrow for carrying loads over rocky, steep, or wet ground. On well-packed snow, a "sled barrow," pushed by one person, can carry enormous loads, even going uphill.[1] Be careful on the downhill side!

Perhaps wheels were discovered rather than invented. A tree trunk will scoot downhill with alarming speed if it happens to lie across one or more short logs that are free to turn like rollers. In fact, this is a good way to maneuver heavy logs around a woodlot, onto a truck, or through a sawmill. The "invention" was probably the isolation of a roller mounted on an axle of some sort. (See the illustration of a "drug" in Chapter 2: Materials.)

The essence of a wheelbarrow seems to be the idea of replacing one man in a two-man barrow with an axle and wheel. Over smooth terrain the wheel could carry more weight than the missing man.

Many old styles of wheelbarrows carried all the weight behind the wheel. This put severe limitations on how much a person could handle. One remedy was to lengthen the rails, giving the worker leverage. But there are practical limitations as the wheelbarrow

---

1. Eric Sloane, *A Museum of Early American Tools* (New York: Wilfred Funk, Inc., 1964), p. 87.

quickly becomes cumbersome and awkward to handle.

The ideal solution would locate the load over the wheel itself, so that the operator can concentrate his energy on forward movement, not lifting. The genius of this is fully realized in traditional Chinese wheelbarrows.[2] In the Chinese design, a framework is placed around and above the wheel, which is very large (fully 3 feet in diameter), so that it's comparatively easy to negotiate the rough roads or paths around farm plots. Very heavy loads—several persons, huge bundles of produce, wood, or goods—can be carried. But the load has to be tied on as there is no handy compartment to dump stuff into.

The modern "contractor's wheelbarrow" is a compromise design that is fairly efficient and quite expen-

2. Hommel, *China at Work,* p. 321; F. H. King, *Farmers of Forty Centuries* (Emmaus, Penna.: Rodale Press, 1974), p. 59.

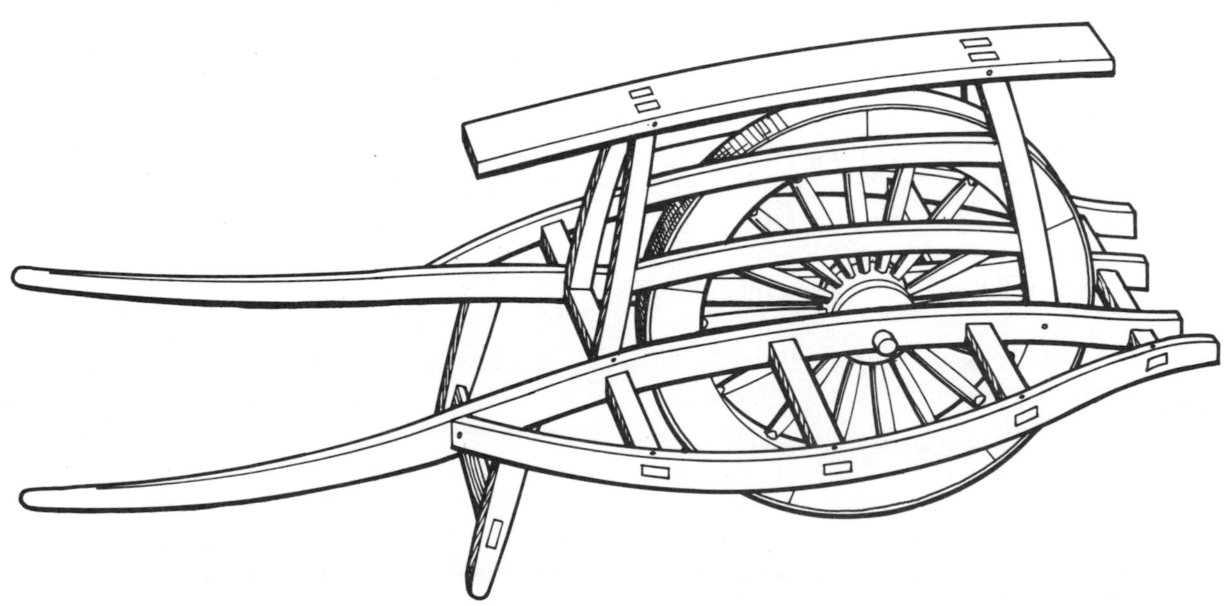

Traditional Chinese wheelbarrow.

sive. The load is concentrated well forward and more or less above the wheel due to the shape of the steel tub.

A far cheaper wheelbarrow, which is also superior for carrying certain types of loads, was used by rural English woodsmen, such as the old charcoal burners.[3] This wheelbarrow had a frame that was basically an X-shape in profile. One pair of rails had the conventional function of housing the axle and forming the handles. A second pair of diagonal poles crossed the rails behind the wheel, forming a platform above the wheel, and a triangulated element for bracing the legs when the wheelbarrow was not in use.

I first saw a wheelbarrow of this type while visiting homesteading friends who had just made one. It could carry five or six hay bales, several hundred pounds of feed, four garden flats, or a huge pile of firewood. The parts were all made of saplings, fitted together like Tinker Toy stubs and sockets. The iron wheel came from a long-dead commercial wheelbarrow, and cost 25¢ at a flea market.

Following are the plans as slightly modified in a version I have built and subsequently used a great deal.

For materials use hardwood saplings or sawn hardwood lumber. I used locust saplings, about 2½ inches in diameter at the base before debarking. Other good saplings include ash, hickory, beech, oak, and yellow pine. Altogether collect 40 feet of straight, knot-free wood. If sawn lumber is your choice, use 2 x 2s. Oak is the traditional wheelbarrow wood.

3. Edlin, *Woodland Crafts in Britain,* fig. 149.

You will also need a few small finishing nails (threepenny), one foot of ¼-inch dowel, one foot of ½-inch dowel (these are easy to make, see Chapter 13: Hay Rakes), some wire, a wheel, and an axle. Old iron wheels are nice looking, often free or very cheap, and they do work quite well. A pneumatic wheel might look "wrong" on a rustic wheelbarrow, but it would work better. For the axle, use a ½-inch bolt, 12 inches long. (The head and threaded end help to keep it in place.)

Construction. With saplings, the first step is to debark the saplings with a drawknife. Look over the wood, choosing the best pieces for the two main rails and the two diagonal rails. Saw out these pieces:

Two main rails, each 70 inches long.
Two diagonal rails, each 52 inches long.
One front brace, 11 inches long, (it should be a stout piece, fully 2½ inches in diameter).
One center crosspiece, 20 inches long.
One rear brace, 18 inches long.
One platform brace, 14 inches long.
Two legs, each 12 inches long.
Two cross braces, each 20 inches long (they may be small as 1½ inches in diameter), or use 1-inch-wide steel straps.
½-inch-thick platform boards, each 20 inches long. (Enough material to cover from front to rear brace—48 inches over-all—is needed.)

Saw the parts to length and lay out the stub and socket joints. The holes are a full 1 inch in diameter, about 1½ inches deep.

To make the stubs, mark out the stub shoulder 2 inches from the end of the piece. With the part in a shaving horse or vise, drawknife down to about a 1¼-inch diameter, forming a rather soft S-curve profile. Then, with the piece in a vise (you can't do it with a shaving horse), drawknife from the end grain straight toward the shoulder for about 1½ inches. Gradually work down to a diameter as close as possible to 1 inch. Remove the waste wood with a sharp knife. Chamfer the leading edge with a spokeshave or knife. Make test fittings in a block of wood drilled with a 1-inch hole.

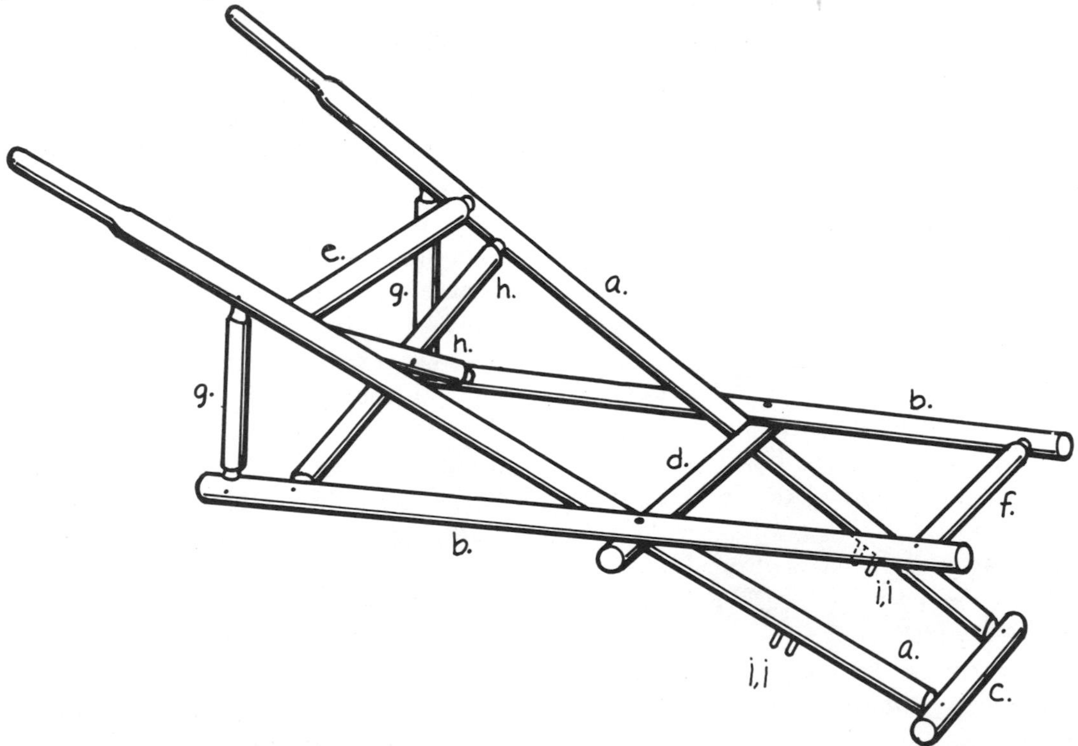

Wheelbarrow framework. (a,a) main rails, 70 inches; (b,b) diagonal rails, 52 inches; (c) front brace, 11 inches; (d) center crosspiece, 20 inches; (e) rear brace, 18 inches; (f) platform brace, 14 inches; (g,g) legs, 12 inches; (h,h) cross braces, 20 inches (or steel straps screwed in an X directly into legs (g,g)); (i,i) dowels to hold axle in place.

Make and assemble in the following order:

The front brace has two holes, each drilled 2 inches from the ends.

Each rail has a stub at the large end. The rear-brace sockets are 18 inches from the handle tips. The leg-brace sockets are 16 inches from the handle tips perpendicular to the brace sockets (facing downward). Be sure to designate left and right rails. Shape the handles. Insert the rail stubs into the front-brace sockets.

Make the rear brace. Fit it to the rails. Drill 1/16-inch pilot holes through the rails into the stubs just above the front and rear braces. Drive a finishing nail through each of these joints. *Leave the head and 1/4 inch of the nail exposed in case the pieces have to be disassembled later.*

Notch the center crosspiece to accept the main rails and the diagonal rails. Locate it 20 inches from the front of the rail stubs, and secure it with 3-inch lengths of 1/4-inch doweling, chamfered along the leading edge to prevent tearing.

Drill sockets 2 inches from the ends of the diagonals for the platform brace and for the legs. Be sure to designate right and left pieces.

Make the platform brace with stubs at each end. Attach it to the diagonals and pin part way through the joint with finishing nails.

Locate the diagonal rails across the center crosspiece, well over the wheel. Pin with a 1/2-inch dowel.

Make the legs. Drill socket holes under the rails after finding location by test fit. Pin loosely. *Note:* The placement of the legs and the rear brace should be reversed from positions shown in photographs. This will give better leg room when pushing the barrow uphill.

Make the cross braces. Locate them by experimentation. If necessary, pull the rails and diagonals into position by twisting tight a cord looped around opposite pieces. These braces may also be made of 1-inch-wide steel straps, drilled, then screwed or even nailed in place.

Drive down the protruding finishing nails, but don't countersink them. At this point the wheelbarrow looks exceeding long. The rail handles must extend well beyond the platform for ease of use. Otherwise the operator's knees would constantly bump into the platform.

Treat the frame with creosote.

Nail on the platform boards. Treat both surfaces with creosote.

The axle carriers are two pairs of 1/2-inch dowel stubs protruding 1 1/2 inches beneath the rails. Their exact location depends upon the diameter of your wheel. Install the stubs and drop the wheelbarrow frame over the wheel and axle. Use extra washers or oversized nuts to help center the wheel.

Twist wire in an X-pattern over the rails and under the axle so that the wheel can't drop off at bumps or ledges. (This works.)

For the next wheelbarrow I make, I'll lengthen the

overhanging platform 3 or 4 inches to put even more load over the wheel. I'll also lengthen the main rails 2 or 3 inches, giving more leg clearance along the handles. A removable bottomless box attached to pegs inserted through the platform brace and the main rails would make a nice addition.

Milking stool.

CHAPTER 16
SWISS MILKING STOOL

LOUISE AND I first saw a Swiss milking stool while living in the Bernese Alps with a cheese-making woodworker friend. The stool differs from a common milking seat in that it is one-legged, and it is strapped onto the user.

Anyone who has milked a cow (or goat) will immediately see the advantages. Cows (and goats) tend to wander and sway around during milking. With this stool, the single leg easily pivots in any direction; the user provides the other legs, forming a triangular base that flexes with the situation. When milking is finished, or if you have to move, the strap holds the seat so that it doesn't need to be carried.

When we began homesteading, I made a replica Swiss milking stool, even though it was to be a year before our heifer freshened. The stool is now in use, twice daily, and as one old-timer around here says, I wouldn't trade it for a pretty penny.

Strapped in place, the stool does look funny. But one soon learns to appreciate something so useful. The buckle is set quite loose so that the stool almost dangles beneath one's buttocks; that way, the leg flops to a vertical position as you sit down.

The traditional design is very simple. The seat is shaped like a rounded-off rectangle—typically measuring 5½ x 11 inches. The top is slightly dished for a comfortable seat. A 1-inch hole is drilled through the center to hold the leg. At each side there's a slot for the leather straps.

The leg measures about 11 inches, including the 1½-inch stub that passes through the seat. The leg diameter tapers from approximately 1¼ inches at the rounded tip to 1⅝ inches at the base, where a shoulder is cut bringing the diameter of the stub down to 1 inch. Sometimes legs are turned on a lathe in a fancy shape. Others are made longer or shorter than 11 inches, depending on personal preference. At the tip of the leg is a dull spike made from a tenpenny double-headed (duplex) nail.

The 1-inch leather straps measure 24 inches and 28 inches (including over-laps for passing through the seat slots and around the buckle).

A wide variety of woods could be used for making this stool. The seat should be a wood fairly easy to shape. The leg must be a hard wood. My stool has an ash seat and a white oak leg. Maple all-around would be handsome. A pine board (or pine split) seat, with a pine limb leg would do the trick.

To make the seat, you need a flat blank measuring 5½ x 11 x 1½ inches. (A so-called 2 x 6 would work fine). Shape to the desired outline with a drawknife, saw, rasp, and/or spokeshave. Dish the seat before rounding the bottom. (The original flat bottom is easier

to hold in place than the ultimate convex shape.)

The seat can be clamped in place, or secured by a holdfast. In either case, the hardware will be in the way, and you risk nicking a gouge in it. You can set the wood into a vise, but it tends to come loose as the work progresses; the curved sides of the seat don't provide a good grip, and woodworking vises are not really made to be pounded on. Another way to hold the wood for this type of carving is against two short pegs driven through the workbench. Or you could use a loosely filled sandbag; this technique borrowed from the metal arts. But the ideal way to hold such a piece is between two dogs: one just protruding above the bench surface, the other on a vise. In this situation, the work is held on the bench top, not between the vise jaws.

To scoop out the concave seat, use a large, shallow gouge, about 1½ inches wide. A bent-style gouge is best. Work inward from the ends. For roughing out, you may need to strike the gouge with a mallet. Finish work is done holding the gouge two-handed, with the left hand close up to the cutting edge, acting as a guide and fulcrum. The gouge must be very sharp. (Refer to Chapter 26: Spoons.) The total depth is about ½ inch—just enough to make a nicely dished seat. Smooth with a curved scraper, or a piece of broken glass.

The convex underside of the seat may be formed with a drawknife, chisel, and spokeshave. Leave a flat circle in the center for the leg to butt against.

Drill the 1-inch-diameter leg hole with a brace and bit.

The strap slots are located 1 inch on center from

each end. A simple way to make these slots is by drilling two ⅜-inch holes, 1 inch apart. Then drill two or three ¼-inch holes in between. Finish cleaning up with a narrow chisel. (Do not drill or chisel straight through; work from both sides.)

The leg may be turned on a lathe, carved with a knife, or shaped with a drawknife and spokeshave on a shaving horse. The piece starts out as a 1¾-inch square, 11 inches long. On a shaving horse, first shape to an octagon. Continue reducing the diameter to 1⅝ inches, slightly tapering towards the 1¼-inch tip. Round off the tip using a rasp and sandpaper.

With a pencil, mark off the shoulder 2 inches from the base. Set the leg in a vise or across the jaw of a shaving horse, and begin to saw (with a backsaw or 11-point crosscut) very shallowly along the line, going round and round the leg. Saw about ¼ inch deep. Take a chisel and, from the end grain, knock out waste wood forming the shoulder. Measure. Then saw and chisel again, bringing the diameter to 1 inch. Saw a slot across the grain, the full depth of the stub. Chamfer the tip of the stub just slightly. Make a small wooden wedge (as explained in Chapter 10: Wedges).

Fit the leg into the seat. Use a mallet, not a hammer. If necessary, shave the stub to fit. (It will protrude slightly.) Apply a bit of white glue to the wedge and drive in place. Trim off the stub with a chisel or slightly curved gouge.

The straps are made of 1-inch-wide leather strips. They may be riveted or sewn around the slots and buckle. (A method of making rivets from nails is de-

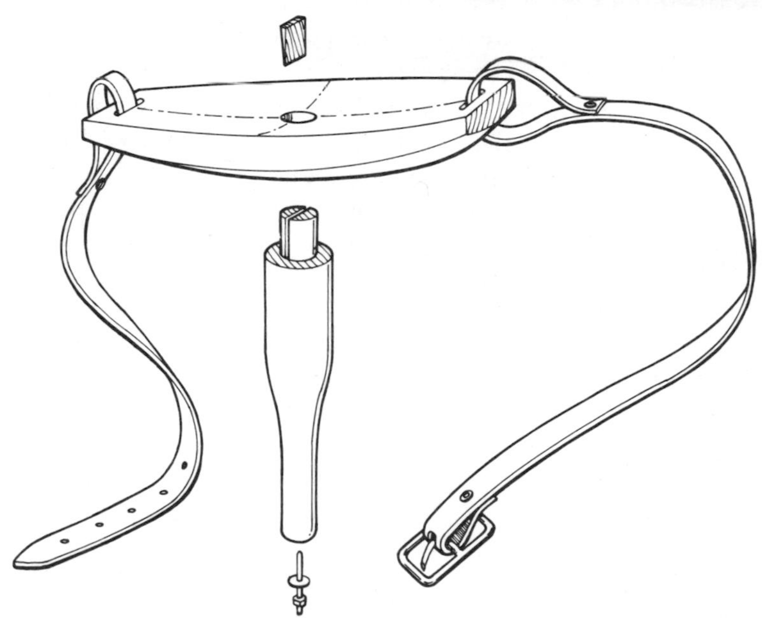

Assembly details.

scribed in Chapter 14: Pitchforks.) Buckle holes may be punched out or made with a hand drill.

The final step, making the spike, is optional, but recommended for barns and milking parlors with wooden flooring. (For milking on concrete floors, use a rubber chair-leg tip. On dirt floors, no special tip is required.) This spike eliminates any chance that the stool could slip when sitting at an angle.

Drill a ⅛-inch hole about 1 inch deep in the center end grain of the leg. With nippers or a hack saw, remove the head of a tenpenny duplex nail, and trim to a length of 1 inch below the remaining head. Round both ends with a file. Insert the nail through a size 0 washer. Tap into the leg tip.

Finish the stool by sanding; then oil or varnish or leave to polish through natural use.

Shoulder yoke.

CHAPTER 17
A HAULING YOKE

ANYONE WHO HAS HAULED buckets of water around soon realizes that a good part of the job is holding the weight out to the sides in a comfortable position for walking. And it's almost easier to haul two buckets than one. This is because a single bucket tends to hang toward the carrier's center of gravity causing it to bump into the legs in a very annoying way. Another problem with conventional hauling is the strain on the grip on the bucket bails.

With a carrying yoke (also called a burden stick or carrier) one still has to haul the weight of those buckets full of water. But it is a far easier task as there's no effort involved in holding the buckets out to each side. Fingers don't cramp up, either. Instead, the weight is distributed evenly over a wide shoulder area, perfectly in line with gravity. The yoke arms hold the buckets a nice distance apart for comfortable hauling.

For some reason, the use of burden carriers seems to have died out in this country. Such devices were common household articles during our pioneer era. I believe Americans don't like to think of themselves as carrying a burden. But I suggest making one and trying

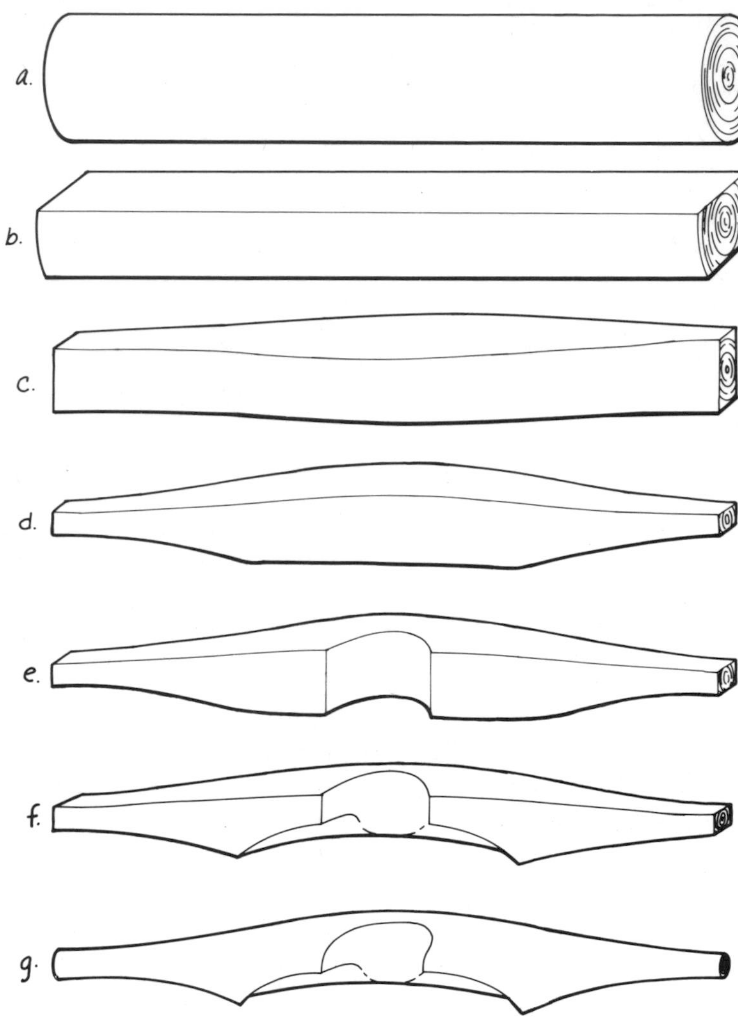

Yoke-carving sequence: (a) round log, 7 to 8 inches in diameter, 38 inches long; (b) top and bottom hewn flat and parallel to each other; (c) top plane hewn to shape; (d) front plane; (e) neck; (f) shoulder; (g) finished yoke.

it if you have to haul water to a cabin, barn, or garden on more than an occasional basis.

Yokes were made by English carvers and turners until recently. And they are commonly seen throughout much of Asia. Yokes can also be used to carry firewood, feed, compost, etcetera.

Material. To make a hauling yoke choose a wood that is easy to carve, fairly lightweight, yet quite strong. Tulip poplar, bass, and pine would be good choices. The only sure way to avoid serious checking is to use thoroughly seasoned wood. (If this is impossible, see special measures in Chapter 27: Dough Troughs.) The yoke shown was made from a poplar log, 7 inches in diameter, 38 inches long. This yoke is just about right for an average-sized person. The dimensions and configuration should be determined by the user in a personal fitting.

Construction. The first step in this project is debarking. Then roughly square the log. Score the top plane by making shallow cuts of equal depth with a hand saw. Hew flat with a hatchet. Repeat on the remaining sides, being careful to make them perpendicular to one another.

Snap chalk centerlines along the center of the top and front planes. Sketch out the upper vertical projection (excluding the neck and shoulder cavities). Saw a series of cuts 3 or 4 inches apart, almost down to the guidelines. Knock out major waste wood using a chisel and mallet. (Work with or across the grain.) Sketch the horizontal projection and shape as above.

Locate the center of the yoke and sketch the neck cavity. Allow 2 inches of wood along the back of the yoke for adequate strength. Make several saw cuts into the neck cavity. Clean out with a chisel. Turn the yoke over and sketch the shoulder cavity. Rough out. Be sure not to work too deeply at this point.

Round out the yoke with a chisel or drawknife, then a spokeshave. A large bent gouge is fine for shaping the shoulder cavity. A large shallow gouge (number 3) is helpful for smoothing the neck cavity. These gouges must be sharp! (Use and sharpening of gouges is further discussed in Chapter 26: Spoons.)

Try a test fitting, checking for pressure points that should be relieved. Go over the outside surfaces again with a sense of achieving minimal weight and graceful contours. Bevel the edges around the neck cavity.

To use the yoke, tie one end of a 3-foot length of stout rope around each yoke arm. Find two forked sticks and secure to the hanging end of each rope. Hook the sticks around the bucket bails. At first one may have difficulty walking with the heavy buckets swinging back and forth. Develop a smooth gliding walk so that the load remains stable.

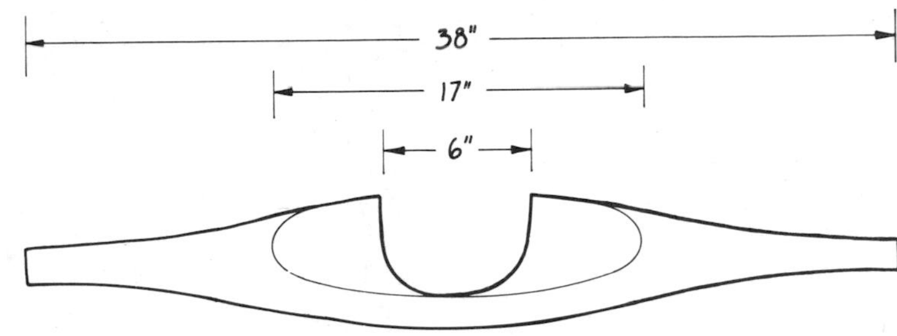

Yoke dimensions from the bottom side.

An old sled with locust runners and pine box.

CHAPTER 18
SLEDS

WORKING WITH DRAFT ANIMALS is one of several potential alternatives to a fossil-fuel-based agriculture. However, keeping and using horses or mules (or donkeys or ponies or oxen) involves a commitment which includes year-round care and feeding, and the mastery of special skills for both man and his farming partners. One must be aware that a 1,000- to 2,000-pound horse can deliver a fatal kick. And there is the risk of accidents from runaway equipment. These are just a few of the details that must be considered.[1] I am not an expert with draft animals, but have worked our place with such beasts for a few years now. Experiences have been good and bad. So far, I'm sticking with our equestrian friends.

1. Helpful resources for hopeful teamsters include: Maurice Telleen, *The Draft Horse Primer* (Emmaus, Penna.: Rodale Press, 1977); George Ewart Evans, *The Horse in the Furrow* (London: Faber and Faber, 1960); Small Farmer's Journal (Junction City, Ore., issued quarterly).

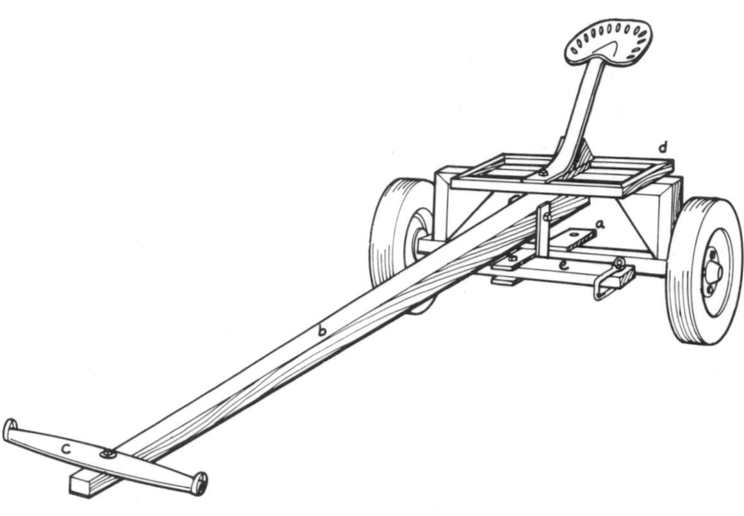

A fore-cart used with with pull-type tractor equipment. Drawbar is at (a). Tongue (b) is 13 feet from neck yoke (c) to end of welded steel box frame (d). Evener (e) is mounted 2 feet in front of axle.

A basic problem that faces most anyone who wishes to work with draft animals is acquiring usable equipment. A few items may be bought new. There is still a lot of old stuff around—once you start hunting. Get a realistic idea of what you need first. A lot of the old farm equipment was made for hitches of three, four, or five heavy horses. The beginner will have his hands full handling one or two horses or mules on far fewer acres than much of the larger old machinery was made for.

Some of the smaller, old pull-type tractor equipment can be adapted for work with draft animals. This is done by rigging up a "fore-cart"; consisting of an axle and a pair of wheels that supports the weight of the equipment. A tongue is attached to the front of the axle, upon which are mounted the equipment hook-up and an old tractor seat to ride on.

The remainder of this section on agricultural implements is about homemade equipment for use with draft animals. These implements are all proven and serviceable. They are easily worked by a single animal weighing 1,000 pounds, or less.

Sleds rate high on our homestead. They can be pulled over rough terrain (which would shake a cart or wagon apart). They do well traversing slopes (where a wagon might tip over). Being low to the ground, they are easy to load up. On the other hand, carts and wagons are far better for traveling on roads, which quickly abrade sled runners to nothing. (You can smell them burn.)

Farm sleds are used throughout the year. We haul

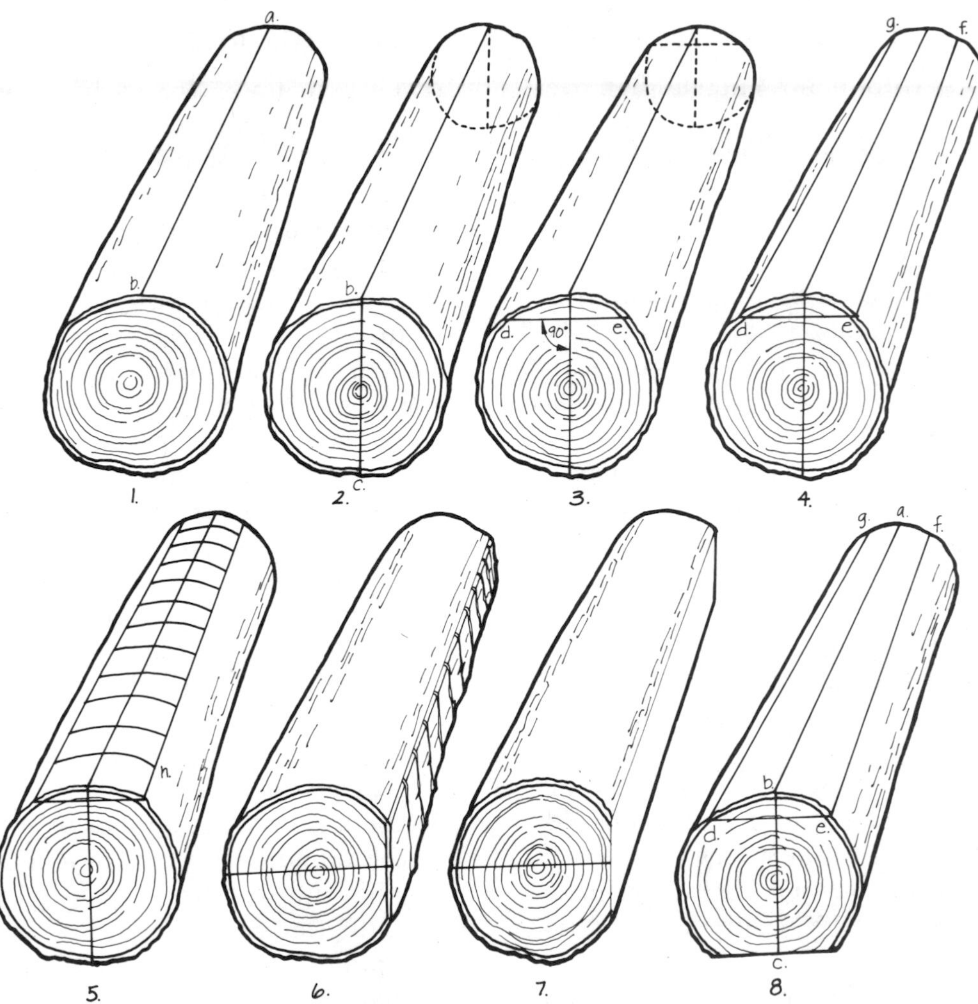

Steps in hewing a log. 1. Snap a chalk line (a,b) along the center of the top of the log. 2. Draw verticals (b,c) on both ends of the log. 3. Draw horizontals (d,e) on both ends. 4. Snap chalk lines (d,g) and (e,f). 5. Score (h) with an axe or saw to the chalk lines, 6. Rotate the log 90 degrees and chop off large chips. 7. Hew to the line with a broadax (or return to horizontal position and use an adze or slick). 8. Rotate the log with flat side down and lay out the opposite face as in the above steps.

firewood, compost, rock, corn, plows, and children over grass, through woods, across streams, over snow, just about anywhere. Huge loads can be pulled in winter over well-packed snow. But then the teamster must be very careful on even slight downhill runs.

Materials. The main elements of any sled are the runners. The wood chosen must be tough, hard-wearing, and weatherable. In addition, it is advisable to locate timber curved to a natural runner shape. Runners can be hand-hewn from logs; or lumber may be bought and appropriately shaped.

In the Southern Highlands, sourwood is the favorite wood for sled runners. Locust and oak are also used. Hewing runners from a curved log is best, as they will be tough and long lasting. The trick is to find two logs with well-matched bends.

While log hewing (for building construction) is a specialized craft in its own right, a few general tips will be helpful for the beginner out to shape a pair of sled runners.

Hewing. To hew a log one needs a very sharp axe (preferably a broadax, although a sharp double-bit will do), two half-log trestles (or two short logs laid flat on the ground), a chain saw or one-man log saw (actually both optional), hewing dogs (or chain and a load binder), a chalk line, and a level.

First snap a line down the center of the log. With the level, scribe or pencil a vertical line from the centerline down each end of the log. This insures that you don't hew a paraboloid. For a runner 4 inches wide, scribe vertical lines 2 inches to each side of the end-center guidelines. Snap a line from the edge intersections of these lines from one end of the log to the other.

Lay the log on one side and secure in place. With a chain saw, crosscut, or axe, score a series of cuts, 4 to 6 inches apart, across the guidelines. With the axe, chop out most of the waste wood. Then rotate the log 90 degrees and hew down to the guidelines. Turn the log to the other side and repeat this process. The top and bottom planes are located by setting a right angle against the original guidelines, then proceeding as with the sides. With a sled, special allowance will have to be made for the curved forerunners.

Shaping runners from commercial lumber is much easier—but not so good. It's difficult to find timber with good grain. And then there is the problem of preventing undue wear at the front ends if they lack a natural curvature. In northern Europe, runners were steamed and bent in jigs.[2] Another approach is to add lengths of 2 x 4 along the bottoms of the runners. This is explained in detail in the section on *half-soles* (see below).

In any case, runners should be shaped green, then set aside to season at least six months before being used. Green runners will wear down before your very eyes.

Because sleds are commonly used over rough terrain, the framework is purposely left flexible, but very well pinned together. In a typical Appalachian sled, the primary crossmember is an oak 2 x 4 mortised into the runners about 6 inches from the front end. A wooden pin, spike, or bolt is driven through the runner to secure this joint. The remaining (secondary) members

2. Viires, *Woodworking in Estonia,* pp. 159-165.

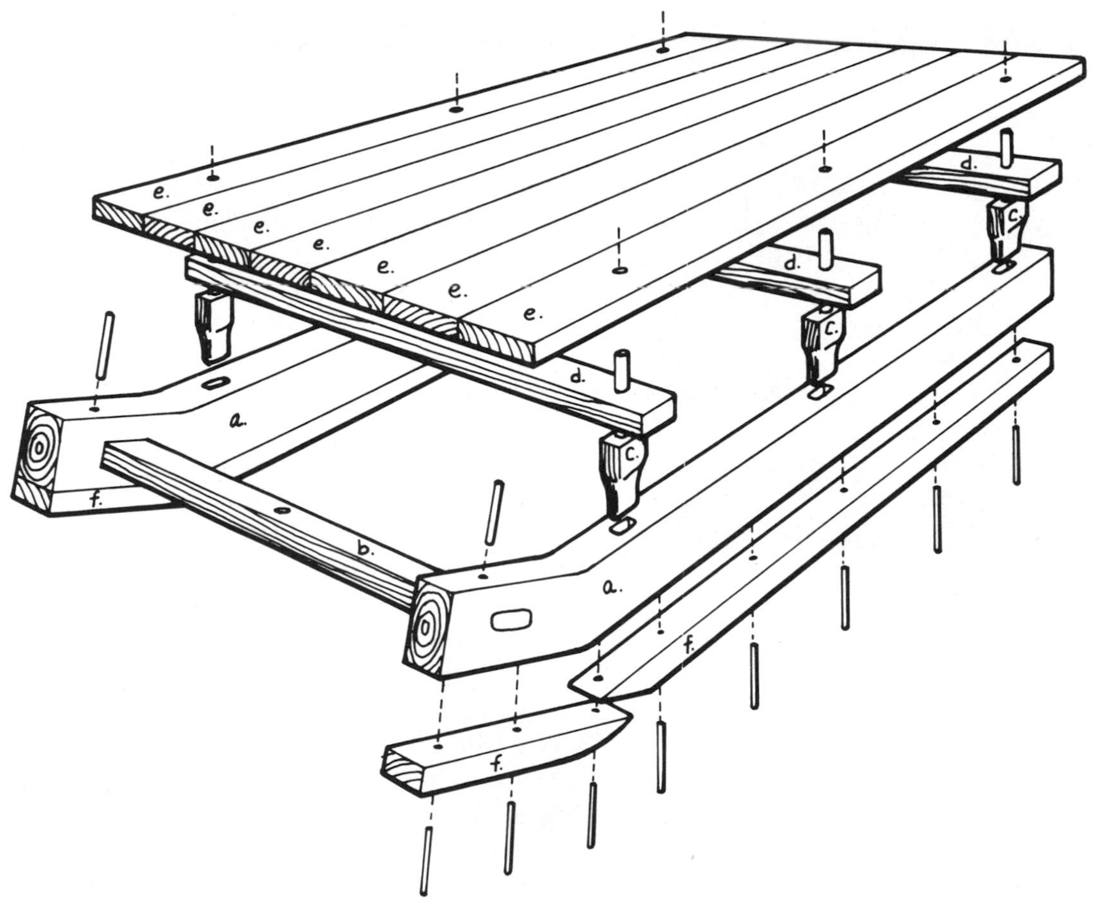

Sled with half-soles. Length 60 to 84 inches; width 42 to 54 inches. Sled parts. (a) runners; (b) primary cross member; (c) standards; (d) secondary cross members; (e) floor boards; (f) half-soles.

Sled parts ready for assembly.

are not attached directly to the runners as this would reduce the sled's ground clearance. Secondary members are fitted to a series of short, double-tenoned *standards* (supports), mortised along the runner tops, centered about 2 feet apart. Standards are generally carved from split-out white or red oak. They can be shaped from an oak 2 x 4, but will be considerably weaker if the grain is not perfectly straight. Standards are usually about 14 inches long.

The standard tenon is 4 inches long. These tenons may be square, but they are usually carved round or oval to fit into holes drilled with a 1½-inch auger. Four inches of the original 2 x 4 are left rectangular to raise the bed above the runners. The upper tenon—6 inches long and rounded—accepts the remaining secondary crossmembers and floorboards, and locates the cargo box in place. Seasoned standards should be fitted into green runners so that they will tighten up during seasoning. (Before the sled is put into service.)

The secondary crossmembers are rough oak 1 x 4s with holes drilled at each end to fit over the top rounds of the standards. At this stage, the sled is overly flexible. To create sufficient rigidity, 1-inch floorboards are nailed side-by-side on top of the secondary crossmembers. The outer floorboards should be bored to pass over the standards.

To complete the sled, a ½-inch hole is drilled through the center of the primary crossmember. A clevis is attached to an open ring, which connects to the singletree, which is hooked to the trace chains, which are linked to the hames, which pull against the collar, which the horse or mule pushes (not pulls!) around the old homeplace.

For most hauling, a bottomless box is set over the floorboards. The easiest way to make such a box is to nail 1-inch side and end boards to 2 x 2s located at the corners. The box is set inside the standards, and held in place by two metal straps, which loop around the front standards. (Electric conduit straps are excellent.) For hauling logs, the box is left off. It's also nice to have a very low box, made of 2 x 6s, for carrying rock and bucked firewood.

Half-soles. Sled runners wear down as they're used. Very old sleds may not be worth fixing up. However, if runners are only partly worn, replacement strips called half-soles can be added on. Seasoned hardwood (usually oak) should be used. To make the runner curve, half-soles are generally in two pieces. One long 2 x 4 is doweled to the runner bottom. A shorter piece overlaps the bottom piece, extending up the curved forerunner. Nails should not be used as they don't wear down with the half-sole, but tend to bend backward and eventually pull out.

Sled runners generally wear to a slightly curved bottom section. This makes fitting new half-soles a troublesome task. Therefore, it's a good plan to put half-soles on a sled before it's ever used. Half-sole replacement over the original square-edged runners is then very easy. (A new sled with half-soles could be used with green runners. However, the various mortises would never tighten to the same degree as well-seasoned runners. Still, this is a reasonable expedient.)

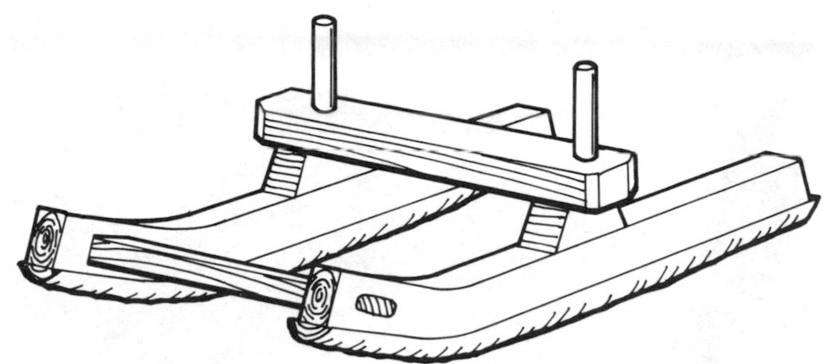

Logging sled with beech half-soles. Log butts are lashed to crossbar; ends drag behind. About 4½ feet long.

Rough locks (chains wrapped around runners) prevent free sliding in snow and ice.

Brakes. Sleds do have problems on downhill runs, particularly over snow, ice, deeply piled autumn leaves, and short, dry winter-killed grass. Depending on slope and ground cover, the sled might speed up and slide into the fetlocks of the horse or mule (that was) pulling it. In dry weather, it's usually possible to pick a route where this won't happen. Years ago, the local farmers grew tobacco and corn on steep slopes of freshly cleared woodland. To bring their crop downhill, they would wrap chain loops around the sled fore standards creating enough friction to avoid runaways. This was hard on the ground, but worked fine on snow. The chains, called rough locks, are about 30 inches long, and are linked together with figure eight links. Be sure to remove rough locks on the level or when climbing grades.

Perhaps the best system is to build a sled with shafts similar to those used on carts for hillside and winter work. With such a rig, the harness includes full britching, and the horse or mule actually controls the slide; the distance to the sled is always held constant.

There are, of course, many variations to this general sled plan. One handy type is a stone boat. This is a small sled, perhaps 30 x 40 inches, consisting of a pair of runners and a primary crossmember with floor boards nailed directly across the runner tops.

Old farms also had many types of man-pulled and pushed sleds. A fair-sized sled load of hay can be man-pulled over grass. "Sled barrows" are easily pushed over snow, even uphill. (Illustrated in Chapter 15: The Wheelbarrow.)

Single-foot or bull tongue. Locust beam and foot with bent oak handles.

CHAPTER 19
BULL TONGUE PLOW

THIS WOODEN PLOW can be used in gardens or small fields with a small draft animal. Unlike a moldboard plow, which inverts the soil, the bull tongue (or single-foot) breaks and aerates without turning the soil over. It's not meant for turning sod (moldboard work) or incorporating mulch or cover crops (best done with a disk harrow). Bull tongues work well for laying out planting furrows, light plowing, and in late fall for harvesting potatoes.

Some bull tongues also had a *coulter* for cutting sod. A coulter is a steel knife-like blade set through the beam in front of the shovel. The coulter was jammed tightly in place through a slot and against the sides of a square loop of iron placed around the beam.

Materials. Wood for the *beam* and *foot* should be heartwood from any tough hardwood. Oak was most commonly used. Mine is locust. These pieces are hewn or sawed from a straight-grain log free of knots. Avoid checks and warping by using well-seasoned timber. The *handles* (made green) are usually oak. However, hickory or ash could be used. The seasoned *stretchers* are cleft hardwood. A few pieces of hardware are needed: a clevis, the shovel (plow point), several nuts and bolts, and two homemade keepers fitted at the handle stubs.

The beam and foot are both made from 3 x 5 stock. The beam is 50 inches long. The foot measures 23 inches overall. The wood should be cross-grained (quartersawn). The exact shape of the beam is not too important. It may be straight, slightly arced, or S-curved. The 3-inch width is maintained the full length, but the depth tapers to 2½ inches at the clevis end. This gives balance to the plow and saves weight. (For tips on shaping, see the section on hewing in Chapter 18: Sleds.) The through-mortise should not be made until the tenoned foot is finished. Bevels along the beam are made after the foot is in place.

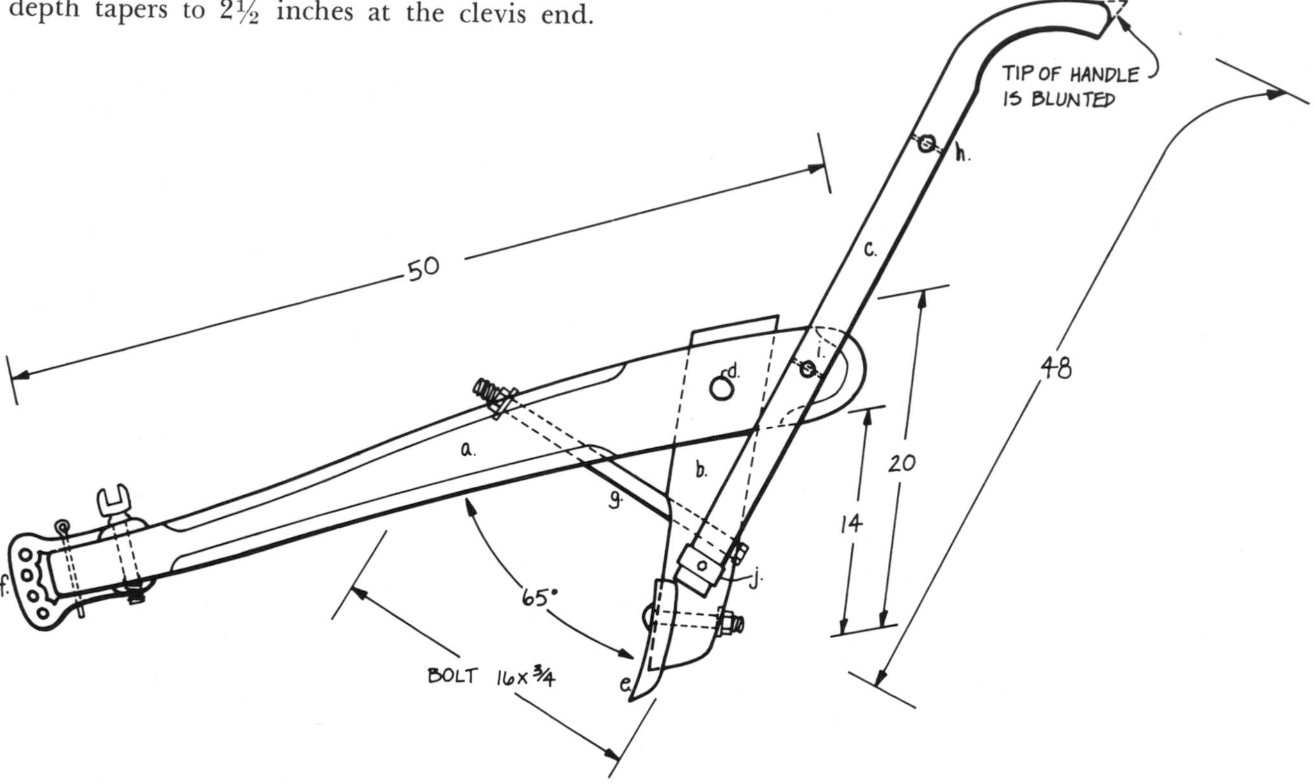

Plow dimensions and components: (a) beam, (b) foot, (c) handles, (d) dowel, (e) shovel, (f) clevis, (g) draw bolt, (h) upper brace, (i) lower brace, (j) keepers.

The foot includes a 1-inch tenon stub protruding above the beam. The tenon is 1 inch wide. (Refer to Appendix I: Mortise and Tenon Joinery.) The angle of the foot to the beam is approximately 55 to 60 degrees. Bore the 1-inch dowel hole that secures the foot to the beam before chopping out the mortise. The long, narrow mortise is made to fit the finished tenon. Locate the dowel hole through the foot $\frac{3}{16}$-inch off center so that the foot is pulled tightly in place when the dowel is inserted. Do not insert the dowel until later.

With mortise and tenon constructed, line up holes for the $\frac{3}{4}$- x 16-inch draw bolt. Drill or chisel washer-sized seats perpendicular to the bolt before boring the actual holes.

Fit the clevis. This may be store-bought, salvaged from an old plow, or made up by a blacksmith. The multiple adjustment feature is a necessity for proper use. Attaching the singletree to an upper hole causes the implement to plow deeper, while the lower holes are for more shallow work.

Disassemble the plow. Chamfer the beam to save weight and eliminate edges that tend to catch or wear. Bevel the leading edge of the foot to match the inside curve of the plow point.

Handles are homemade, or store-bought. These are 2 inches wide, 1 inch thick, and 48 inches long. Handles may be fashioned in either of two ways.

The simplest technique is to find saplings that are more or less straight for a 3-foot section followed by a bend of 20 to 30 degrees. The handle is carved out using a hatchet, drawknife, and/or carving knife.

The clevis.

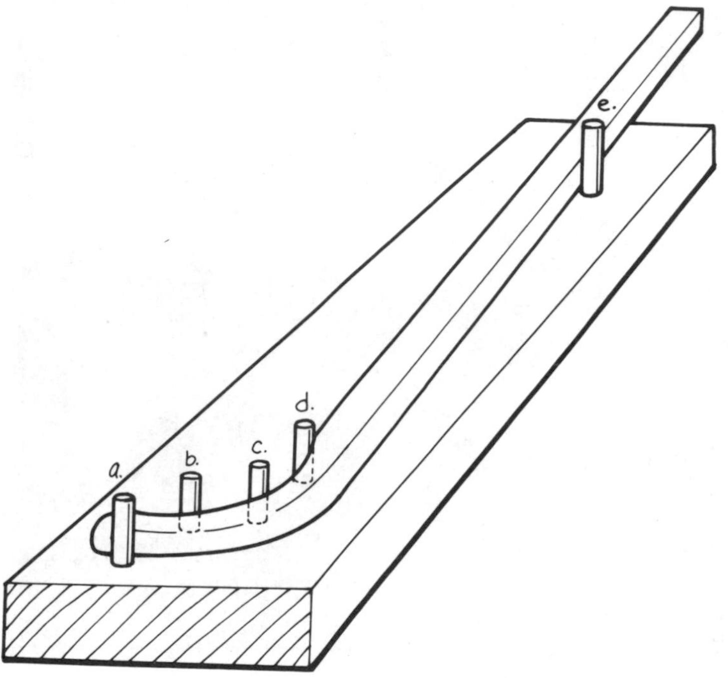

Bending a plow handle. Handle is inserted between pegs (a) and (b), bent around (c) and (d) and secured in tension by removable keeper peg (e).

The other method involves splitting a log and shaping a 1⅛ x 2-inch piece, 48 inches long, which is rounded at the handle end. This is boiled, then inserted in a bending jig. A simple jig can be made by drilling a series of 1-inch holes through a stout piece of timber, tracing the curve of the handle. Hardwood pegs are fitted in the holes. The jig is held in a vise or nailed to the floor. After boiling, the handle is bent in place around the pegs, then held in position by fitting a keeper peg in place. The handle is adequately set when it can be removed with no pressure against the keeper peg.

Commercially bent handles may arc as much as 60 degrees. But without special equipment, bending should be limited to about 30 degrees. It's also possible to use this bending method with handles carved from straight green saplings.

Fitting the handles. Assemble the foot and beam and secure with a draw bolt. Drill a 1-inch hole through the butt of the beam. Shape the 12-inch lower brace: 1 inch thick in the middle tapered to ¾ inch at the ends. Insert. Hold one handle in position against the foot and across the brace. The lower end of the handle must be trimmed to a compound angle. This is outlined by scribing a line the same thickness as the maximum gap of the handle butt held against the foot. The compound angle may be sawn or shaped with a chisel. (I recommend chiseling.) Be sure to cut these angles in pairs for right and left handles.

Reposition the handles against the foot and lower brace to determine the location and angle of the ¾-inch holes. Bore holes and fit handles onto lower braces. Stubs of the braces should extend approximately ⅜-inch beyond the handles. In place, the handle grips should be 22 to 26 inches on center.

Clamp or lash the ends against the foot. Bore a 5⁄16-inch hole through both handles perpendicular to the foot. Fashion two metal keepers from pieces of 1-inch strap iron, each 3 inches long. Drill ¼-inch center holes. Secure keepers and handles to foot with a ¼ x 6-inch bolt. Do not tighten yet.

The center of the upper brace is 1 inch in diameter tapering to ¾ inch at the ends. Locate ¾-inch holes using the brace as a guide. Disassemble handles to bore holes. Reassemble with upper brace in position. Tighten the ¼-inch bolts.

Bore ¼-inch holes through junctures of upper and lower braces and handles. Secure with ¼-inch dowels, paring any protrusion flush with the handles. Bore and dowel a ⅜-inch hole through the beam and lower brace.

Pin beam and foot. Shape a 6-inch-long, 1-inch dowel from hard, well-seasoned wood. Taper one end. Insert it through the offset holes of the beam and foot by pounding it into place with a wooden mallet. Saw off the protruding tapered stub.

Position the shovel, and drill hole through the foot. Bolt it in place.

Finishing. Treat the plow with a mixture of 2 parts linseed oil to 1 part turpentine. The threaded ends of the shovel bolt and ¼-inch lower handle bolt can be protected from damage during use by slipping short lengths of plastic tubing over the stubs.

The foot.

A-harrow.

CHAPTER 20
SPIKE-TOOTH A-HARROW

HARROWS CONSTITUTE A BROAD RANGE of farm equipment used for cultivation, disking, clod breaking, seed bed preparation, etcetera. A spike-tooth harrow is used after disking to level out furrow irregularities, and again after broadcast-seeding to skiffle the seed under cover. The harrow may also be used for very early weed cultivation with hardy seedling crops such as corn or sorghum.

This type of A-harrow was commonly made and used by farmers of the Southern Highlands. It's easy to build, rugged, and quite efficient. Only one draft animal is needed to pull it.

The harrow consists of a timber A-frame punctured with iron spikes. The handle is used to lift the harrow if the spikes become entangled with weeds, and for assistance in turning at the end of rows. Sometimes a heavy rock is placed on the head to help keep the harrow level as it's pulled along.

Materials. The *legs* are rough-sawn oak 3 x 5s, 72 inches long. The *cross bar* (also a 3 x 5) is 56 inches long. At the apex, the legs are bolted to a 3 x 5 *head,* 14 inches long, to which the draft clevis is attached. Just

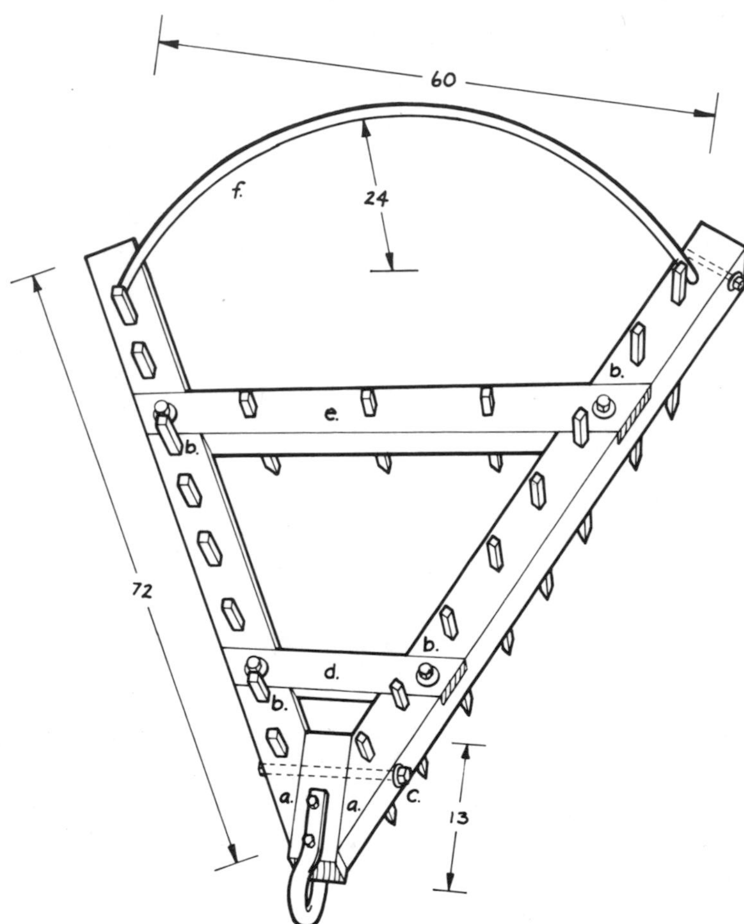

Leg angle (a) is 27 degrees. Half-laps (b) are 63 degrees. Main bolt (c) is ¾ x 14 inches. Two x four brace (d) equals 28 inches. Three x five brace (e) is 56 inches. Sapling handle (f) measures 90 inches tip to tip.

behind is a 2 x 4 oak *brace,* 28 inches long. The *handle* is a bowed hickory sapling 96 inches long. (Any tough, bendable wood will do.) The 10-inch spikes are ⅝-inch square in cross section.

Construction. The simplest way to build the harrow is to begin by sawing the timbers to correct length. The angle at the head is 54 degrees, or 27 degrees for each leg. The fastener is a ¾-inch bolt, 12 inches long, passing through each leg and the head piece. The single bolt allows the head to angle upward somewhat. The tilt helps to keep the harrow flat on the ground, and relieves some stress on the frame during rough use. Recesses are chiseled or bored into the leg sides so that the bolt end, nut, and washers are drawn together parallel to each other. These are angled 63 degrees.

The crosspiece and brace are joined by half-laps to the legs, also angled 63 degrees. Each leg joint is secured by a single ½-inch bolt with 2-inch cast-iron masonry washers between nut and timber. The 2 x 4 brace is set into half-laps sawn in the legs, then secured with ½-inch bolts and flat washers.

The handle is set into 1-inch diameter holes drilled through the legs at an angle canting approximately 15 degrees inward. After shaping, the sapling tips are forced into the sockets. Two small pilot holes are drilled diagonally through the legs into the handle. Eightpenny nails are driven to within ¼-inch of their heads (for easy removal in case replacement is needed). Double-headed nails would be better.

To help resist splitting, a ½-inch carriage bolt is

run through horizontal holes drilled 3 inches from each leg end. Large flat washers are used.

This A-harrow has nineteen square spikes. There are eight along each leg spaced 8 inches on center, and three across the bar at 12 inches on center. The spikes are driven through ½-inch holes drilled through the frame. For general work they are set to protrude 5 inches beneath the frame. Depth may be adjusted for various conditions.

The traditional A-harrow clevis is made from ⅝-inch diameter rod, some 28 inches long. Nine inches of each end are flattened to a 1-inch width. The center is bent into a C-shaped loop having a 5-inch outside circumference. Two matching ⅜-inch holes, 6½ inches on center, are drilled through each flat end of the clevis, and likewise through the wooden head. The clevis is then attached with ⅜-inch machine bolts.

In some countries similar harrows are made with hardwood spikes. The spikes should be well seasoned so that they are tough and will not work loose with age. Hardwood spikes might be 12 inches long, and 1¼ inches in diameter. Carving them as rough, irregular polygons would help to maintain a tight fit. Suitable native woods include locust, heart of oak, hickory, hornbeam, and mulberry.

A typical drag.

CHAPTER 21
DRAGS

ANOTHER TYPE OF HARROW is called a drag. Many types of drags have been made, and they are still used by tractor farmers. Drags are useful for breaking down clods caused by bottom and turning plows, and for the final smoothing of a field before drilling or broadcasting. When a roller is not available, a drag can be used to firm down a seed bed (as for small grains).

Several types of drags are commonly used by farmers in our area. The one that I like is built from two 3 x 8 oak *runners,* 60 inches long. There is also a 1 x 4 *head brace* and two 1 x 4 *diagonal braces.* A ¾-inch hole is bored through the center of the head brace to accept a screw-pin clevis. A 1 x 2 *cleat* is attached along the top side of the second-to-last dragger to provide some footing for riding on the drag. (This adds needed weight and makes the job easier.) The frame is put together with common nails, but the draggers should be pegged.

A nice feature of this drag is that the bottoms of the runners are sawn into a series of ratchets to which the

Drag made from old sled runners.

draggers are pegged. This results in a rigid unit. The dimensions may be modified for different uses. One old mule can easily pull me, the drag, and a number of rocks that we might stop to pick up as we drag along.

A similar drag may be made from a pair of old sled runners. Remove everything but the tenoned main crosspiece. Then peg overlapping 1 x 8s across the bottom.

Drags may also be made of poles or small logs. Some farmers saddle-notch a row of saplings to the bottom of two curved poles that approximate the bend-shape of sled runners. Another common rig is simply a series of three to five logs, perhaps 60 inches long, linked parallel to each other by short lengths of chain.

Maude with her poke.

CHAPTER 22
POKE

POKES ARE OLD-TIME CONTRAPTIONS used to restrain animals from breaking through fences. Most pokes consist of some kind of neck yoke, to which a wooden poker is attached. This extends out in front, getting in the way when the animal wearing it begins to push against fences. The general encumbrance of the poke also tends to eliminate thoughts of jumping.

For a long time, I thought that such things existed only in storybook form. But one day, while I was telling Neighbor Glady how our younger mule kept getting loose, he remarked "Well, Andrew, you need one of them things we used to call a poke." Glady climbed up into the loft of an old crib, rummaged around, and soon located an ancient-looking, now broken poke. He said, "You remember Old Beck, Andrew. She was terrible for bursting fences." So I made a mental note of how the poke was put together, and then went home to make one.

Pokes used to be made in different ways, for many types of farm stock. Edwin Tunis's book *Frontier Living* illustrates several for cattle, horses, and hogs. In *A Museum of Early American Tools,* Eric Sloane depicts a goose poke! I would hardly call a poke a tool,

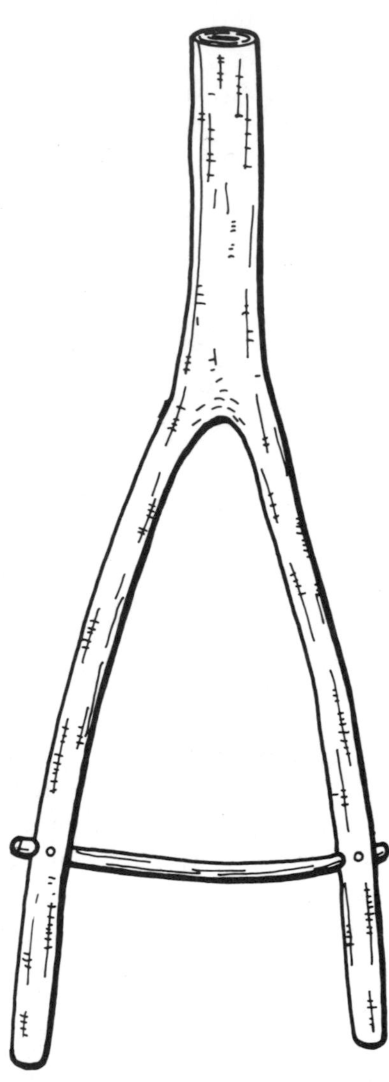

Cow poke.

but the one I made did help to break our Maude from her bad habit.

This poke consists of three parts: yoke, crosspiece, and poker. The yoke is made of a tough, flexible wood so that it may be bent to pass around the animal's neck. The piece is cleft green from a straight-grained, clear piece of white oak or ash, 48 inches long. (Maude uses a 19-inch collar. Modify dimensions to your friend's requirements.) About 10 inches of each end are shaped to a round cross section gradually tapering from just under 1 inch to 1½ inches in diameter. The middle section, between the 1½-inch points, is flattened into a wide, thin band, approximately ⅜ inch thick and 1½ inches wide.

The crosspiece may be any semiround chunk of hardwood, 12 inches long and approximately 2½ inches in diameter. Drill 1-inch holes through the crosspiece 2 inches from each end. Then drill another hole, 1 inch in diameter, in the center of the crosspiece. The third hole is angled 120 degrees in relation to the yoke. This will cause the poker to angle downward so that it will tend to slip under a fence rail or wire. Drill ¼-inch holes perpendicularly through the three larger holes. Chamfer the edges.

The poker can be about 22 inches long. Pokers generally take a curved shape so that they angle downward from the crosspiece, then level out toward the tip (when Beastie is standing head-up). The poker should be well-seasoned, stout hardwood, such as oak. The diameter is up to 2 inches just before fitting into the crosspiece. The small socket is used so that the poker will break if much force is put against it. This is a safety precaution. The tip is also well blunted.

The yoke is bent into shape after the other pieces are made. This is done by ladling boiling water over the middle part of the thin band-shaped section. While still hot, carefully bend the yoke in half and insert the tips into the crosspiece end holes. If the yoke doesn't bend nicely, thin down the central section. Reheat and rebend. Leave the yoke in place for a few days so that it seasons permanently to the bent shape.

Fit the poker tightly into the central hole. Redrill the ¼-inch hole through the poker stub. Drive a ¼-inch dowel through the crosspiece securing the poker in place. With an awl (or nail), mark the center points where the yoke fits through the end holes. Remove the yoke and drill ⅜-inch holes at these points. If necessary, dress the yoke tips so that they easily fit in and out of the crosspiece. Use ¼-inch bolts with washers and wing nuts for these connections.

Finish with linseed oil for protection against the weather.

In use, the poke tends to dangle downward allowing full freedom for grazing. Our mule broke one or two pokers, I think while rolling. ("Wallering," they call it around here.) In close quarters a poke is somewhat dangerous, like horns, so it should be taken off each time the animal is brought indoors.

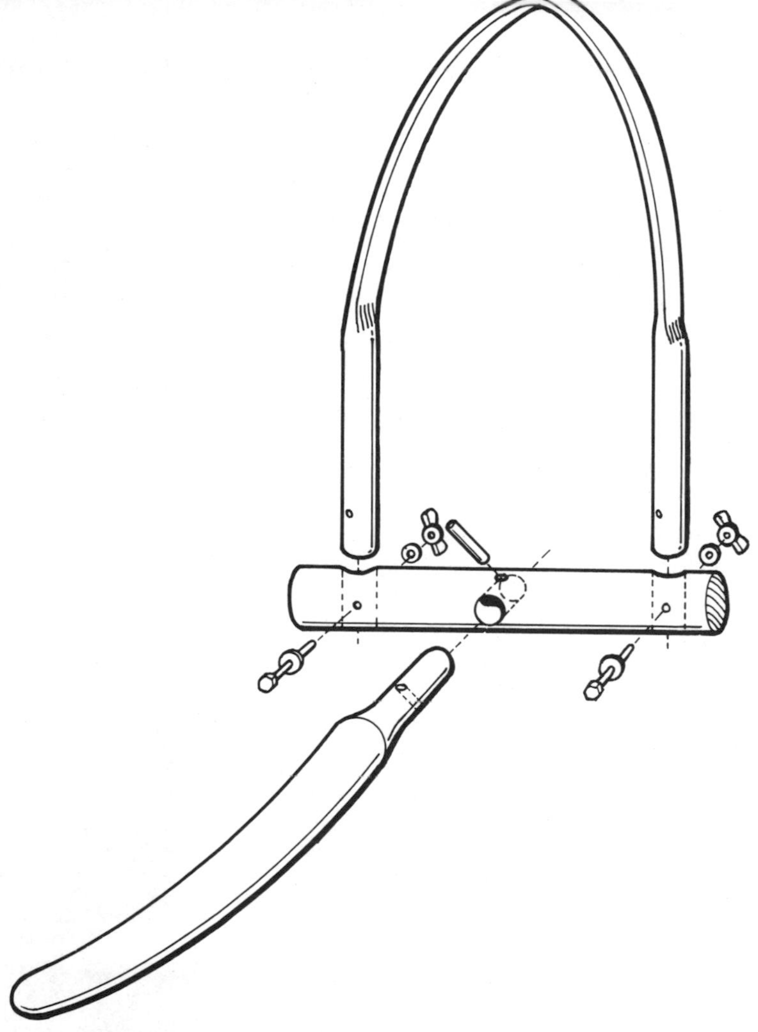

Mule-poke details.

A basket maker of Kentucky.
Used by permission of the Doris Ulmann Foundation and Berea College.

PART IV
HOUSEHOLD CRAFTS AND FURNISHINGS

Homemade brooms.

CHAPTER 23
BROOM TYING

ONE OF THE FIRST SIGHTS that Louise and I saw in Switzerland a few years back was two or three workers sweeping out a village square with huge, picturesque twig brooms. Such brooms, called "besoms," are not a tourist attraction. They are traditionally used throughout much of Europe and Asia. In Greece, our nearest neighbor used a similar brush-broom to sweep around her house several times a day—a good idea with chickens running loose. But we never knew how effective these besoms are until tying one and trying it out. Besoms are unexcelled for coarse sweeping, such as around patios, or out on the sidewalk, or among the chips and shavings of a woodworking shop.

The craft of tying brooms has changed very little since ancient times. Most commonly favored are birch twigs, although heather, broom sedge, and other materials are often used.

A professional "broom squire" in England will buy a stand of young birches (seven to ten years old). Felling is done in winter or early spring, before the leaves are formed. Twigs are collected, then the trunks and branches are sawn up, sorted, and bundled for sale as

Smoothing a broom handle.

firewood. Carefully tended birch coppices have been continuously harvested for centuries.[1]

Materials. The home craftsman can easily collect ample material for making a single besom by simply cutting twigs from scrub birches often found along waysides. Look for finely divided twigs that are more or less straight. Twigs can be gathered any time of year, but in spring or summer the leaves will have to be stripped by hand. This is too time-consuming for quantity production. After collecting, tie the twigs in a loose bundle to season several months in a sheltered place having free air circulation.

In the meantime a broomstick should be cut and seasoned. Commonly used are saplings such as ash, hazel, and linden. In the eastern United States sourwood has always made a favorite broomstick material. Handles from worn-out commercially made brooms can be recycled.

Besom handles are 2½ to 4 feet long. They should be barked after harvesting to prevent rot, then set aside to season. A green handle would shrink and come loose from the broom head.

The besom maker also needs some kind of tough, pliant tying material. Traditionally, a variety of ties were used including hammered ash splits, hickory and linden bast (see Chapter 24: Berry Boxes), cleft oak stems, hazel and willow twigs. Brambles (blasphemy vine) can be used fresh and green; the prickles are easily removed with a sharp knife. Nowadays, most broom makers use wire ties. Wire is far easier to tie than

1. Jenkins, *Traditional Country Craftsmen*, pp. 76-81.

natural materials, which are also time-consuming to collect and prepare.

The broom squire's tools are a pliers, hatchet, and a drawknife. A chopping stump is also needed.

Method. The first step in besom making is gathering the seasoned materials together. Sort the twigs into two piles—large and small. Discard poorly shaped or brittle twigs.

Gather a handful of large twigs and arrange so that the tips are even. The stems should run parallel to one another. Hold onto this bunch and proceed to add finer twigs around the core by rolling the bundle back and forth across your lap. Stop at the desired size.

To tie the broom, secure a strand of tying material to a fixed hook. Make the first tie about 4 inches below the butts of the shortest twigs. Wrap the broom head round and round, continually pulling against the tie for a good tight fit. Cut and secure with a square knot. Use the pliers to tighten knotted withes or other bulky tying material. Wire is much easier to handle than bast, brambles, etcetera.

Make a second tie 4 or 5 inches below the first one. Even off the twig butts by trimming with a hatchet against a chopping stump.

With a drawknife or hatchet, sharpen a long slender point on one end of the broomstick. Insert the shaft into the center of the twig bundle. Bang the heel against a stump several times to drive the broom head tightly into place. Bore a ¼-inch hole between the ties. Secure the head with a dowel driven through this hole. (Or hammer a finishing nail through the broomstick at

Sewing home-grown broomcorn into a continuous bundle.

Softening the broomcorn with boiling water.

the same point.) Trim the twig tips to an even length with a hatchet. Drill a hole through the end of the stick so that the besom may be hung on the wall when not in use. This helps to maintain straight sweeps. Tie a third thong about one foot above the broom tip. This may need to be sewn in place.

As would be expected, there are many variations in making handmade brooms. The wide variety of possible materials also include Scotch broom, dyer's broom, butcher's broom, Spanish broom, and many types of straw. Traditional Chinese brooms are made with bamboo splits or millet straw.[2] Broomcorn (a relative of sorghum) makes fine light-duty household and hearth brooms. Cultivation is similar to edible corn.[3]

Some craftsmen prefer to assemble brooms around the pointed broomstick. In this case, the sweeps (generally domestic broomcorn) are first sewn together like a mat. Boiling water is poured over the stems. The softened stems are then wrapped around the broomstick and tied tightly as possible. Twine or decorative string may be used.

Flat household brooms are tied like round brooms. The sweeps are pounded into a flat, fanned-out shape with a wooden cudgel, then held in place with a simple clamp consisting of two sticks that are hinged at one end and bolted with a wing nut at the other end. The shape is permanently secured with several stitches passing through the sweeps just below the clamp.

2. Hommel, *China at Work,* p. 309.
3. Louise Langsner, "Grow Your Own Brooms." *Organic Gardening and Farming,* (Emmaus, Pa.: Rodale Press, Inc., June 1976) pp. 80-82.

Broom Tying

French besoms are often made with very long sweeps. After assembly these are leaned against a wall forming a permanent curve in the broom head. In use, these are held almost parallel to the ground, with the sweeping being done by the sides of the sweeps.

Tying softened broomcorn around a pointed broomstick.

Poplar bark huckleberry boxes.

CHAPTER 24
BARK BOXES

by LOUISE LANGSNER

THE STORY GOES, as we are told by our neighbors, that an old-time mountaineer invented the bark box when he came across a large huckleberry patch in the woods and needed a container. He went to the nearest young tulip poplar, peeled off a section of bark and quickly laced it together with a bramble thong. Instant berry box. Folded from a single piece of bark, it was cylindrical, with a unique, concave eye-shaped base. Similar bark vessels are also credited to the Cherokee, who more than likely taught the early settlers.

The tree that yields this handy bark is the yellow poplar (*Liriodendron tulipfera*), or the tulip poplar. This species enjoys wide distribution over the eastern third of the United States and southern Ontario. On young trees the bark is fairly thin (about ⅛-inch) and relatively smooth. Its grey, brown, and green mottling is often overlaid with a fascinating collage of lichen. With age, the peeled bark turns to a rich umber. Older trees have quite a different appearance, as the bark thickens and becomes deeply furrowed with a slight spiral pattern.

What makes poplar bark such a good material for

Bark-working tools.

berry boxes is that it can be peeled from the tree trunk in one piece. In addition, it is pliable and may be folded and shaped while green. Drying renders the bark tough and durable.

Because the bark of young trees is needed, this is a good use for thinnings in an overcrowded stand of poplars. However, the bark may be peeled from older trees, up to 10 inches in diameter, though considerably more elbow grease is required in working it.

Bark slipping is a summertime phenomenon. We have successfully peeled poplar poles from May through mid-July here in the mountains of North Carolina. While poplar bark is most commonly used for huckleberry boxes, other barks will work too. These include mountain magnolia, ash, bass (linden), and paper birch.

Instructions are given here for a traditional Cherokee huckleberry box, about 6 inches in diameter and 15 inches in height. Adjustments can be made for other sizes or proportions.

Choosing a tree. A pole 3 to 4½ inches in diameter will make a berry box 5 to 7 inches across. It should be fairly straight, and at least 30 inches long for each 15-inch container. Look for smooth bark without large, unsealed knotholes.

Felling. Before felling the tree, saw through the bark in a ring. This prevents the bark from tearing. Make every effort to fell and handle the pole gently; bruised or torn bark is wasted.

Peeling the bark. Cut the poles to length before peeling, or merely ring the bark at appropriate intervals. Mark a 30-inch section and slit it open with a sharp knife. A "good" tree will easily slip out of its skin. If not, carefully ease the bark loose with pressure from your fingers. The bark should peel easily in places where scar tissue has formed over dead knotholes, and this creates very interesting designs.

Scoring. Leaving the slipped bark around the pole (slit downward), mark the point midway between the ends and points 2½ inches from the midpoint toward each end. Then chalk a line from the slit edges through the midpoint. Using this centerline and the points marked on either side of it as guides, draw an eye shape 5 inches across the widest section. Score about half-way through the bark along this outline. At the point of intersection, the lines should just cross, forming a very small X. The angle formed by these scores coming together is slightly less than 90 degrees.

Setting up. Remove the bark from the pole. Hold down both points of the "eye", cup a hand around one side and lift. Then lift the other side; the base curves up and inward by itself. Overlap the sides 1 inch or so—to get the desired diameter—and hold it in place. Spring clamps are convenient.

Assembly. One may lace the box together with bramble, as many an old-timer has done (scrape off the thorns). However, a superior material is found in the bast (inner bark) of a young hickory, cut during late spring or early summer.

To obtain bast, fell a hickory sapling no more than 6 inches in diameter. With a drawknife, carefully remove the outer bark, which is rough and hard. Score a series of strips, about 1 inch wide, through the smooth

Slipping bark from a sapling.

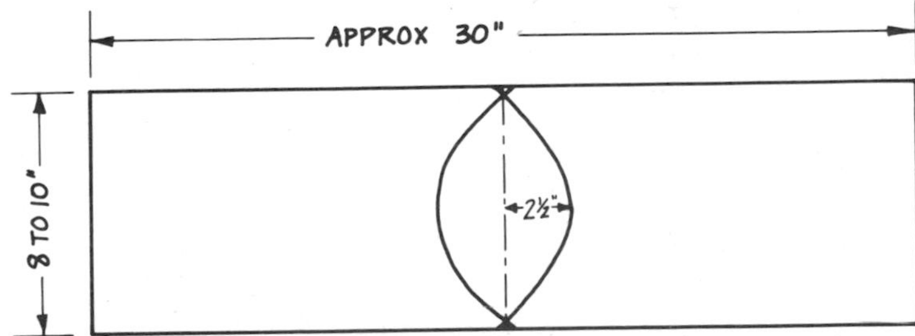

Scoring a bark box. Cuts should cross just before the edge and converge at an angle slightly less than 90 degrees.

Scoring the bottom.

Peeling hickory bast (inner bark) used for lacing.

Lacing a berry box.

Making a large wastebasket.

inner bark. (A snapped chalk line makes neat guidelines.) The leathery inner bark easily peels off. It may then be cut into narrow thongs; 60 inches is a good length for most lacing work. Hickory bast can be rolled up and stored for an indefinite period. When needed, soak in water and the pliancy is restored.

To lace the berry box, mark holes on both sides of the overlapping seams so the stitches will make an X or a diagonal slash pattern. Drill holes with a 7/16-inch auger bit, as the fresh bark is easily cracked. This is easily done with two people—one holding and the other boring. The holes can also be made with a sharp, narrow-pointed knife, but it's important to be careful or the bark might tear.

After lacing the sides, fit a sturdy inner rim to hold the shape as the bark dries. The rim may be a hoop made from a flexible rod of willow, hazel, birch, or pine, or an oak or ash split may be used. Lace the hoop tightly and secure the thong ends in place.

The box is complete, except for a shoulder strap or belt loop for ease of carrying. Hang in a well-ventilated place to cure until the bark is hard and dry.

White oak basketry (top l. to r.): egg basket, garden basket; (bottom l. to r.): market basket, pack basket.

CHAPTER 25
WHITE OAK BASKETRY

by LOUISE LANGSNER

THE WHITE OAK (*Quercus alba*) is traditionally the most common source of basketry material in the southern Appalachians. Trees used in other areas for making similar splits include ash, buckeye, and white pine. A prime basket-tree candidate has a 4- to 6-inch diameter, a straight, clear section of trunk measuring at least 4 to 6 feet, with no knots or other visible imperfections. Although much folklore exists regarding where the best trees grow and when to cut them, our own experience has verified no hard and fast rules. We have found good and bad trees on south slopes as well as north, east, and west; their quality has not seemed to correspond to the season harvested. Our search for basket trees has only helped to convince us that many trees of the same species—even specimens of relatively the same age standing side by side—will often grow very different from one another.

One tentative generalization is that a slow-growing tree (with fine growth rings) makes a good basket tree. This is because to procure the stuff of basketry, it is necessary to split the wood more or less along the annual rings. Hence, the narrower the rings, the finer the splits.

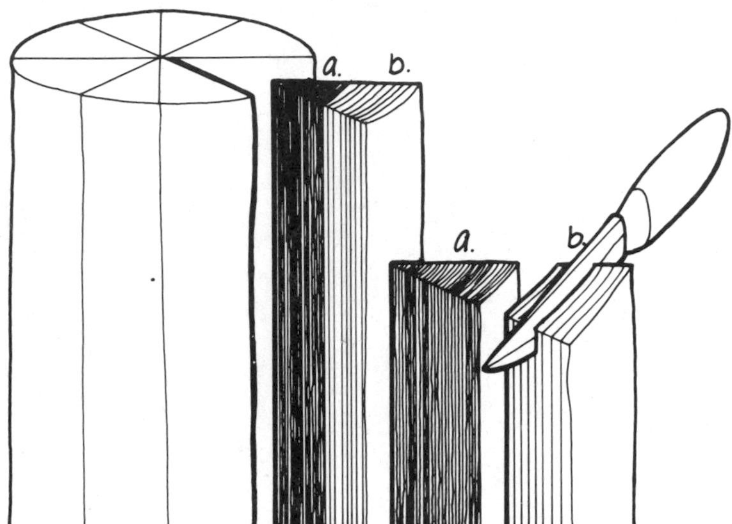

White oak splits. Heartwood (a) is generally discarded. Sapwood (b) is split into halves, followed by quarters, eighths, and occasionally sixteenths.

Working the tree into splits the same day it is felled is advisable. If this is impossible, submerge the bole in water to keep it from drying out.

Making splits. Using froe, wedge, and maul, split your section of oak in half, then into quarters, and finally into eighths. (For cleaving instructions refer to Chapter 14: Hay Forks.)

Remove the bark with a drawknife. Cleave off the heartwood, which may be saved and worked into handles, rims, or (possibly) splits. Square the remaining section of sapwood to uniform cross section.

Drive a knife blade into the end of the sapwood section, tangential to the center growth ring. Rotate the blade to begin the split, then continue separating the two halves with your fingers. If the split begins to run out, i.e., veer off from center course, increase pressure on the *thicker* side. Sometimes the wood fibers must be pared a bit with a knife to keep the split running evenly. Repeat splitting until sapwood sections are in strips 1/16- to 1/8-inch thick.

Splits may be smoothed further with a spokeshave or carving knife. If splits are not to be used directly, coil them in bundles and hang to dry.

Preparation for basket making. Sort splits according to size. In general, ribs are thicker than weavers, rims thicker than ribs, and handles thicker than rims. Approximate measurements are: weavers 1/16- to 1/8-inch thick, ribs 1/8-inch, rims 3/16- to 1/4-inch, and handles 1/4- to 3/8-inch. Some baskets have ribs and weavers of the same weight; dimensions of all the members will vary to suit the design and function of each basket.

Making white oak splits.

Splits are worked in a damp condition. Heavy splits must be soaked until pliable; very thin ones need only be dipped in warm water. Do not leave weavers under water once they are softened. They will absorb too much water, shrink as they dry, and result in a loose and weak basket.

Cut rib splits to length. Cut weavers to desired width. (Spiral weave requires grading.)

Tools. In basketry, fingers are the most important tool. Also helpful are a knife, heavy-duty scissors, small screwdriver for tapping down weaving, and spring clamps and clothespins.

General design. Make a sketch, or have an idea in your head of what you want the finished basket to look like. Take into consideration the qualities of your materials, as well as usefulness, strength, and shape.

Every tree yields splits of different qualities. Some are fine and smooth, others rough and thick. Flexibility and workability vary, though a short soak in hot water helps to minimize difficulties. Very thin splits are more suitable for a small, delicate basket, while heavier ones work well for a large, sturdy design. Select splits compatible with the size and purpose you intend.

Purposes are many. Baskets are useful for marketing, berry and fruit picking, gardening, storage of yarns and wood and sewing, egg gathering, fishing, and carrying light, bulky loads (among other things). For each job, various characteristics are desirable and should be incorporated into the planning of your basket.

Basket strength relies on a combination of factors. One, of course, is the weight (thickness) of the splits, though all good-quality oak splits are very tough. Spacing of the ribs also determines structural strength; the closer the ribs, the stronger the basket. A sturdy, well-attached rim provides stability. Since the outer and inner rims are sewn to the top weavers, these weavers must be held in place adequately by folding over the ribs and doubling them back upon themselves. This structural integration is necessary, as the handle would otherwise tend to pull the rim loose.

Though shape does correspond with the above elements of design, it is also a matter of personal preference. One may look at traditional baskets for inspiration and examples of good design. Whatever the choice, it is important to pay close attention to the shape as you weave. The base should be symmetrical, and the ribs evenly spaced. After the ribs are bent up to form the sides, the first inch or two of weaving determines what shape the basket can become. Curved sides are more easily shaped with narrow weavers (½ inch or less) than with wider ones. A measuring tape is helpful for keeping tabs on where the shape is going. Some basket makers weave around wooden forms.

SQUARE OR RECTANGULAR BASE BASKET

Ribs. Determine rib length by adding one dimension of the base (length or width), plus twice the height of the sides, plus 4 to 6 inches to fold over, plus 1 inch for curve allowance. Shaving down the last 3 inches of both ends of the ribs makes it easier to bend them over at the rim. The number of ribs depends on the size

The base of a square-bottomed basket.

Weaving the sides.

of the base and the width of the rib splits. An uneven number of ribs makes it possible to center the handle. Ribs should be soaked in water until pliable.

Base. For a large basket, it is helpful to clamp one set of ribs (the warp) between two blocks of wood while weaving in the other set. With chalk, mark on each rib the base dimensions from center. Then weave the two sets of ribs together, aligning the chalk marks. Measure to check that the base is square.

Bend ribs up to form sides. Tie them in place by looping a cord around the ribs if they are too springy.

Weaving. Take a weaver (dampened with a sponge) of sufficient length to reach all the way around the base, plus overlap. Begin weaving in the middle of one side, placing the end over the first rib, under the next, and so on around the four sides. When the two ends meet, they are joined by overlapping for a distance of four ribs. Spring clamps or clothespins are helpful for holding this first weaver in place. Starting the second weaver on the opposite side from the first, i.e., so that the overlapped ends of successive weavers alternate from one side to the other, also helps to keep the latter from sliding up. Complete one round with each weaver, reversing the under-over pattern with each successive round. Press each weaver down as tightly as possible with your fingers or the flat of a screwdriver blade. Weavers may be pieced if they are not long enough to reach. This does not weaken the basket.

Shaping. You may allow the basket to take a round shape, or crease the weavers at each corner to keep them square. Increase or decrease the length of each weaver to pull the sides inward or outward. Continue weaving to the desired height.

Top edge. Ribs should extend 2 inches above the last weaver. Soak the top edge of the basket by placing the basket upside down in hot water until the ribs may be bent easily. Fold each rib over the top weaver (forward or backward as required) and tuck the end through two rounds of weaving.

Handle. Shape the handle from a sapling or piece of cleft oak. The thickness should be determined by the basket's size and use. The ends are tapered. Pour boiling water over the wood before bending it to shape (or shape green). Insert the ends of the handle through the weaving down the entire distance of the sides. The handle may be notched beforehand or pegged in place after the rim is secured.

Rim. Select two stout splits, each about ¼-inch thick, for the inner and outer rims. Fit them around the top edge of the basket and clamp in place. Sew around the rims with narrow splits or strips of hickory bast (refer to Chapter 24: Bark Boxes).

The finished basket should be given a protective finish of raw linseed oil and turpentine mixed 2:1.

ROUND BASE OR SPIRAL WEAVE BASKET

Ribs. Select splits of adequate length and weight. A 10- or 11-inch-diameter base requires about eighteen ¾-inch ribs. Chalk mark the center and base on each split. The base is more easily and tightly woven if begun with half the total number of splits. Carve the

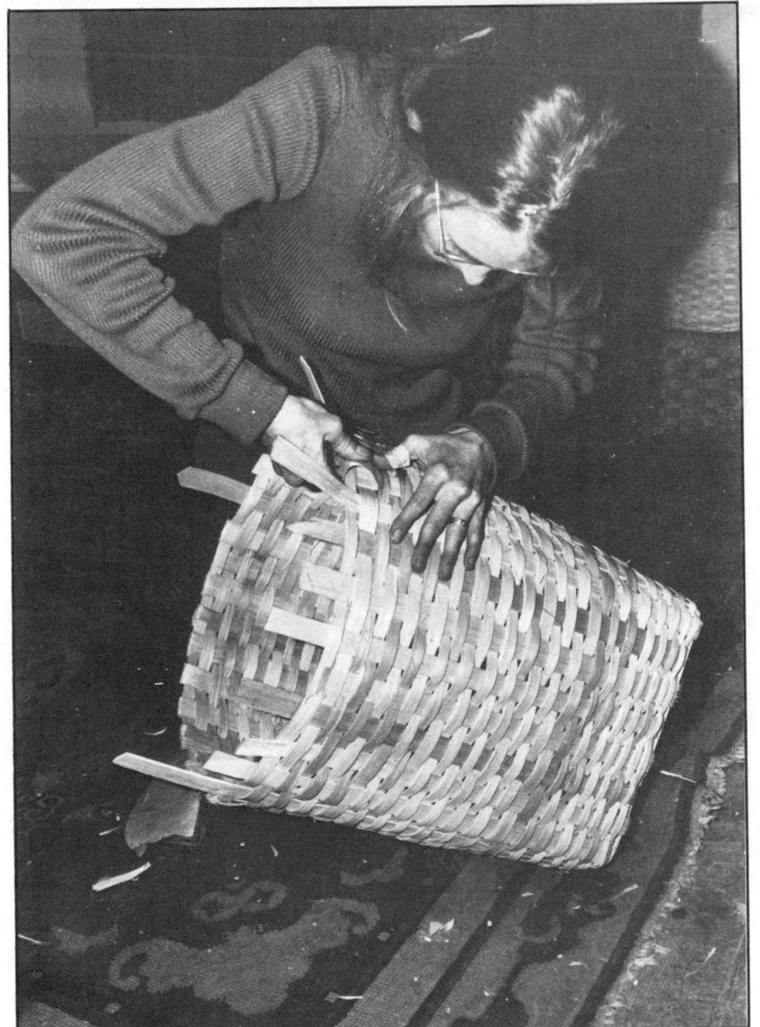

Folding ribs over the top weaver.

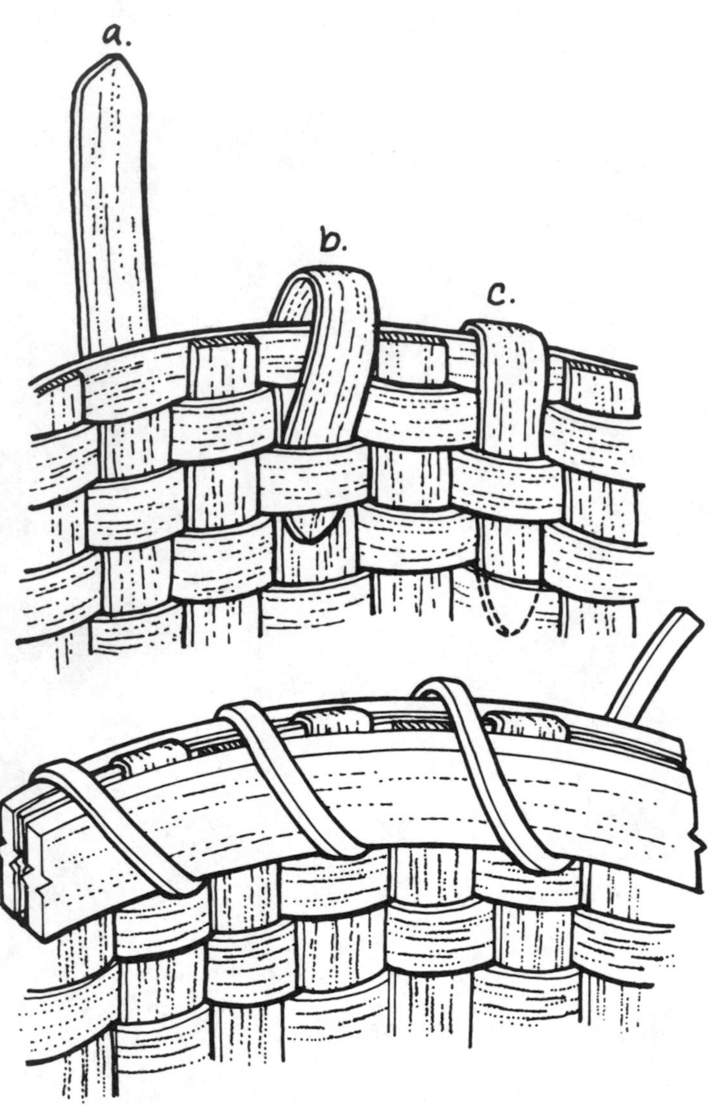

Cross section of basket rim. Tapered rib (a) is bent over the top weaver (b) and under the third and fifth weavers (c,d). Inner rim (e) and outer rim (f) are lashed in place by spiral binding (g).

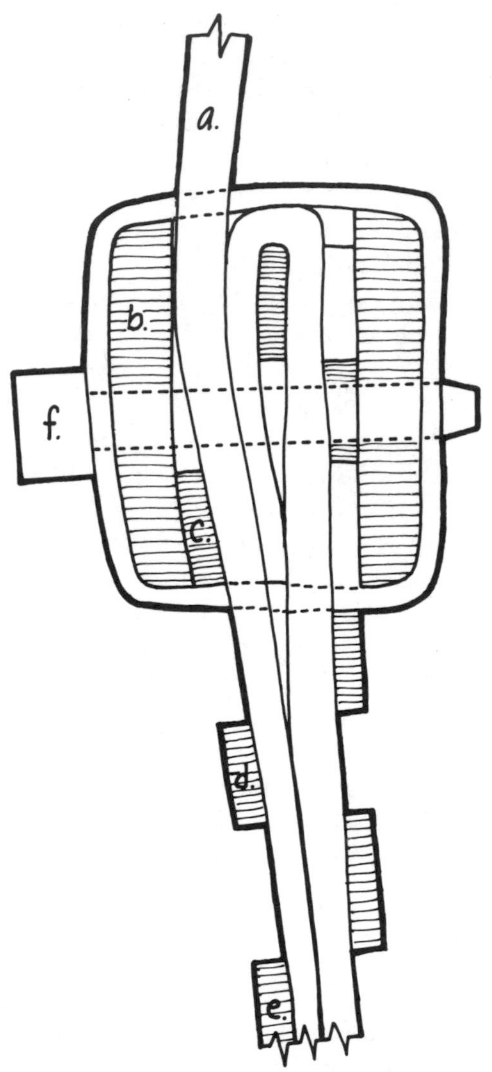

Tapered basket handle (a) is forced inside rim (b) and weavers (c,d,e), then pinned in place with peg (f).

center section of each rib thinner with a knife. Soak all ribs until pliable.

Lay the first set of ribs across each other so that they cross at the center and radiate like spokes of a wheel. Secure the "wheel" to a block of wood by driving a small nail through the center.

Weaving base. Select long flexible weavers 3/16- to 1/4-inch wide; dampen before using. Because there is an even number of ribs, weaving must begin by "chasing," i.e., working two weavers more or less simul-

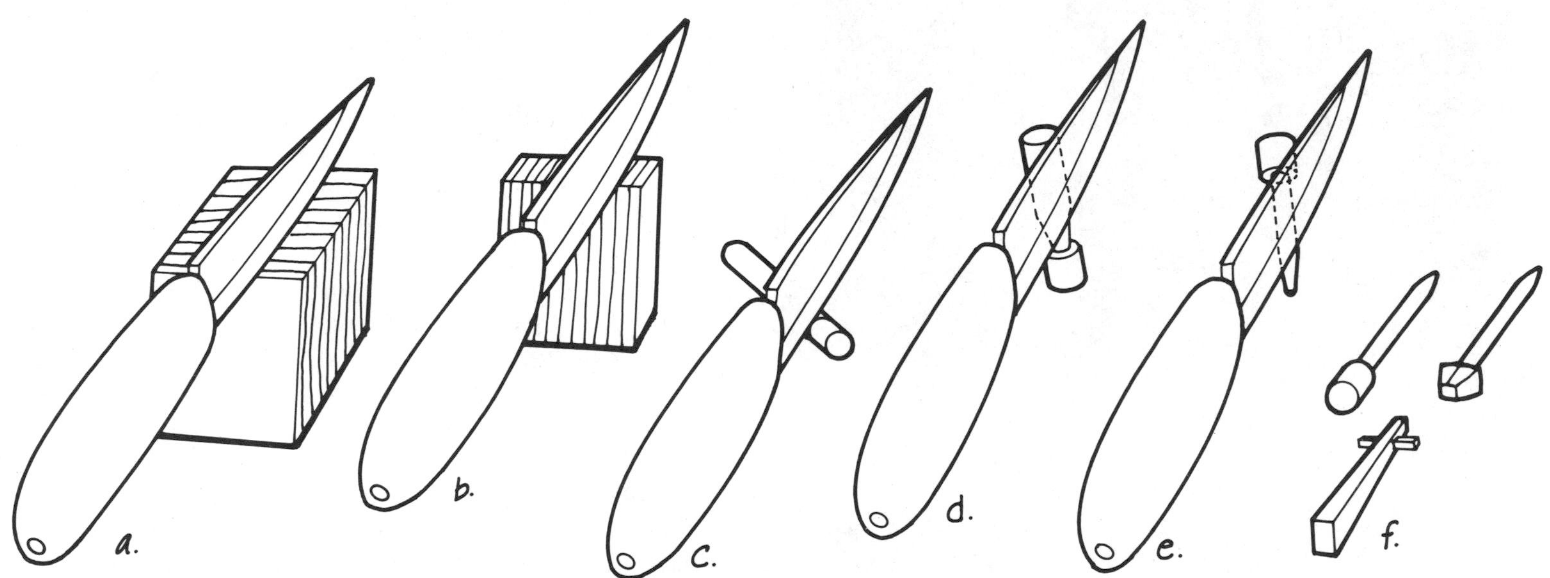

Carving basket-handle pegs. A section of split-out heart-of-oak (or similar hardwood usually salvaged from the stove-wood pile) is crosscut to 1½ inches. A carving knife is placed ⅜ inch from one edge (a) and struck by a hammer to split off a thin slab. This is split again (b) to a ⅜-inch square. The head is shaped by carving to an octagon, then rounded. The base is started by pressing the knife down and around the head (c) ⅜ inch from the crown. Sides are started by carving directly into the base cut (d), trimming down to 5/32-inch diameter (e). The tip is pointed to facilitate installation. Illustration (f) shows three styles of finished pegs—plain cylinder, chamfered button, and a thin wedge that is secured by a secondary peg just within the basket rim. Pointed tips are trimmed after insertion through hoops and handle. Any sharp carving knife can be used.

Beginning a round basket, working with two weavers simultaneously.

taneously. This seems confusing, but it is not difficult. Bend the first weaver in half and catch it around one rib as close to the basket center as possible. Weave one end of the folded split around through the ribs, using the under-over pattern, all the way around the basket's circumference. At this point take over with the other end of the weaver. Weave once around, then change back to the first. When this first split runs out, overlap a new one the distance of four ribs.

Adding ribs. When the base has spread out enough, remove the nail and tack the second set of ribs on top of the first. Offset the new set of ribs so that the original and additional ribs alternate.

The odd rib. In order that the weaving may proceed with one weaver only, an odd number of ribs is necessary. Otherwise, the weaver would always go under and over the same ribs. The odd rib allows you to continuously weave under and over and have the pattern alternate on each row. The odd rib may be added by splitting one of the original ribs down the center. An alternative is to insert an extra rib into the weaving. In either case, tuck in the end of one of the existing weavers and continue weaving with a single split until the base reaches the desired diameter.

When the base is large enough, tuck the end of the weaver securely under a rib to finish.

Setting up. Before bending the ribs up to the sides, check that they are sufficiently pliable to take the 90-degree bend without cracking. If the ribs seem stiff, pour boiling water over them at the edge of the base, then bend into place.

To begin weaving up the sides, insert the tapered end of a split into the base alongside a rib. Pull it around and weave through the ribs counterclockwise.

As with the base, the sides are woven in a continuous spiral. To minimize the lopsided effect, start weaving at the bottom edge with very narrow splits and increase width gradually with consecutive splits. The first inch or two of weaving is the most important stage with regard to the final shape of the basket. The angle of the ribs is more or less determined at this point.

Sides. As one split is finished, join in another by overlapping the distance of four ribs. Press down each round of weaving firmly and check that ribs are spaced evenly. Shape as you work. As the weaving nears the desired height, let in splits of decreasing width. Taper the final weaver so that the sides of the basket are of uniform height all the way around. Two inches of ribs remain.

Rim and handle. Follow directions given for the square-based basket.

Foot (optional). This is a ¼-inch-thick split bent into a hoop and fastened around the edge of the base to give the basket greater stability and protection from wear. Bend the split to fit the circumference of the base. Clamp it in shape. Make marks on the hoop to correspond with the space between each rib. Carve a notch at each mark. Sew the foot to the bottom of the basket, running a thong of hickory bast around each rib and through the notches.

Preparing the second set of ribs. The two sets are woven together, forming a composite bottom.

Setting up.

ROUND FRAME BASKET

Handle and rim rings. Two stout splits or small saplings are used for the frame (consisting of handle and rim). Both ends of each are tapered down in thickness and shaved flat. The two rings (oval or round, depending upon design) are then formed and secured with tiny nails.

Frame. Fit one ring inside the other. The rim is horizontal and the handle is vertical. Nail or tie the two rings temporarily in place. If the handle ring passes outside the rim ring, it must be slightly larger to keep the shape round. If not, the basket will be slightly melon shaped.

Tying frame rings. Very thin and flexible splits are used to tie the handle and rim. Tie one side, then the other, lapping far enough to give a hold for the first ribs. This creates a "God's-eye" pattern.

Placing of ribs. Ribs are cut in pairs of equal length (one for each side of the handle ring) and are incorporated as the weaving progresses. The first few pairs are inserted into the tying. Taper both rib ends.

Weaving. Tuck the weaver end into the tying and begin weaving with two or three pairs of ribs. The weaver is worked back and forth, looping around the rim at each edge. Additional ribs are added as space opens for them.

Shape. The rib length (as well as rim shape) determines the basket shape. This structure is versatile and may be a perfect half-sphere, oval, rectangle, or melon shape, depending upon variation of ribs.

Rim and handle for a round-frame basket.

Tying a round-frame basket. Continue in a counterclockwise direction for five or six rounds.

Starting the weave on a round-frame basket.

Adding ribs.

Nearing completion.

Round-frame baskets.

Homemade spoons.

CHAPTER 26
SPOONS

SPOON MAKING combines function and aesthetics in a household object appreciated by almost everyone. The variety of spoons is wide: dainty sugar spoons, hearty soup spoons, pot stirrers and ladles, cream skimmers for the dairy, and many more. Regional traditions developed spoons of favorite shapes in many areas. There is a quality of perfection in the best spoons, yet there remains the opportunity to change and modify each one made.

Spoons for soup and porridge should have a nicely hollowed bowl, with the stem curved upward at a comfortable angle. Our Swedish friend, Wille Sundqvist, makes very fine, small spoons with a straight front edge offset at an angle: useful for scraping one's dish clean at the end of a meal. Cooking and batter spoons are more or less flat, with shallow bowls. Dairy spoons and dippers tend to be deeply carved, with the stem at a steep angle to the rim of the bowl. A hook at the end of the stem is convenient for hanging on a pot, storage rack, or basin—besides being attractive.

Spoon making is also excellent training in the fundamentals of woodworking. Hatchet work and carving techniques are developed along with precision gouge work. The study of proportions, functional and

Stages in spoon carving.

Spoon-carving tools.

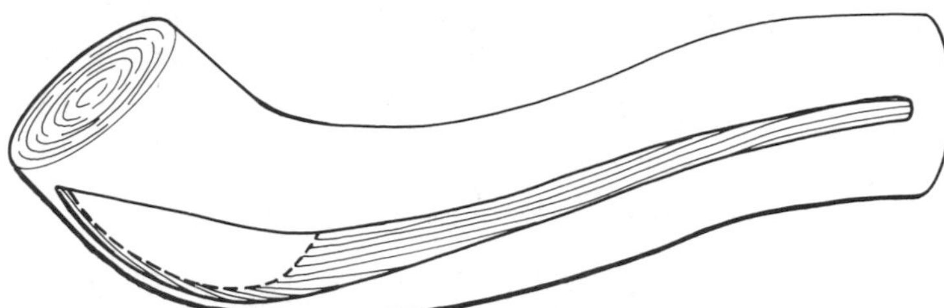

Locating a spoon in a crooked limb. Front edge of the bowl should not intersect the pith.

aesthetic, are beautifully combined; I consider spoons small sculptures. Of course the final test of a spoon is in how it works and feels in one's hand and mouth.

Spoon making provides a fine opportunity for experimenting with different woods, including that from many smaller varieties such as dogwood, holly, rhododendron, and mountain ivy (*Kalmia latifolia*) which is sometimes called "spoon wood."

It is good winter and evening work, and an excellent pursuit for nomadic craftsmen. Only a few tools are used and no workbench is needed. Suitable materials can be found most anywhere.

Evening spoon carving may be done without electricity. Wille says, "The light shines in the dark." Ah! Much work can be accomplished in the dim of dusk, taking advantage of the low-angle lighting. A single-point source, such as a kerosene lamp, is adequate, and will reveal slight surface undulations and imperfections better than diffused incandescent lighting. Spoons may be sanded sitting by the wood heater or fireplace after supper chores are finished when one is too lazy to do much else. Much of the work is done by feel, gauging the thickness with one's thumb and forefinger.

Materials. A wide variety of woods are suitable. English spoon carvers traditionally worked with sycamore, although holly and beech were commonly used. Swiss woodworkers favor maple. Scandinavian carvers use birch, birch root, and sometimes juniper. Some other appropriate woods include dogwood, laurel (rododendron), and the fruit woods.

The wood may be worked green or seasoned. Green

Splitting out blanks.

Shaping with a Kent hatchet.

wood is easiest to carve, but must be set aside for seasoning before final finishing.

Spoons can be carved from saplings, limbs, or billets split from larger logs. A curved spoon may be shaped to take advantage of the crook in a limb. It's sometimes possible to shape a spoon from wood growing in a natural concavity around a knot. Logs are first sawn to length, then split into quarter sections which are further split into cross-grained billets.

Roughing out. A coarse saw of some sort is used to crosscut the wood to length. An appropriate splitting wedge is simply an axe or hatchet with a wide blade. A long-handled maul is used to drive the "wedge" for splitting out billets.

Spoon blanks can be shaped in different ways.

An experienced wood craftsman should be adept at precise hewing work. The hatchet used is generally quite light, always very sharp. Broad hatchets, sharpened on one side, take the best bite. An ordinary hatchet may be ground with an asymmetrical bevel if much shaping work is to be done. Work in small, fine cuts, supporting the piece against the end of a clean hardwood stump.

An easier way to shape the blank is with a turning saw (such as the one described in Chapter 8: Bow Saws). Sketch the pattern with a soft pencil. Place the wood in a vise. Saw on push or pull strokes, depending on how the saw is held. Remove the piece and sketch out the profile. This is also sawn (somewhat oversized) to shape.

The square edges of a sawn blank are quickly

beveled with a carving knife. Only rough out; leave the blank greatly oversized. The concave bowl is hollowed before much work is done on the exterior bowl or stem.

Safety first! The carving knife must be razor sharp. An axe may be the most dangerous hand tool, but it's even easier to get sliced up with a carving knife. As I write, the five stitches in my left thumb testify to this. Carvers should learn to hold tools so that accidents are avoided. The photographs of Wille demonstrate different positions for effective, safe knife work. Carve with a slicing action. Keeping the bevel flat against the wood gives best control.

Hollowing the bowl. Spoon carvers have developed many hollowing techniques. As mentioned in Chapter 1: Basic Tools, Welsh craftsmen, along with many nomadic northerners, use various crooked knives. My Swiss teacher, Herr Kohler, clamped the blank in a vise, and then went at it with a bent gouge and maul. Very fast. A small adze can be used for hollowing the larger dippers and ladles.

Commonly used gouges measure ⅝ to ⅞ of an inch across the channel. The bevel should be ground flat, then whetted to a keen, absolutely flat, edge. Use an Arkansas slipstone held flat within the channel for removing the burr. The exterior junction of bevel and channel should be rounded to facilitate a scooping action. A ¾-inch spoon gouge is also useful, especially for deep dippers and ladles.

Wille teaches a method which is safe and efficient. The piece is held in one's left palm, with the thumb well

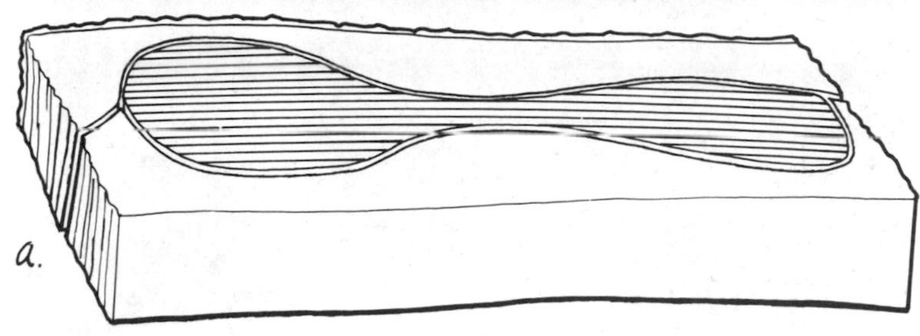

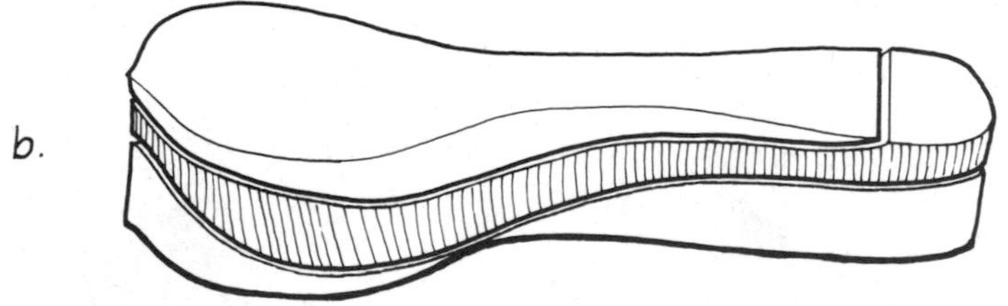

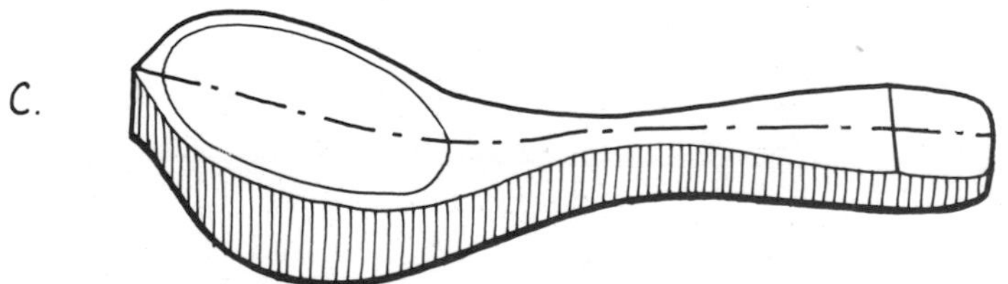

Sawing a spoon from a split billet.

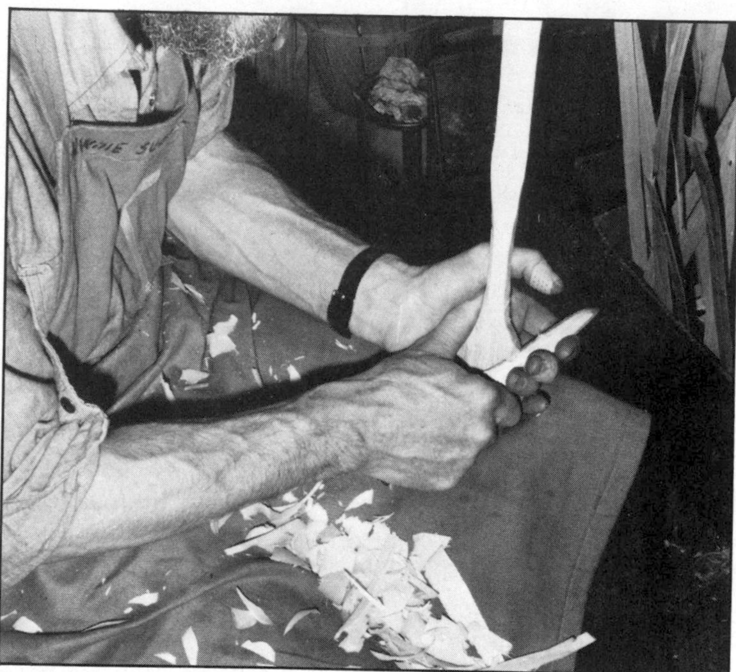

Two-handed carving technique results in extra strength and control.

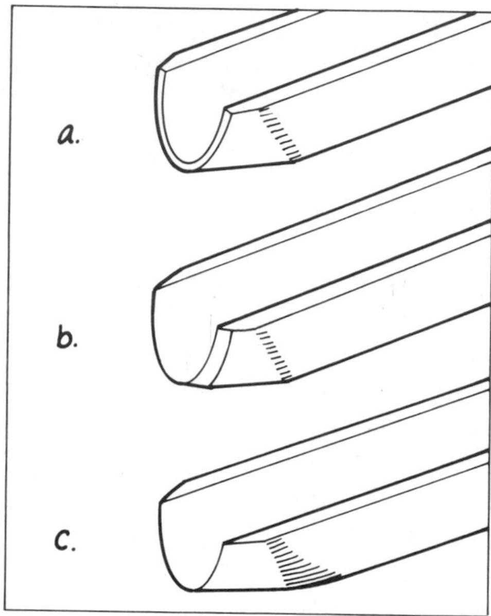

Sharpening gouges begins with proper shaping on a grindstone. A fine-grit electric wheel may be used; however, be very careful not to overheat—indicated by a blue edge and hot steel. Grind from the base toward the edge. A hand-cranked wheel is safer, but requires an assistant for turning. (a) illustrates a new gouge from the factory—slightly exaggerated. The expedient approach (b) is grinding a sharp, somewhat obtuse, bevel across the edge. In (c) the entire bevel has been ground to a finer angle than the original shape. The meeting section of bevel and channel has been rounded to give clearance for scooping work. Grinding is followed by hand whetting; first on a fine India stone, then with an Arkansas slipstone (with a rounded edge). Use light oil to float off particles of stone and steel. Rock the gouge sideways, back and forth, maintaining the proper bevel angle. Remove the burr with the Arkansas slip held flat inside the channel, rubbing lightly back and forth.

extended. The gouge, which must be very sharp, is grasped dagger-style along the shank, close to the cutting edge. The extended right thumb is the only digit that contacts the gouge handle. The heel of the right hand is butted against the piece being worked. The left thumb presses across to the right palm or the channel of the gouge. In this position one has great leverage and slips are virtually impossible.

The bowl is hollowed with a series of fine sweeping movements, generally working across the grain. Stubborn places are worked with shallow cuts or with an angled slicing motion. Variations of the hand position are improvised for working at different angles. But the left thumb always remains as a fulcrum and safety point while the heel of the right palm is held against the work.

The leading edge of the bowl should not be too steep, because the excessive end grain makes a weak wall. Do not carve the edges too thin. A moderate rim provides a margin of safety and adequate material for nicely sanded contours. A very thin edge is likely to chip during use. Work for smoothly curved sides and a thin bottom.

The exterior is carved to create a bowl with thin sides, front, and bottom, but a comparatively heavy rear section for balance and good attachment to the stem. This work is done with a carving knife. (Wille uses Swedish knives made by Frosts.) Welsh carvers often use a spokeshave for exterior work.

The stem may be plain and straightforward or elaborate and decorative. In any case, it must be well balanced and comfortable to hold, besides having ade-

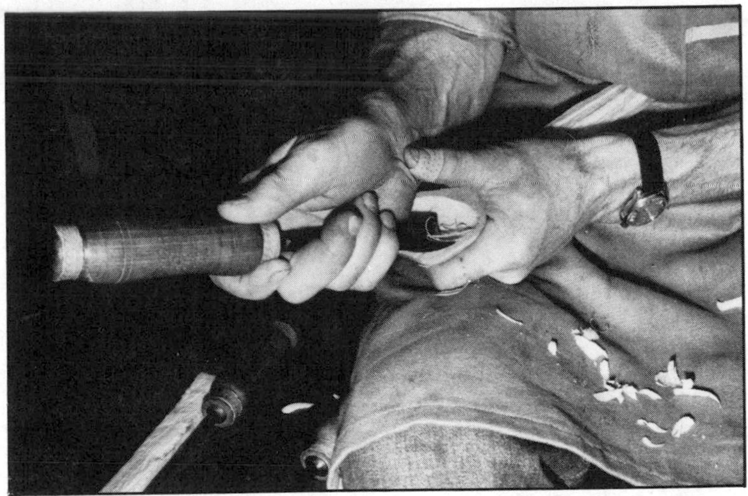

Gouge technique, with left thumb serving as fulcrum and safety.

Hollowing the bow.

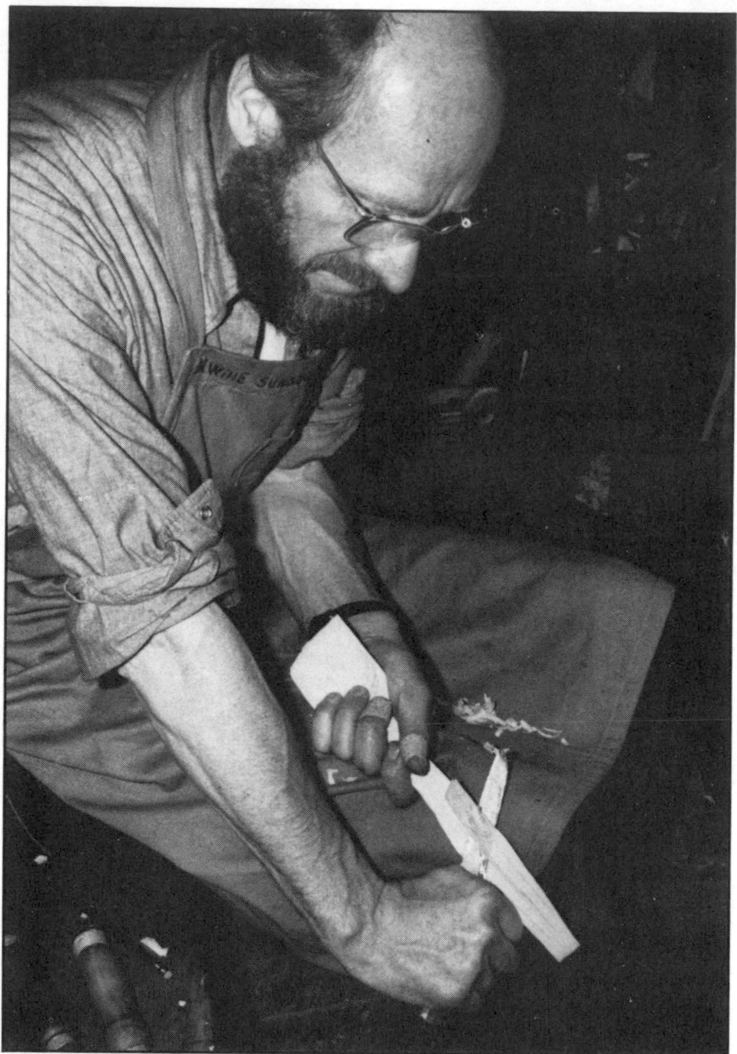

Carving outward with a slash angle.

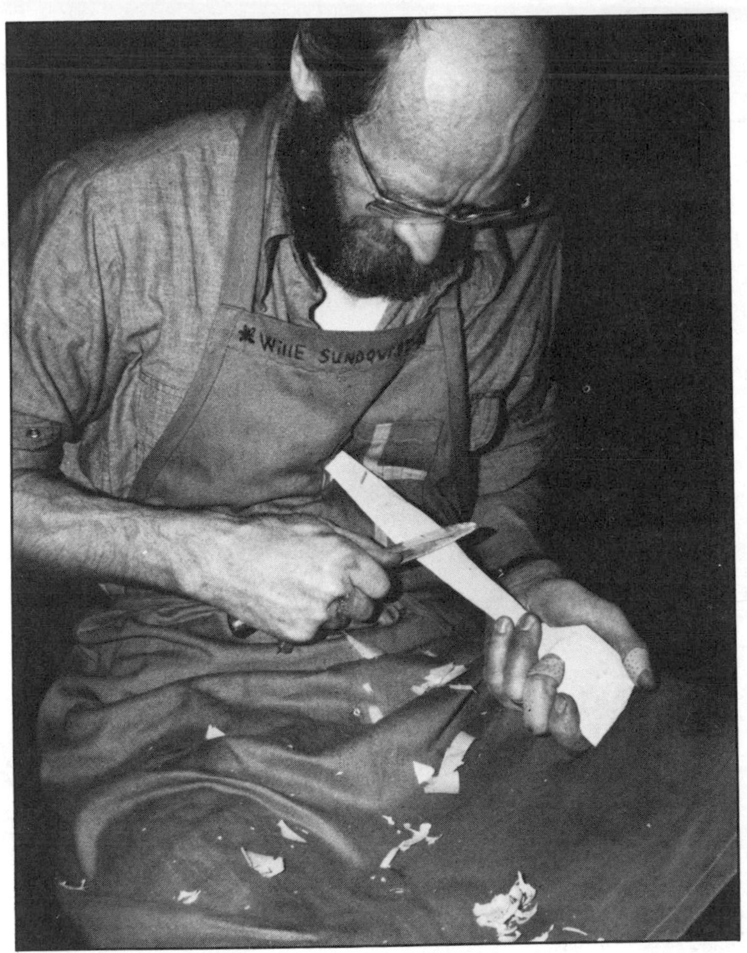

Working inward.

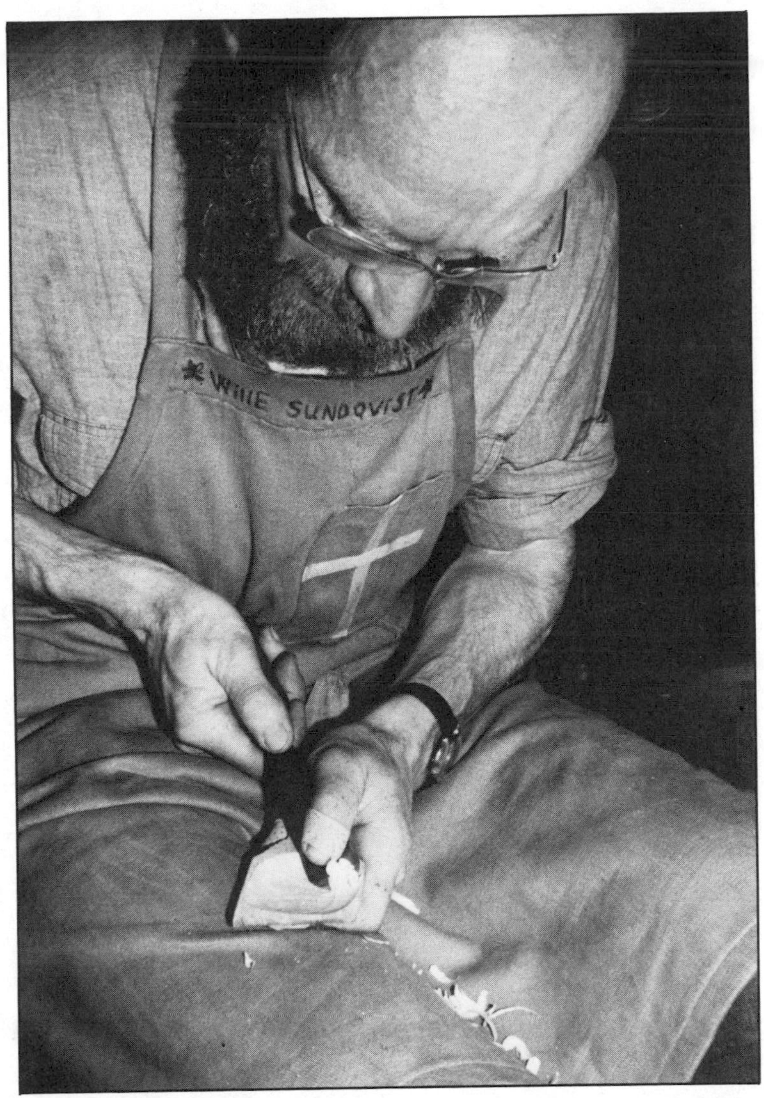

Trimming the lip.

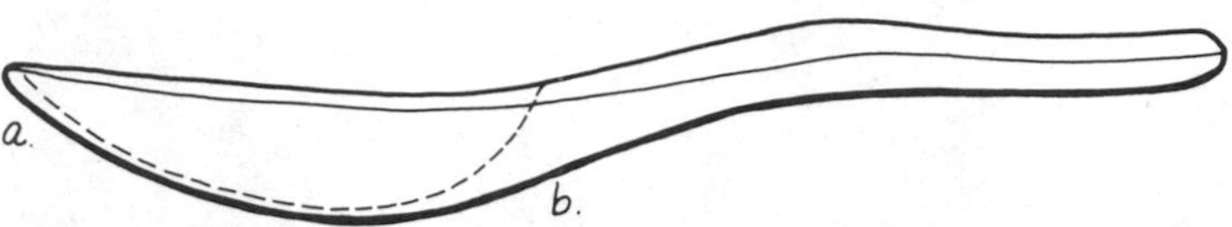

Shallow angle (a) along the leading edge minimizes weak end-grain. Be sure to provide adequate support at the meeting of bowl and stem (b). The sketch illustrates a small porridge spoon.

quate strength. Work for good proportions and a pleasant feel.

Finishing. Carving should be carried out to a practical degree of smoothness, thin shell, and pleasing proportions. The spoon is set aside to season, approximately one week. Final gouge and knife work will be easier on some seasoned woods.

The spoon is sanded, beginning with 80-grit paper, working through medium and fine grades. High-quality emery cloth is the most effective abrasive. Garnet paper is good, followed by aluminum oxide. Flint types are comparatively ineffective on hardwoods.

A deep, rich finish is created with several coats of straight linseed oil, rubbed in with a coarse cloth until a penetrating and hardening heat is generated. Space coats a day apart and wait a week before using. After washing (scalding water but no soap, please) a "nap" may come up on some woods. Sand again with well-used, fine sandpaper and reoil.

Dough trough.

CHAPTER 27
DOUGH TROUGHS

CARVING VESSELS DIRECTLY from a log is a craft of great antiquity that has an archetypal appeal for many woodworkers. Craftsmen of many indigenous cultures have reworked naturally hollow logs for grain containers and bee gums. The magnificent 6-foot "talking drums" of Africa were made by a continuous charring and scraping process. Sea-going boats and wooden bowls have been patiently carved by craftsmen of every continent. The famous watering troughs of Alpine Switzerland are still being made.[1]

In our travels we have seen large dough troughs being used in many Turkish farmhouses. The trough described below is a traditional Scandinavian pattern, learned from Swedish craftsman Willc Sundquist. This vessel is somewhat different from typical early American dough troughs—the profile is considerably lower and the interior contour is more bowlike. (American versions often have a flatter bottom.)

Materials. Hollowware may be carved from any fine, close-grained wood of neutral taste. Bowl carvers often favor extremely hard woods, such as Osage orange. However, due to their size, dough troughs are generally made from softer woods. Most favored is linden (also

1. Langsner, *Handmade,* p. 160.

Hollowing tools.

known as bass, or lime in England), followed by buckeye and poplar. In Sweden birch is commonly used. Harder woods, such as maple, beech, or apple make fine hollowware, but work is more difficult. Barnyard watering troughs are generally carved from pine, which will hold water and take inclement weather for many years.

After felling, the trunk should be sawed into bolts the lengths of the anticipated carving projects. These are moved to any airy shed, then split in half. Everything possible must be done to avoid checking and splitting. The end grain of green bolts should first be coated with roofing asphalt, or use latex paint, followed by polyurethane varnish, aluminum paint, or melted paraffin.[2] Do not make hollowware from wood that develops end checks.

Most carved hollowware is made from a log section split in half. A round slice makes a strong vessel, but the shape crosses the grain at difficult carving angles.

Tools. The basic hollowing tool is a small, curved hand adze. *It is imperative that the cutting bevel is ground on the exterior edge.* Commonly found curved adzes with an interior bevel must be reshaped for hollowing work.

An ideal adze head measures less than 6 inches long. The curved lips should be very deep so that lateral chips won't break away during cross-grain hewing. A short, stubby handle—about one foot long—is best for work on household-sized wares. Larger handles tend to get in one's way.

---

2. R. Bruce Hoadley, "Drying Wood," *Fine Woodworking,* vol. 1, no. 5.

The adze shown is somewhat of a compromise tool. This adze was manufactured with an interior bevel and a hammering peen. The bevel was laboriously reversed and the peen sawn off. The altered head is 8 inches long and is a little too heavy for one-handed use. A 15-inch handle is fitted and provides sufficient leverage.

A few other tools are also used. External shaping is done with a well-sharpened hatchet (preferably a broad hatchet beveled on one side only). A large bent gouge and mallet are used after preliminary adze work. Final interior smoothing is done with a wide, shallow gouge. I have found a reshaped spokeshave, ground with a slight lengthwise curve along the sole and cutter, to be very effective for exterior detailing. A large wedge and maul, two planes (jack and scrub), and a drawknife are also used.

Technique. Select a log 10 to 15 inches in diameter, and crosscut a section 15 to 25 inches long. Use a wide-bladed axe, hatchet, or timber wedge and wooden maul to split the log into halves.

The shape of the Swedish vessel is particularly suited to hand work as the low profile requires minimal work into the grain. Proportionately deeper troughs require steeper sides, making interior and exterior work considerably more difficult. For this style, plan a total height of 4 to 5 inches. (However, the same principles of design and technique may be adapted to deeper vessels.)

Sketch the base line across the two ends, parallel to

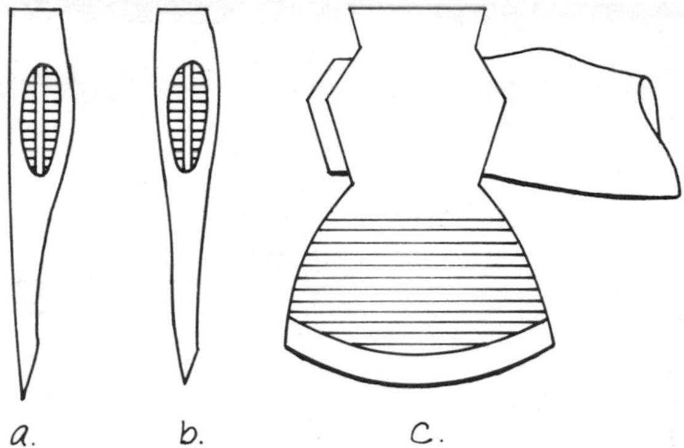

A broad hatchet (a) is beveled on one side; the other side is very slightly convex from poll to cutting edge and is filed absolutely flat to remove the burr caused by sharpening. For hewing, a standard hatchet may be reground with asymmetrical bevels (b). Contrasted to "camp hatchets," the Kent hatchet (c) is forged with a flat band across the beveled side.

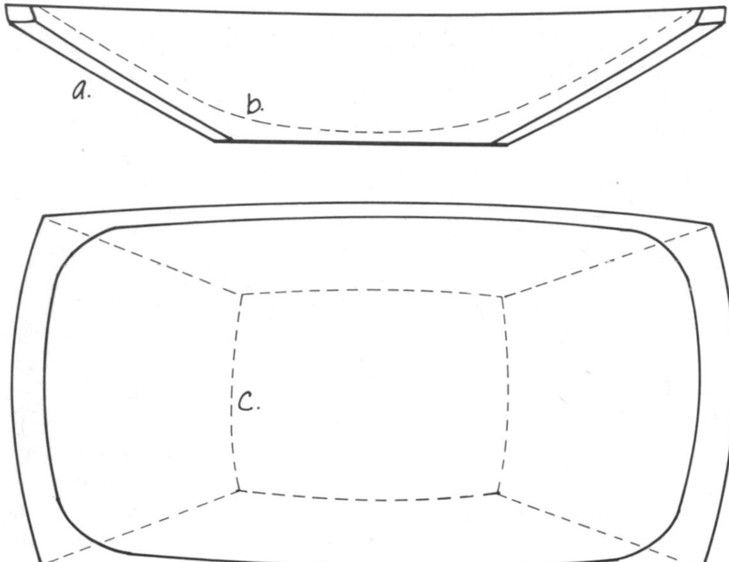

The ends (a) of the dough trough are hewn at 30 degrees or less. The gently sloping interior with rounded bottom (b) is fully accessible for adze and gouge work. (c) indicates the base.

Hewing the bottom.

the rim. Place an end on a cutting block and rough out the bottom with a sharp hatchet. Hew to within ¼ inch of the guidelines.

Secure the block upside down on a workbench with adjustable vise dogs; or set against two protruding pegs or a cleat. Continue leveling the bottom by planing. A scrub plane quickly brings excessive waste wood to the guidelines. Finish smoothing using a jack plane with the blade reground to a fine convex arc (1/16 inch overall).

Turn the block over and mark the outline of the trough interior. The overall shape is that of a rectangle with rounded corners. Leave a full inch margin at the ends but come within ⅝ of an inch along the sides. A wide-nib flow pen will mark on green wood, and can be used to make highly visible guidelines that won't rub off.

Hollowing. Nail a short 2 x 4 cleat to the floor (or to one end of a 2 x 4-foot piece of plywood). Place the trough block against the cleat and go to it with the adze. Alternately, use the illustrated notched chopping log of Swedish origin.

For most work, hold the adze with both hands. With a small adze, double-grip the handle with interlocked fingers, or grip it with one hand and reinforce the grip by grasping the wrist with one's free hand. This is vigorous work.

Start out by chipping a depression across the middle. Continually reverse the block so that cutting is with the grain and into chips from the opposite side. Work for a shallow angle at the ends, with somewhat steeper sides, and a nicely rounded bottom. A beginner's

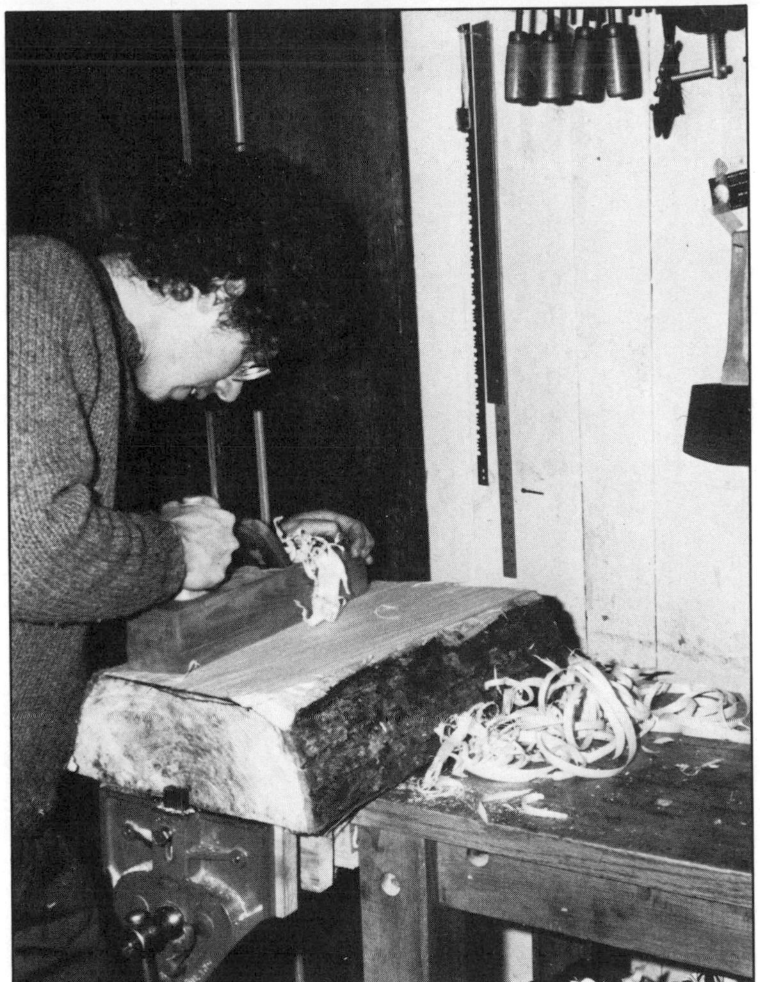

Planing the bottom.

Beginning adze work.

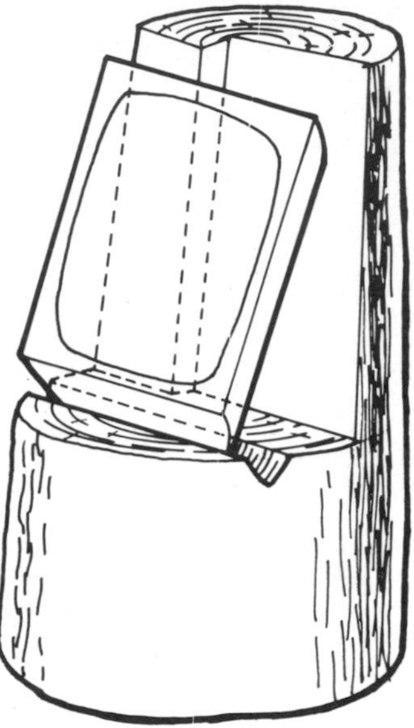

Swedish device for holding a dough trough while adzing out the interior.

tendency is to work too steep an angle. This results in a flatter bottom, which can be attractive but is more difficult to smooth out. Be careful with that adze. It's fast and potentially dangerous. Work to within ⅝ inch of the bottom and ¼ inch of the guidelines.

Hollowing continues at the workbench. Chunks of waste are removed to the guidelines with the large bent gouge and heavy mallet. For good control and easy cutting, the gouge should be sharpened with an absolutely flat bevel and razor-sharp edge. Grind (round) off the area where the bevel and back meet to create clearance during scooping.

Be sure to maintain the shallow angle along the ends and the nice, concave bottom.

Fine work is done using the gouge two-handed. Hold the blade quite close to the edge with your left hand acting as a guide and fulcrum. Apply smooth, controlled force to the handle with your right arm and appropriate wrist action. Final paring work is done with the wide, shallow gouge, also two-handed. A "spoon gouge" may be used to get into finer-radii curves of deep-sided work.

The rim is leveled with a drawknife, held bevel downward. Work from midsides toward middle ends. Use a slicing action, with a drawknife diagonal to the rim. A large amount of leveling results in a smaller cavity. This can be brought back to overall dimensions by additional gouge work.

External shaping begins by outlining the trough sides along the rim. The traditional shape is a bowed rectangle, with angled corners. Shaping work begins

Maintain shallow sides and curved bottom.

Working with a chisel and mallet.

Hewing the sides.

with the broad hatchet. Hold the trough edge-side down across one end of a *clean* log block. Start out chopping the corners, working toward the middle of each end. The low-angle profile results in a small, graceful base; do not chop too steeply into the wood. Begin to hew out the sides. Always work with the grain. Leave a ¾-inch vertical edge along the ends. As the trough develops, hew finer, with more careful slices. Stop axe work within ⅛ inch of the final shape.

Continue paring the outside with the modified spokeshave. Ends may be smoothed with the trough dogged to the workbench. Straddling a low bench, such as a shaving horse, is ideal for trimming down the sides. Rim details are done with a long narrow carving knife.

Finishing. Dough troughs carved from green wood are liable to crack during subsequent seasoning. One way to minimize this risk is to slow down and even out dehydration by alternate periods of exposure and storage in a sealed container. (I use plastic garbage bags.) Internal moisture is wicked toward the surface at night, evaporated off the next day. Mexican wood carvers store green ware in damp sawdust.

Seasoned troughs are sanded or scraped smooth. A finish of vegetable oil or raw linseed oil and spirits of gum turpentine mixed 2:1 may be rubbed into all surfaces.

Trestle table with walnut top and oak legs.

CHAPTER 28
A FARMHOUSE TABLE

FOR ME there is no better symbol of farmstead living than a solid wood table, laden with homemade breads, cheese, garden salad, pitchers of milk, and inviting benches along each side. Every meal should be a harvest celebration. And aesthetic appreciation of woodenware, pottery, and furniture is an important element.

This trestle table has two massive *legs,* one at each end, mortised and tenoned into wide feet. The tabletop is supported by *rails,* also mortised and tenoned to the legs. The rails and feet are secured by two dowels driven through each of the four joints. Lateral stability is achieved with the single *trestle,* tenoned through mortises in the legs and held rigidly in place by removable *keys* wedged through tapered slots in the protruding tenon stubs. A unique feature of this design is that the framework can be quickly disassembled so that the table can be stored, moved, or expanded. Still, it is extremely sturdy and should last for generations of daily use.

The dimensions should suit your needs and the room where the table will be used. Our trestle table is

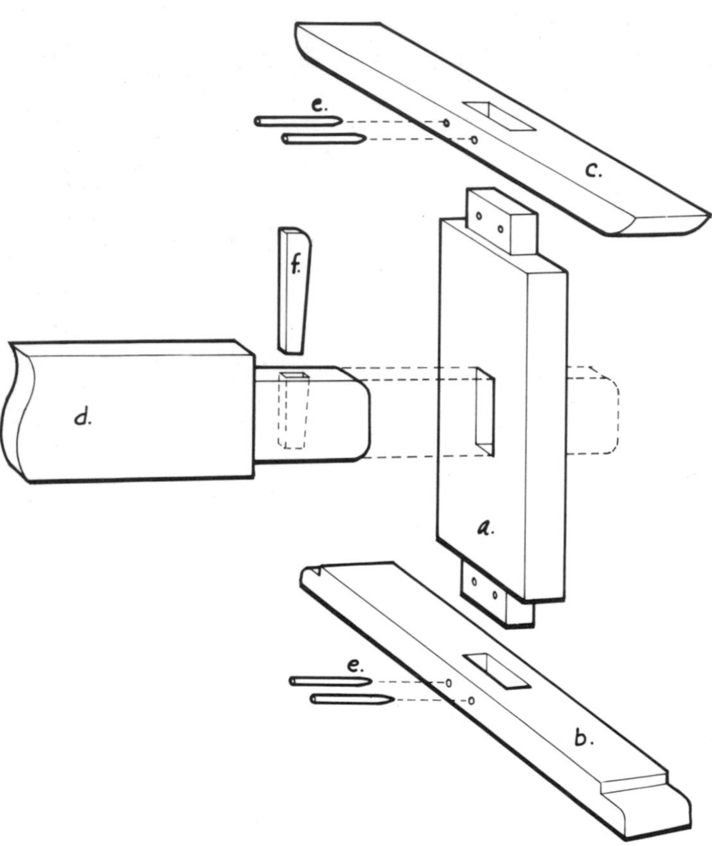

Trestle table details, dimensions to be modified to individual requirements. In this case, leg (a) is milled to 2½ x 9 inches; foot (b) is 2½ x 5½ x 30 inches; arm (c) is 2 x 5 x 30 inches; trestle (d) is 2 x 8 inches. Chamfered ⅜-inch dowels (e,e) are 6½ inches long, then trimmed flush after placement. The tapered key (f) is ½-inch thick and 10 inches long.

28 inches high, 32 inches wide, and 72 inches long.

Materials may be separated into frame and tabletop. Hard or soft woods can be used. The frame is massive, but the simplicity and proportions result in grace and elegance.

The legs and feet were made from oak bridge timbers, originally 3 inches thick, and dressed to 2½ inches. The legs are 9½ inches wide, and the feet are 5½ inches wide. The rails are planed 2 x 6s and the trestle is a planed 2 x 8. Both oak. The tabletop may be made of hardwood or softwood boards, 1 to 2 inches thick. For our table I used 1-inch thick walnut.

Construction. The framework is built exactly like the lathe discussed in Chapter 12. (Technical details are covered in Appendix I: Mortise and Tenon Joinery.)

The tabletop boards are edge planed, first with a jack plane, then a 24-inch joiner's plane. The boards are matched in an order that best conceals small discrepancies amongst them. They're also numbered with a pencil, and slash marks are drawn across the top as a guide for assembly order.

The next step is optional: marking holes for the dowel pins. A 6-foot table should have four or five dowels between each board. Guidelines are first made across all the boards at once. Use a sharp pencil and carpenter's 24-inch framing square. Mark lines across board edges with pencil and a small try square. The easiest way to indicate the center point for boring is with a marking (or mortise) gauge, set at dead center. Scratch marks guiding the gauge along the top edge of each board.

Assembling the leg.

Table framework.

Fitting a tapered key.

Secure each board in a vise and bore $\frac{3}{8}$-inch holes $1\frac{1}{4}$ inches deep, at each cross point. To insure straight holes use the try square held against the side of the board and on top of the edge. Commercially made dowels are fine for this use. Saw into 2-inch pieces and slightly taper each end. Saw a shallow groove the length of each dowel to allow excess glue and trapped air to escape during installation.

Gluing up is the touchy part of this operation. The workshop should be cleaned, sawdust swept out, obstructions and old debris cleared away. Gluing requires room for the tabletop, long clamps, and your own movement. Use white glue or plastic resin glue, which is an old-fashioned powder glue that's mixed with water. This glue sets up slowly and is very strong once hardened. You will need four to eight bar or pipe clamps (or the homemade type explained in Chapter 11: Workbench). Pinch dogs are useful for holding board ends together and in alignment. Gluing up can be done using the table frame as an assembly bench.

Apply glue along the inside edge of the first board. Put a little glue on each dowel and tap into place. Fit the second board to the first. Tap snug with a mallet. Repeat the procedure until the top is assembled. Begin clamping from the center of the tabletop. Alternate clamps on top and bottom of table. Alternating clamping sides tends to cancel bowing in either direction. Use clamp pads or small blocks of wood between the clamps and the edges of the tabletop. Check for flatness as the clamps are tightened. Use a reliable straightedge and sighting sticks. (These are two accurately sawn sticks, typically 1 x 2s, as long as the project is wide. One is placed along each end. Any parabolic warp is easily detected by viewing the top edge of the two sticks from one end of the table.)

Pinch dogs, if used, are driven into the end grain of adjoining boards.

The clamps should be quite tight, but not extremely so; otherwise too much glue will be driven out. Wipe off excess glue squeezed to the top and bottom surfaces before taking a well-deserved rest break. Allow the glue two or three days for thorough setting before removing the clamps.

The tabletop is attached to the frame with lag bolts. Countersink holes through the arms for lag bolt heads and flat washers. Be careful not to bore the pilot holes too deep. (Stanley depth gauge No. 47 is dandy for this purpose.)

Go over any bumps and ridges with a finely adjusted plane. Small irregularities can be smoothed with a cabinet scraper, hand-held scraper blade, or a piece of glass.

If the ends are straight, then simply smooth with a block plane. To prevent cracks and chipping, work inward from each corner. Ragged ends should be sawed off straight, then planed as above.

The tabletop is next sanded with successively finer grades of abrasive paper. Some folks like to let a kitchen table acquire its own finish through use over the years. A rubbed-in linseed oil finish gives a rich effect and allows the surface to age at the same time. Varnish or urethane gives more protection; several coats of urethane makes a tabletop practically scratch-proof. Satin urethane does not have quite the plastic look of gloss and semigloss finishes, but the table will never have the beautiful quality of a plain one carefully used for many years. Your choice. (Refer to Appendix II: Wood Finishes.)

Dining bench.

CHAPTER 29
A DINING BENCH

THIS SMALL BENCH is typical of many examples made by early American craftsmen. A similar type is still commonly seen in farmhouses of central and northern Europe. It is characteristically made of four boards plus two small wedged "keys." No glue, screws, or other mechanical fasteners are used. The bench seat is fastened to the legs with haunched mortise and tenon joints. Length may vary from two to ten feet (with a middle leg fitted on the longer versions).

Oftentimes such benches are decorated with scrollwork cut around and within the legs and trestle. The version shown is more closely related to a quite plain and functional Shaker pattern.

Materials. The bench is made from softwood or hardwood lumber that is flat and well seasoned. Pine, birch, and maple are typical choices. The boards may be ¾ to 1 inch thick. On some Shaker benches, the seat is ⅞ inch with legs and trestle ¾ inch. For a 2-foot bench, all four components can be taken from a single 8-foot board, 11½ inches wide, with generous waste wood to spare. Knots need not be avoided if they are sound and do not interfere with the joinery.

Construction. Although simple in design, the bench demands precision work in order to fit properly

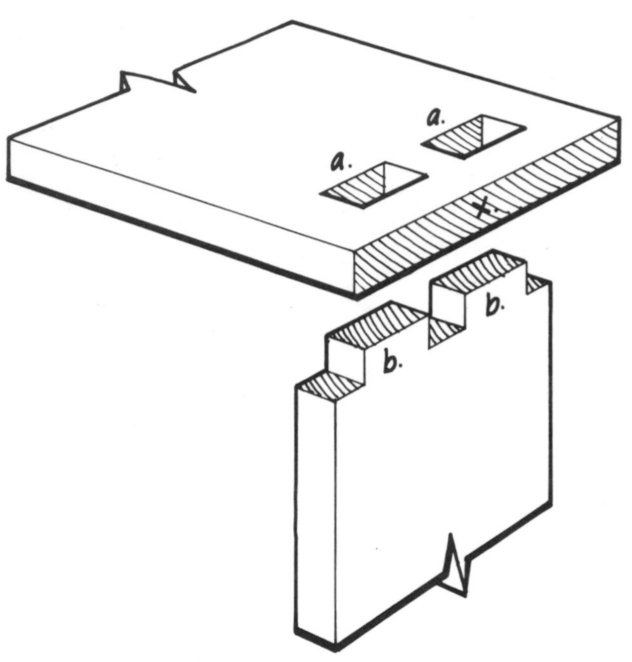

Haunched mortise (a,a) and tenon (b,b). Used for joints where a single, wide mortise would result in severely weakened end grain.

together. The mortise and tenon joints are set at angles and this calls for extra care in marking out and cutting. The twin mortises run across the grain at the bench ends leaving a divider running with the grain in between. One wide mortise crossing the grain near the edge would weaken the bench and probably break through under stress.

A simpler variation can be made using perpendicular legs rather than the inclined legs as illustrated. If this is done, the bench seat is secured by the twin mortise and tenon joints with foxtail wedges. (See Appendix I: Mortise and Tenon Joinery). The legs and trestle are joined with the removable keys as shown.

The first step is laying out the legs. Locate the best face and side and pencil mark with traditional inverted "e" and "v" joined at the common edge. Lay out the shape with sloping sides, the cutaway for feet, and any decorations. Do not cut out or shape until later. Square-sided boards greatly facilitate laying out the mortises and tenons. (The leg shoulders are 9 to 10 inches across.) The mortise for the trestle should terminate 2 to 3 inches below the shoulder line of the twin tenons. In the pictured bench, the legs are angled 8 degrees from vertical. Five degrees would be adequate. The bench height is 17 inches. There is no need to add extra leg length for the slight incline, as this adds a minimal but confusing and unnecessary consideration.

Mark out the tenon shoulder 1 inch below the upper edge. (Excess wood is trimmed after assembly.) Use a sliding bevel to pencil angled sides, then mark inside area of shoulders. The haunched tenons are 2 inches wide each, with a 1-inch space in between. Saw out the tenons, being careful to stay on the waste side of the marked lines.

Mark out the trestle mortise on the leg face with a standard square. (The leg sides are still parallel.) Then transfer the markings to the back by scribing a line across the edge, using a sliding bevel, set to an 8-degree angle, as a guide. Extend the edge marking across the back using a standard square as a guide. Drill and beat out the mortise.

The next step is making the trestle. The tenon shoulders are angled at the same 8 degrees. Note that these tenons are located off-center. The upper shoulder is greater to provide sufficient end grain above the mortise in the legs. Half-inch wide slots are beat through the tenons just within the fit of the legs. These are given a slight outward angle, ⅛ inch, to secure the keys that hold the legs in place.

Make the keys. (Detail discussion in Chapter 12: Spring-Pole Lathe.)

Assemble the legs and trestle.

Lay out the seat from the bottom side. Space the haunched mortises to correspond *exactly* to the distance between the tenons measured from shoulder to shoulder. Transcribe lines along sides of seat angled inward at 8 degrees. Beat out haunched mortises.

Assemble bench. Chisel excess waste off the protruding seat tenons. Disassemble. Cut out the feet, scrollwork, decorations, etcetera. Taper the legs. Trim off the seat corners and sand exposed edges. Finish with linseed oil, varnish, or leave plain.

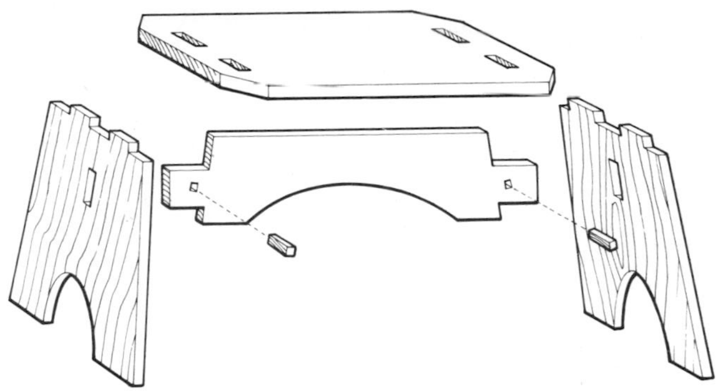

Bench construction. The pattern is easily expanded to seat several persons.

Whisks.

CHAPTER 30
PINE WHISKS

IN OUR INDUSTRIAL CULTURE resources are often manufactured to the point where there is little (if any) recognition of the raw material. In doing so, obvious uses of natural forms are often overlooked. This was not the case in a preindustrial society where anything not used as found had to be carefully handcrafted with simple tools.

Examples of using naturally shaped materials are these kitchen tools made from the junction of a whorl of pine limbs along the stem of a young sapling. Traditional Scandinavian cooks stirred their potato porridge with such a stick ending in a crown of cut-off limbs. The stick also makes a great egg beater. For stiff egg whites, place the handle between palms and rub back and forth spinning the whisk one way, then the other. The Swiss *Senn* (mountain cheese maker) uses a similar whisk, only larger, to break and stir the curd of his renowned *Alpkase*. In Appalachia, a similar type of stick was sometimes hung from the hearth or ceiling and used as a pot hanger.

Making these whisks is an easy and satisfying task. It's also a great project for kids or folks with very

Sawing off base of a pine whorl.

limited woodworking experience.

Materials. Several types of pine grow a full whorl of limbs each year and it's usually easy to locate thick young stands or scrub that need thinning. A sapling 7 or 8 feet tall will often provide materials for two or three whisks. Look for trees with evenly formed whorls growing in stands that need thinning.

Tools. The only tools needed are a saw and a penknife or small carving knife. To make the cheese whisks (with upturned beaters) you will also need string or wire.

Method. Cut the sapling any time of year. Make whisks within four weeks—while the wood is green and bark easily workable.

With the saw, cut sections just below each whorl of limbs. Egg and porridge beaters are then cut at 8- to 12-inch lengths. Cheese whisks may be 18 to 24 inches long.

For a beater, trim limbs to a 1-inch length. Remove all the bark on stem and limbs with the penknife. Cut out *all* the gooey pulp-like stuff at the base of the whorl. Set the beater aside to season (one or two weeks). Clean rosin off your hands and knife with paint thinner or other solvent.

Once seasoned, sand the beater with coarse, then fine abrasive paper. Smooth around the base so that food doesn't stick where the limbs attach to the stem.

In making a cheese whisk select a larger whorl with even, well-developed limbs. Trim the limbs to about 12-inch lengths. Very small, fragile limbs should be removed. Shave off all the bark and gooey stuff around the whorl. Bend the limbs upward and back crossing

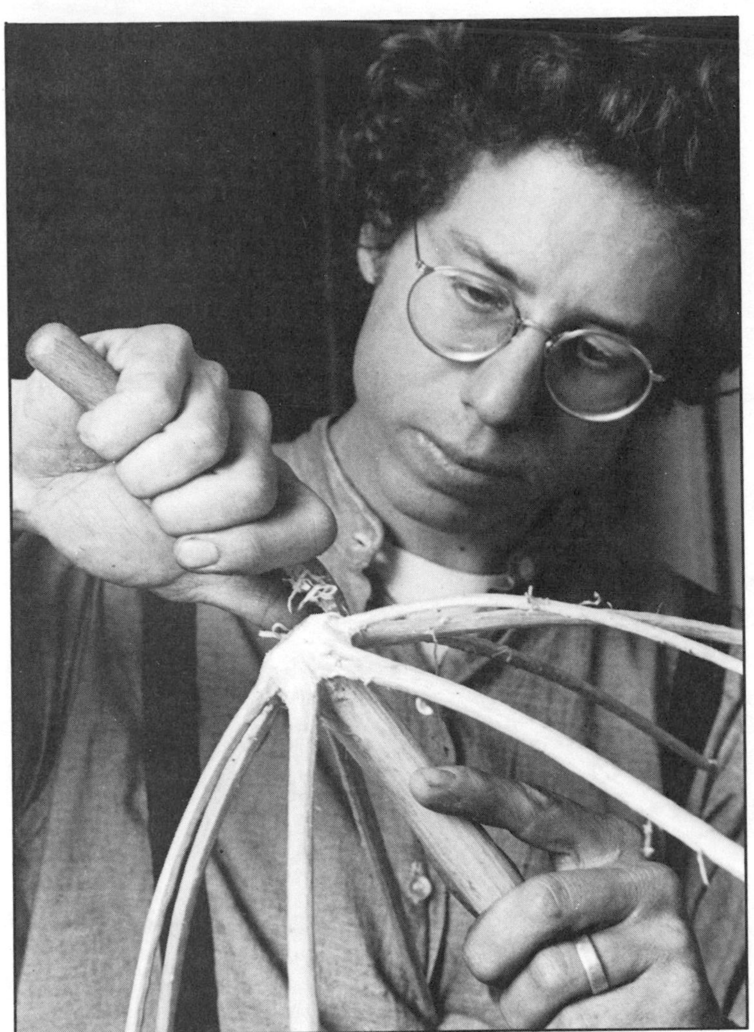

Trimming a cheese whisk.

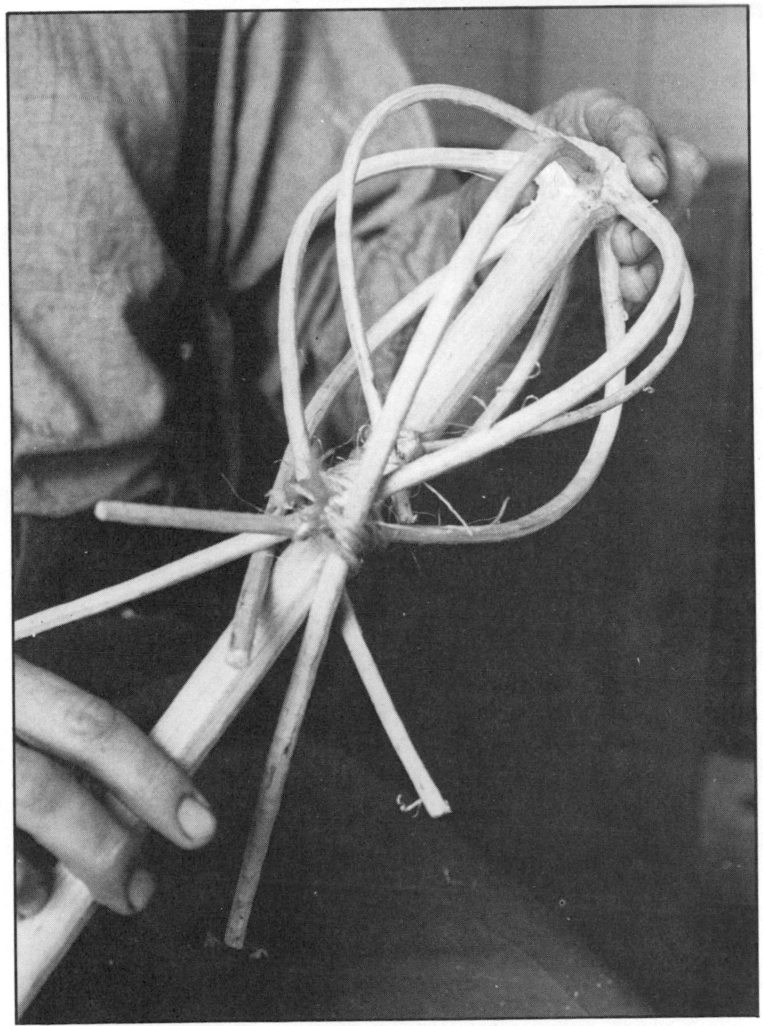

Tying the whorl to season.

the stem. Begin with the thinnest limbs, tying all in place with a continuous string. Season the whisk about two weeks.

The seasoned whisk will feel much lighter than the green sapling. Cut off the knotted string. Trim the limbs to a pleasing shape. Sand the whisk, being especially careful around the base of the whorl.

Pot hangers are made in much the same manner as egg beaters and cheese whisks. Use a stouter whorl found closer to the base of the sapling used for the smaller items. Use a hatchet to trim the limbs to 6- to 10-inch lengths. The stem may be cut anywhere between 1 and 2 feet long. Strip off the bark and remove weak or crowded limbs. Carve a V-notch on the upper edge of each limb to hook pot latches, hot pads, strainers, or whatever. Sand smooth in two or three weeks. Drill a hole through the stem tip and attach a thong loop for suspending the hanger from the ceiling or fireplace mantel.

APPENDICES

Mortise and tenon joinery.

APPENDIX I
MORTISE AND TENON JOINERY

The terms mortise and tenon refer to woodworking joints created by fitting a projection from one piece of wood into a hole in a second piece. The two elements are generally secured with a dowel, wedge, or glue. This is the basis of joinery and timber frame building construction techniques. Refinements of the mortise and tenon include dovetails, slip joints, and other specialties of furniture makers. In most cases, the country woodworker does well enough with a simple shouldered tenon and through mortise.

Handcrafted mortise and tenon joints are always made in matching pairs. Even if a number of identical parts are needed, slight variations will occur in the making. Code pairs and matching sides from the beginning of work. A good system is to punch coded dots on matching parts, e.g., . / ., . . / . ., etc.

While it's possible to make these joints in nearly any piece of wood, working on stock with square sides is far easier. Planed (or surfaced) lumber is more likely to be square than rough-sawn boards. Large dimension work (such as building construction) can be done on rough timbers, but for finer work, the surfaces should

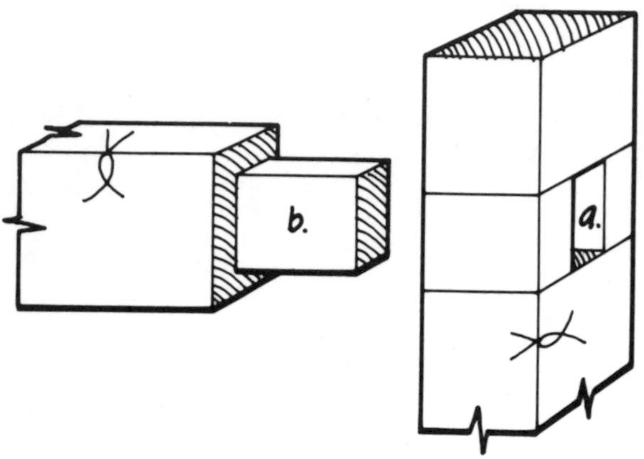

Typical mortise (a) and tenon (b) joint.

be dressed. A jack plane with a slightly convex ground blade ($\frac{1}{16}$-inch arc) will quickly work down most rough-sawn or split material. Oversized wood can first be reduced to approximate size with a scrub plane.

The first step is to examine the wood to determine the best face and side of each piece. Traditional pencil marks—an upside down cursive "e" on the face, and an upside down "v" on the side are scribbled joining each other along the common edge of the chosen face and side. All measurements are then made from one end of this edge. By keeping a single reference point, parts will line up even if the wood is slightly warped.

Generally tenons are made first. It's advantageous to have the finished tenon on hand to check measurements before making the matching mortise.

Tenon measurements are marked out with a well-sharpened pencil. Use the same ruler for all measurements, preferably one with a square end (not a slide or movable hook). It's surprising how much variation may be found from one ruler to another. Right angles should be marked with a large set square. Combination (or sliding squares) tend to be inaccurate; also the leg is too short unless the lumber is exceptionally straight. For large tenons (such as in making a workbench) use an 18- x 24-inch carpenter's framing square. It's a good idea to mark out tenons slightly long, trimming to size after assembly.

From the edge of the chosen face and side, mark out the tenon shoulder. The other face is aligned from the best side, while the back side is marked from the best face. The tenon cheeks are penciled in at this time as a guide for the depth of cut along the shoulder.

Secure the material in a vise or clamp with the best side up and best face forward. For large tenons, a carpenter's crosscut saw may be used. Finer work requires a reinforced backsaw or a miter saw. Carefully saw along the waste portion. Start the cut by drawing the saw toward yourself several times. Make a shallow kerf across the far corner and top, then angle the saw downward along the best face, without sawing further on the back (unseen) face. Stop just before the check line. Reverse the piece (left to right) and saw down the "back" face using the kerf through the best face as a guide to keep the saw in line. Reversing the sawing direction insures straight cuts without using a miter box or guide blocks.

Using the same technique, saw out the shoulders along the back side, front face, and back face.

Next saw out the cheek sides. For large tenons, use a 4½-point rip saw. Continue to reverse sawing direction, working downward at an angle so that the exact location of the saw along the unseen back part of the cut is always in alignment. It's possible to "steer" to the right or left for corrections by sawing at a very acute angle to the board. Saw down the faces in the same manner.

Sometimes the cheek waste wood will not drop loose because the cuts don't come fully together somewhere in the middle. It may be necessary to carefully resaw either kerf until the waste wood comes free. If only a few strands hold on, the piece may be broken out by hand pressure.

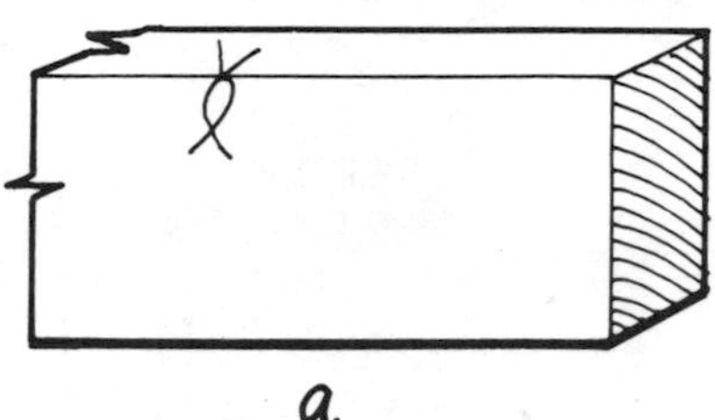

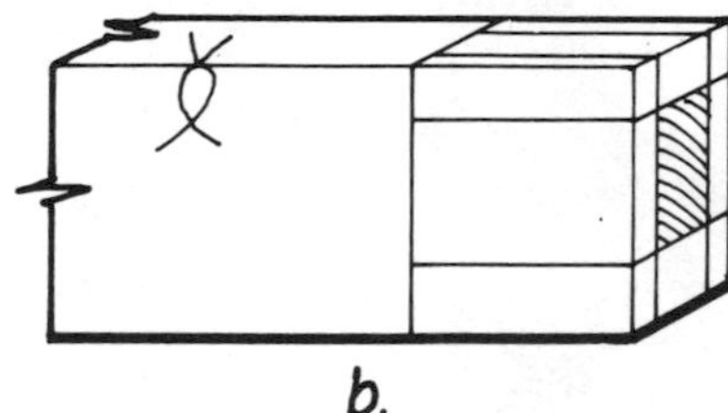

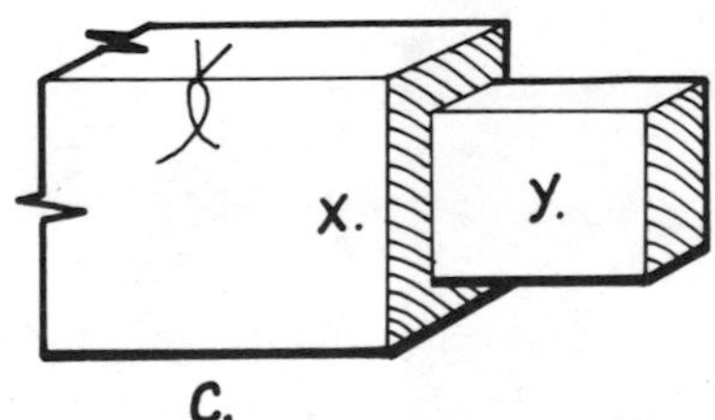

(a) Traditional marks for best face (*l*), and best side (*v*). Marking out is done from the common edge. (b) Marked-out tenon. Use sharp pencil. (c) Side view of tenon with shoulder (*x*), cheek (*y*).

Sawing out a tenon.

The tenon is cleaned up by paring with a sharpened chisel. The inside shoulder angle often needs attention, and a bit of work may be called for along the face and sides. Check the dimensions against original specifications. Make sure that the tenon is square. Pare with the grain direction so that the chisel does not run out of control into the wood. With a spokeshave or chisel, chamfer a slight bevel along the outer stub so that fitting into the mortise will be eased.

Mortises are marked out following the finished dimensions of the paired tenons. Marking should be done with a mortise gauge or a knife, preferably one sharpened along one side only. Pencil lines are hard to follow and scratch awls break out rough lines. As with tenon work, mark from the joining edge of the best face and side.

Secure the work to a bench with a piece of flat waste wood between it and the benchtop. Use a hold-down or C-clamp. Alternately, a wood vise can be used. But with a vise there is generally more vibration and the wood may slip during hard beating. This is also hard on the vise, and there is risk of damaging a chisel by striking through the mortise onto the screw or guides.

The traditional method is to beat out the mortise using a sharp, stout chisel (a mortise chisel or a heavy firmer chisel) and a mallet. First chisel straight down along the outline. Begin along the end grain dimensions. Set the chisel into the knife-scribed marking, with the flat side out. Strike sharply (once) with the mallet. The slight resulting groove will prevent chips from splintering outside of the mortise dimensions.

Next chisel from the center gradually creating a V-groove extending to the outlines. The chisel should be held so that the bevel edge faces down; this will cause it to scoop out waste. (Facing up, the chisel tends to dig in and tear the wood fibers.) Turn the piece over about halfway through. Never chisel straight through as the wood will probably break away or crack on the back side. Repeat the chiseled outline process and removal of waste wood on the reverse side.

To remove wood more quickly, most mortises are started by boring a series of holes well within the chiseled outline. Do not drill straight through; turn the work over and counter-bore to avoid the possibility of wood breaking as the bit emerges.

After the cavities of both sides meet, beat out the remaining bulk. Then pare down the sides by turning the chisel flat against the mortise walls. Usually hand pressure will provide sufficient force and greater control than using a mallet. Use both hands, one for downward pressure, the other as a guide. Work with or across the grain, never against it.

Ideal mortises have perfectly straight walls. In practice this may be hard to achieve. This is especially true for long, deep mortises, or when working with rough-grained woods. It's annoying to try to fit a tenon into a slightly convex-walled mortise. It's sometimes a good idea to pare the walls just perceptably concave. Pare from each side so that the outer edges are preserved. Check with a straightedge placed against the wall; it should not rock on a bump but rest flat against both outside edges. Make sure that the corners are clean and

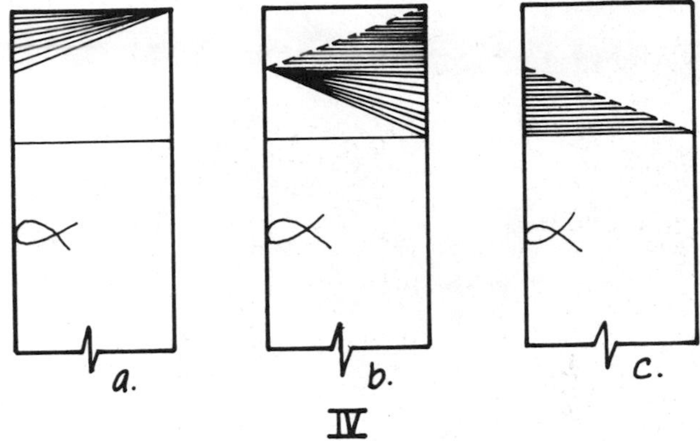

Progression for sawing out a tenon cheek. Sawing direction alternates from left (a), to right (b), to left (c).

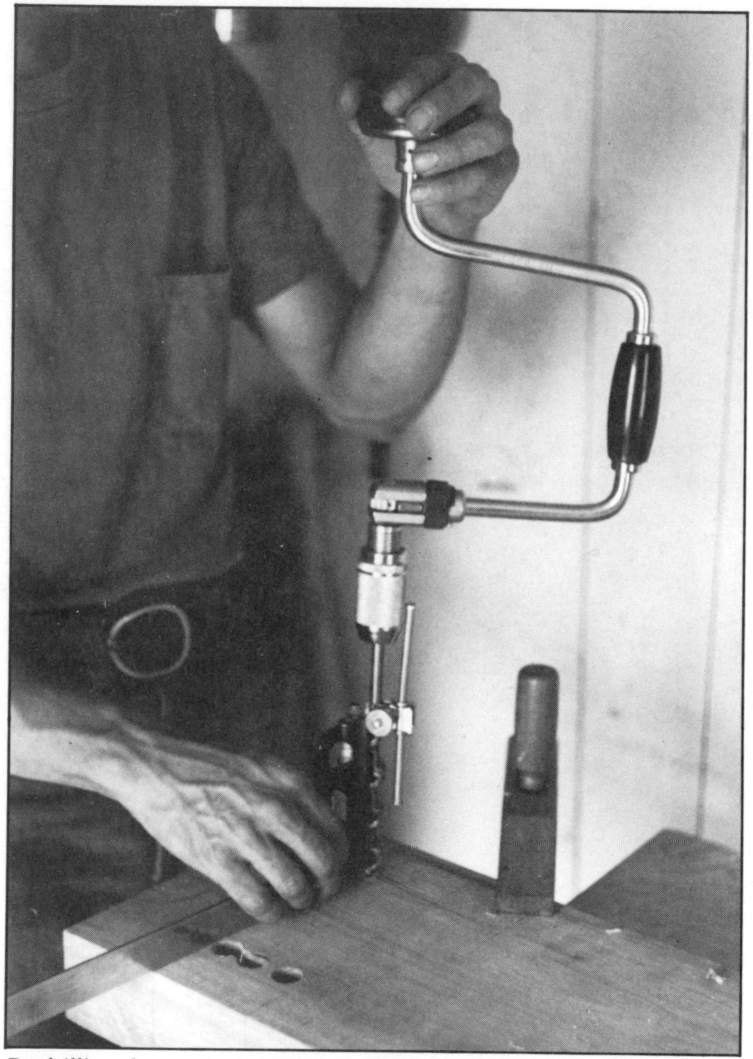

Predrilling the mortise holes. Depth gauge contacts surface before cutter emerges on reverse side.

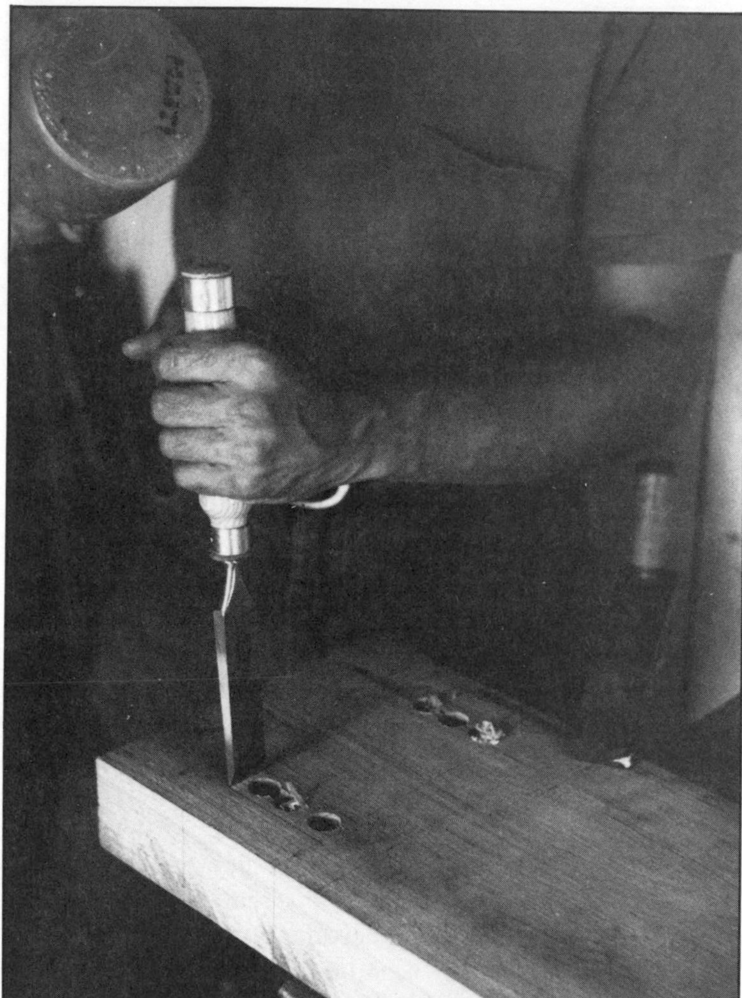

Outlining the mortise with chisel bevel inwards.

straight or the tenon will not fit.

If everything is perfect (or too loose!) the mortise and tenon will slip together without any trial fittings. Often, however, the tenon seems too large and the mortise appears too small. Be careful in making adjustments, as it's easy to pare off in the wrong places resulting in a sloppy fit.

The first step in troubleshooting should be remeasurement of all dimensions and checking of right angles. Make sure that there are no bulges along the mortise walls or across the tenon cheeks. Check for clean inside corners. If necessary, tenon shoulders can be pared slightly inward. The cheeks must be flat. A mechanic's feeler gauge, perhaps set at .005 inch, will help to locate obstructions within the joint. If the fit is too loose, the joint may be tightened up by inserting thin wedges or shims from the back side.

A common method of fastening mortise and tenon joints is with a wooden dowel passing through both elements. In such cases it's best to drill the dowel hole through the mortise piece before working on the actual mortise. (Drilling after mortising can result in wood tearing loose as the auger breaks into the mortise cavity. Usually this has no effect on function of the joint.)

After the mortise and tenon are fitted, mark the hole center on the tenon and disassemble the joint. With an awl, mark another center ⅛ to ¼ inch toward the tenon shoulder. Drill at the relocated mark. Reassemble. Drive a chamfered dowel through the hole. The dowel will tighten the joint as it passes through the off-center tenon hole.

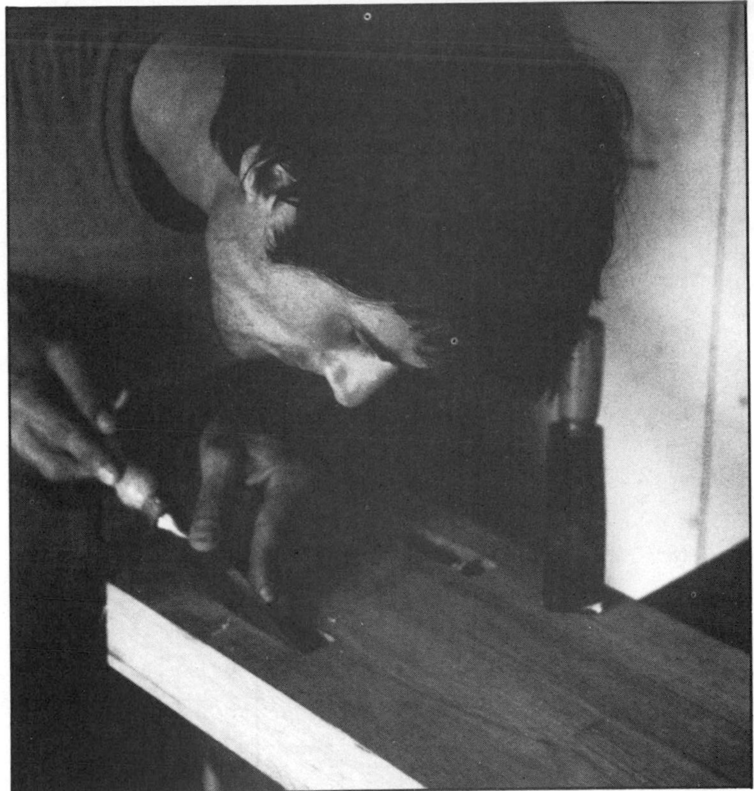

Paring the walls.

Another effective method of fastening mortise and tenon joints is with a "key": a thin wedge driven through a tapered auxiliary slot on the outside stub of an extended tenon. The beauty of this technique is that the joint may be quickly disassembled. (Details on keyed joints are in Chapter 12: The Spring-Pole Lathe.)

A permanent mortise and tenon joint may be secured with a foxtail wedge. In this variation, one or two slots are sawn through the tenon to the shoulders. A little glue is applied to the sides of wedges made for the particular joint. (Refer to Chapter 10: Wedges.) For a through mortise, the joint is assembled and then the glue-smeared wedge is knocked into place with a mallet and trimmed flush to the mortised member. In a blind mortise care must be taken not to make the wedge too large. The wedge is just barely started into the slot. Then the joint is assembled (with glue) and the wedge tightened up as mortise and tenon are knocked into place.

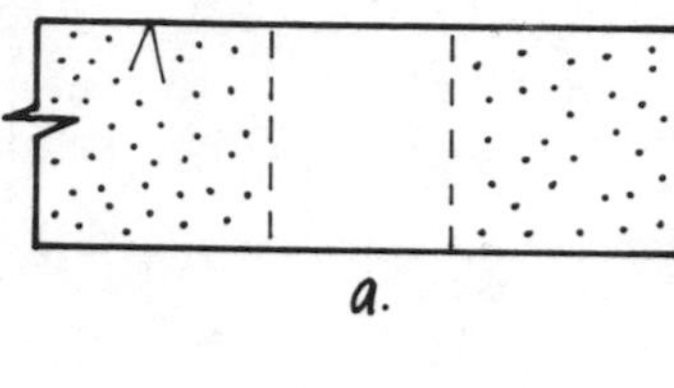

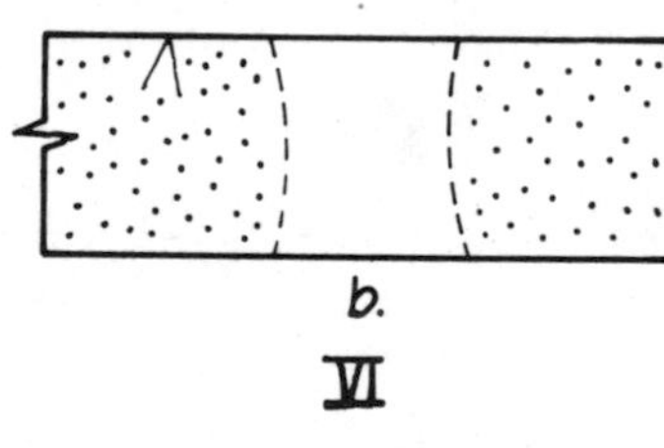

VI

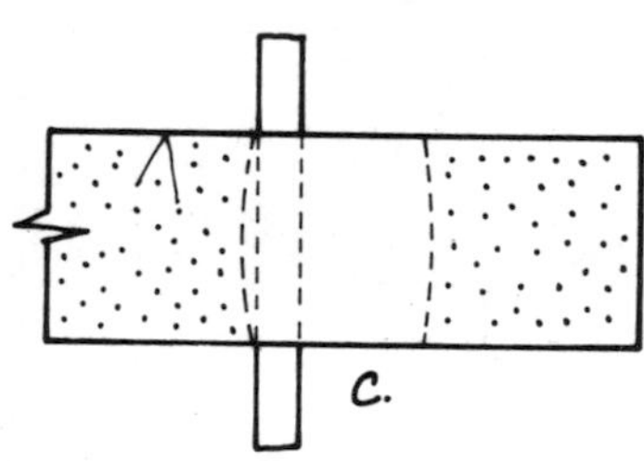

Mortise interior: (a) perfect mortise; (b) convex walls won't accept properly sized tenon; (c) slightly concave walls are acceptable. Use a straight edge to check for bumps.

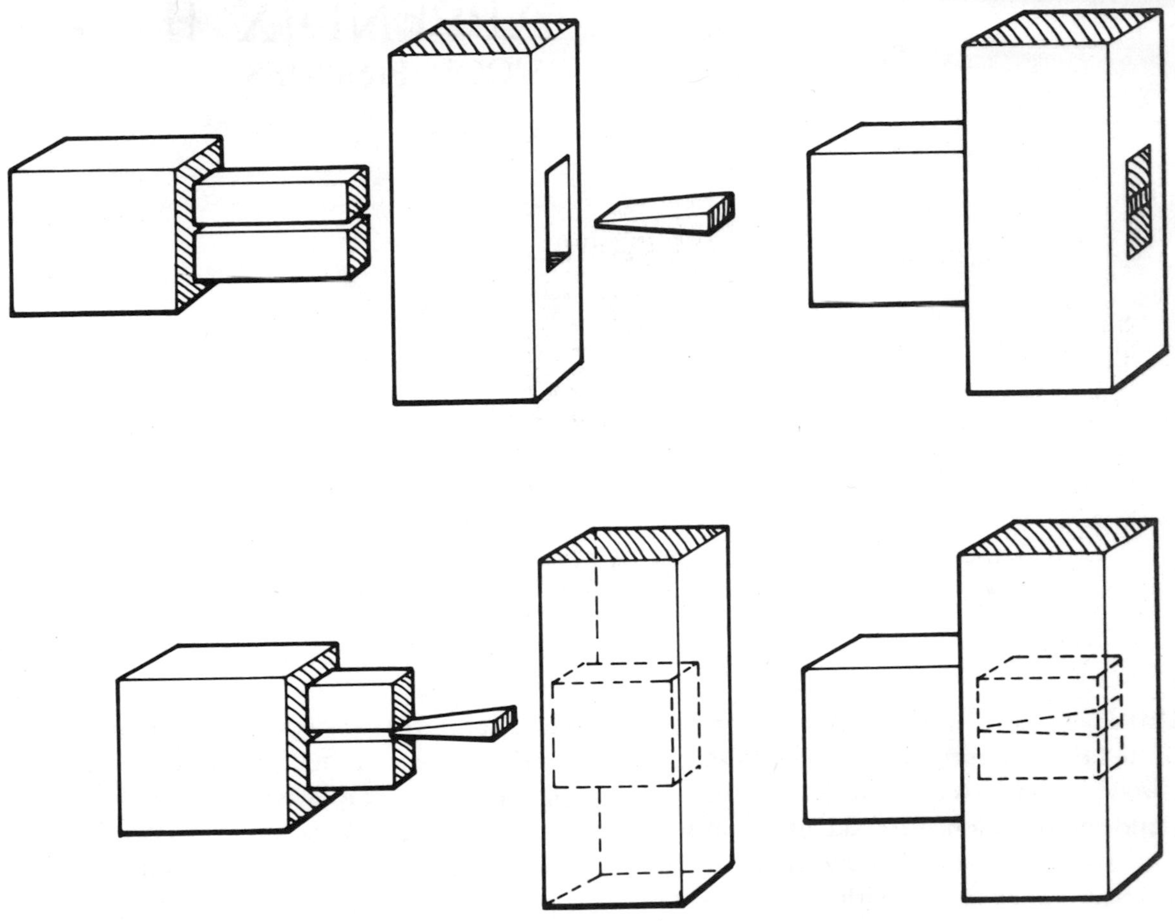

Mortise and tenon joints secured with foxtail wedges. Top: Through mortise with wedge inserted after fitting the tenon. Bottom: For a blind mortise, the wedge is started before insertion of the tenon. In each case, the wedge is glued.

APPENDIX II
WOOD FINISHES

Country craftsmen have always taken a simple, straightforward, functional approach to wood finishing. Much very fine woodwork is given no "finish" at all.

In Switzerland the tradition is to take great care of woodenware and buildings, allowing aging to occur naturally. The great *Baurnhauser* with their massive overhanging roofing, combining barn and farmhouse in one structure, discolor, or rather take on new coloration, over the centuries, with little actual deterioration of the timber. (In fact, painting wooden buildings is a cosmetic, cultural obsession having no relation to preservation. Dry rot sometimes occurs beneath painted surfaces that cannot adjust naturally to atmospheric conditions.) The Swiss cooper applies no finish to his pine milking pails, cream keelers, or butter churns. The magic quality of these tubs results from a gradual impregnation of butterfat over decades of use.

With hardwoods, I generally use a raw linseed oil finish. Contrasted to paints, varnishes, urethane, and other synthetic resins, linseed oil is easy and safe to use. Oil finishes can be applied with the cheapest brush, and there is no problem of cleaning up after yourself. (Just brush out until semidry.) There are no toxic vapors requiring a spray booth equipped with exhaust fans, or the use of a gas mask. Most oil finishes are safe for food containers and around small children. Tung oil, however, is poisonous. When using oil, dangerous, highly volatile (and expensive) thinners are avoided. Clothes don't get ruined. Drips and splashes are absorbed into the wood. There is no need to be concerned with dust or other stuff adhering to the finish.

Linseed oil brings out the natural beauty of wood. Through handling and age oiled woodwork acquires a patina and a unique beauty of its own. Oil finishes are not cosmetic. They don't crack or chip. Instead, oil is absorbed into the wood, acting as a moisture stabilizer and replacement for the original sap. Periodic applications of oil should be applied, as in oiling leatherware. The old finish is never stripped away. Simply clean off dirt and add a fresh coat.

Preparation for oil finishes consists of planing or scraping and sanding until surfaces are clean and smooth. Eighty-grit garnet paper works for most projects. Aluminum oxide paper is definitely a second choice, and flint papers are virtually useless for work on hardwoods. Fine work requires sanding with a progression of finer abrasives, ending with a piece of well-used 220-grit paper.

Small flaws can be filled with a homemade wood putty consisting of sanding dust from the project mixed with shellac or varnish. This makes a better color match than commercial "wood dough."

I generally use raw linseed oil mixed two parts oil to one part spirits of gum turpentine. The thinned mixture (which isn't any cheaper) gives good results. It dries faster, penetrates somewhat better, and seems to polish up faster then straight oil. For fine finishes warm the mixture by placing a container of it in a pan of hot water. Apply the oil and rub with a coarse rag. Repeat about twelve hours later.

Household woodenware, such as spoons, are sanded very smooth, then coated with straight warm oil and rubbed until a penetrating and hardening heat is generated. Repeated treatments over a period of several days result in a deep lustrous finish.

Open-grained woods, such as red oak, should first be sealed by adding an equal part of varnish to the linseed oil–turpentine mixture. (Three parts varnish, 2 parts oil, 1 part turpentine.)

Occasionally I use satin varnish or urethane finishes. For instance, it's a good idea to give a hard, wear-resistant finish to some tabletops. Oil finishes give no resistance to abrasion. Several thinned coats of matte urethane are applied, 12 to 24 hours apart. (Timing depends on relative humidity.) Between each application I sand very lightly with well-worn, old sandpaper. This gives a slight "tooth" so that each layer adheres to the next. It's important to clean the brush thoroughly with three baths in paint thinner after each application. This work is done in a well-ventilated, dust-free area.

There are also a number of proprietary oil finishes on the market. Compared with linseed oil, these are rather expensive. Watco oil is known for its penetrating and hardening qualities.

I never use stains. Wood has its own unique quality and it is absurd, if not offensive, to pretend that pine is walnut. For some things, such as a wheelbarrow, I simply "finish" with a few applications of creosote. Some woodsmen use old motor oil.

Raw linseed oil and spirits of gum turpentine are available at most hardware stores, as is creosote. The price in gallon cans is quite reasonable.

APPENDIX III
USES OF USUALLY USELESS WOODS

Before the takeover of technological economics, trees and shrubs were valued for many uses that have since been superseded by synthetics and highly manufactured products that must be purchased. The following list, by no means complete, gives some examples from traditional handcrafts of Europe and North America.

Bark (The term "bast" refers to inner bark, generally hickory or linden.)

baskets—poplar, birch, linden (bast)
canoes—birch
thongs—hickory (bast), linden (bast), tulip poplar (bast)
paper—birch
rope—linden (bast), elm (bast)
tanning—oak, birch, alder
roofing—birch (underlayment for sod), linden (bast used for shingles in Russia)

Roots

thongs—spruce

stands—pine
bearings—pine (Swiss butter churn)
ship timbers—larch, oak (Great Britain)
maul—dogwood, hickory
spoon—birch (Scandinavia)

Twigs and rods
baskets—willow, hazel
brooms—birch
rope—birch (Scottish highlands)

Limbs
bucket hooping—pine, birch, willow
spoons—apple, pear

hooks (clothes, harness, etcetera)—laurel, oak, etcetera
mauls—hickory, apple, beech, hornbeam, maul oak

Vines
thongs—blasphemy vine (brier for broom tying, etcetera)

Bushes
rake tines—mulberry, lilac (Finland)

Scrub trees
spoons—laurel, mountain ivy
hooks, brackets, etcetera—laurel

APPENDIX IV
TOOL SUPPLIERS

Many of the tools needed for country craftwork can be found in tool boxes, dusty attics, garage workshops and barn sheds. Drawknives, broadaxes and the like also show up in "antique" stores and Saturday auctions. If not badly corroded, these can be cleaned up and put to use. Due to a resurgent interest in traditional handcrafts some tools that were out of production a few years ago are now available again. I suggest shopping around, then buying the highest-quality tools available; slowly as you need them.

Reliable mail order sources include:

Woodcraft Supply Corp., 313 Montvale Ave., Woburn, MA 01801. Traditional and modern hand tools. Used tools at the sales room. Catalog 50¢.

Frog Tool Co., Ltd., 548 N. Wells St., Chicago, IL 60025. Hand woodworking tools. Catalog 50¢.

Silvo Hardware Company, 107–109 Walnut St., Philadelphia, PA 19106. Brand name tools and hardware. Catalog $1.00.

Cumberland General Store, Route 3, Box 479, Crossville, TN 38555. Homesteader gear including hand tools, work harness, and some horse-drawn equipment. Catalog $3.00 refundable.

The Ben Meadows Company, 3589 Broad St., Atlanta, GA 30341. Forestry supplies such as axes, peaveys, etcetera; 490 page catalog $3.00 refunded on $25.00 order.

Carl Heidtman, Box 140309, 563 Remscheid 14, Germany. Chisels, gouges, and carving tools. Minimum order, about $50.

Zip-Penn, Inc., Box 179, Erie, PA 16512. Chain saw chains, parts, tools, etcetera. Free catalog.

ANNOTATED BIBLIOGRAPHY

Blandford, Percy W. *Country Craft Tools.* London: David and Charles, 1974. (A survey of tools used by woodworkers, blacksmiths, thatchers, basket makers, etcetera. Written by a craftsman.)

Child, Peter. *The Craftsman Woodturner.* London: G. Bell & Sons, Ltd., 1971. (Turning carefully explained by a master craftsman.)

Coggin, J. K. *et al. A Manual on Sharpening Hand Woodworking Tools.* [reprint] Danville, Ill.: The Interstate Printers and Publishers, Inc., n.d. (Originally prepared as a text for vocational-agriculture students. Good, basic information.)

Edlin, H. L. *Woodland Crafts in Britain.* London: B. T. Batsford, Ltd., 1949, 1973. (A classic work organized by wood varieties and their uses.)

Goodman, W. L. *The History of Woodworking Tools.* London: G. Bell and Sons Ltd., 1962. (An academic approach with emphasis on axes, planes, and saws. Many country craft tools not covered.)

Hall, Walter. *Barnacle Parp's Chain Saw Guide.*

Emmaus, Pa.: Rodale Press, 1977. (A recommended manual on buying, using, and maintaining chain saws.)

Hoadley, R. Bruce. "Drying Wood" in *Fine Woodworking,* vol. I, no. 5.

Jenkins, J. Geraint. *Traditional Country Craftsmen.* London: Routledge and Kegan Paul, 1965. (Country crafts with emphasis on social history and tools used. Excellent.)

Mackie, B. Allan. *Building With Logs.* [published by] B. Allan Mackie; P.O. Box 1205; Prince George, B.C.; Canada V2L 4V3. (Text on chinkless construction by an experienced builder and teacher.)

Mercer, Henry C. *Ancient Carpenters' Tools.* The Bucks County Historical Society, 1929, 1975. (A survey of everyday and exotic tools, mostly American, but with some from Europe and Asia.)

Nish, Dale L. *Creative Wood Turning.* Provo, Utah: Brigham Young University Press, n.d. (A general course on using wood lathes.)

Schneider, Richard C. *Crafts of the North American Indians.* New York: Van Nostrand Reinhold Co., 1972. (A craftsman's manual. Crooked knives, stone pecking, leatherwork, basketry, beading, ceramics, even corn husk dolls.)

Sloane, Eric. *A Museum of Early American Tools.* New York: Wilfred Funk, Inc., 1964; [paperback] New York: Ballantine Books, Inc, 1973. (An inspirational collection. Many ideas but few details.)

Viires, A. *Woodworking in Estonia.* Jerusalem: Israel Program for Scientific Translations, 1969; [American edition from: U.S. Government Printing Office, Washington, D.C.] (My favorite book on country and village woodworking, covering history, sociology, techniques, tools, and woodcrafts typical of northern Europe.)

Wright, Dorothy. *Baskets and Basketry.* London: David and Charles, 1959, 1974. (Excellent on willow basketry.)

Zimmerman, M. H. and Brown, C. L. *Tree Structure and Function.* Springer Verlag, 1971.

OF RELATED INTEREST

Agricola, Georgius. *De Re Metallica.* London: The Mining Magazine, 1912; [reprint] New York: Dover Publications, Inc., 1950. (Originally published in Latin in 1559; the theory and technique of prospecting, mining, assaying, and smelting rare and common metals; with hundreds of excellent woodcuts of tools, simple machinery, period work clothes, etcetera.)

CoSIRA. *The Thatcher's Craft.* Wimbledon, England: Council for Small Industries in Rural Areas, 1961. (A model text on thatching.)

Drew, James M. *Blacksmithing.* Saint Paul; Webb Book Publishing Company, 1943; [reprint] Seattle: The Shorey Book Store, 1975. (A basic text written by a former instructor in blacksmithing, School of Agriculture, University of Minnesota.)

Hommel, Rudolf P. *China at Work.* New York: The John Day Company, 1937; [reprint] Cambridge: The M.I.T. Press, 1969. (A great classic work divided into sections on tools, agriculture, clothing, shelter, and transport; fascinating from cover to cover.)

Langsner, Drew & Louise. *Handmade.* New York: Harmony Books, 1974. (Shelter, crafts, farming, and cuisine garnered during a year's wanderings through rural districts of Europe and the Near East.)

Morse, Edward S. *Japanese Homes and Their Surroundings.* Originally published in 1886. [Paperback reprints] New York: Dover Publications, Inc.; (and) Rutland, Vermont: Charles E. Tuttle Co., 1972. (Another classic describing carpentry and houses of farms, villages, and cities in nineteenth century Japan.)

Schumacher, E. F. *Small is Beautiful.* New York: Harper and Row, 1973. (The economics of handcrafts and small-scale intensive farming as a sane and practical life for mankind.)

Sturt, George. *The Wheelwright's Shop.* Cambridge: Cambridge University Press, 1923, 1974. (Beautifully written memoirs with historical and technical material woven in.)

Williams, Christopher. *Craftsmen of Necessity.* New York: Random House, Inc., 1974. (A tour of functional rural crafts from Eurasia and North Africa.)

INDEX

A

Abrasive stone, for sharpening axes, 48
Adze, description of, 9–10
    use in making dough troughs, 254
Ambrosia beetle, in oak wood, 18, 146
Apple, for mauls, 74, 78
    for tool handles, 90
Arkansas stone, for sharpening, 13, 48, 69
Ash, 16, 20
    for bow saws, 84
    for hay rakes, 139
    for pitchforks, 146
    for tool handles, 90
    for wheelbarrows, 166
Axes, cold weather use, 45
    description of, 8–9
    handles for, 90–96
    proper "hang" of, 96
    sharpening of, 47–49
    in woodshed, 38–39

B

Bark, for boxes, 217–22
    harvesting times, 18
    as woodworking material, 16
Basketry, white oak, 225–39
Basket splits, 226
    making with drawknife, 68
Basswood, bark use, 16
    for yoke, 178
Bast, hickory, as lacing material, 16, 219
Beech, for mallets, 74, 77, 90
    for wheelbarrow, 166
    for workbench, 108
Beetles, making of, 78
Bench, dining, construction of, 269–71
Bench rest, to hold wood on workbench, 116
Bending, of wood, 84, 154–55, 194
Besoms. *See* Broom tying
Birch, bark, use of, 16
    for dough troughs, 254
    for tool handles, 90
Block knife, description of, 6
Bone, as material of knife, 4
Bow saws, 28
    construction of, 83–84
Box elder, 22
Boxes, of bark, 217–22
Boxwood, 22
    for mauls, 74
Brake, for cleaving, 149
Broom tying, 211–15
    materials for, 212, 214
Bucking, of felled tree, 33
Bucksaw, 28
    construction of, 84–86
Bull tongue plow. *See* Plow, bull tongue
Burden stick. *See* Yoke

C

California laurel, 22
Cant hook, for moving felled logs, 35
Carrying yoke. *See* Yoke
Chain saw, use for felling, 28–29
Checking, proper seasoning to prevent, 74–75
Chinquapin, golden, 22
Chisels, handles for, 97–98
Cleaving, 148–49
    tools for, 10–11
Clubs, making of, 75
Colt's foot, on axe handles, 91
Conifers, 16
Coppice, establishment of, 23
Coulter, for plow, 191
Crooked knife, description of, 4–5
Crosscut saw, for felling, 26–27
Cross-grain lumber, 19
Crotches, as problem when splitting wood, 42–43
Cudgel, 7
    making of, 75–76
Cutting, tools for, 4–7

D

Deciduous trees, 16
Dining bench. *See* Bench, dining
Doe's foot, on axe handle, 91
Dogs, for holding wood on workbench, 116
Dogwood, for mauls, 74
    for spoons, 243
    for tool handles, 90
Dough troughs, 253–61
    tools for, 254–55
    woods for, 253–55
Douglas fir, 16
Drags, construction of, 201–2
Drawknife, description of, 6–7
    sharpening of, 68–70
    use of, 67–68
Drop-forging, of axes, 9

E

Ear plugs, worn with chain saw, 30

F

Face gauges, use in making pitchforks, 150–51
Felling, 25–35
    controlling direction of fall, 30–32
    technique for, 29–32
    tools for, 26–29

Felling axe, 25–26
Felling cut, 32
Felling time, effect on wood's quality, 17
Fencing posts, pointing, 50–51
Files, handles for, 98
mill, to sharpen axes, 47–48
saw, to sharpen saws, 27
Finishes, wood, 290–92
Firewood, splitting wood for, 39–46
Flint, as material for knives, 4
Fore-cart, for use with draft horses, 182
Froe, description of, 10–11, 160–61

G

Glue, plastic resin, 266
Gluts. *See* Wedges
Go-devil. *See* Splitting maul
Gouges, handles for, 97–98
for spoon-making, 245–46

H

Hafts. *See* Handles
Half-soles, for sled runners, 187
Hammer, 8
Handle clamp, description of, 92
Handles, 89-99
axe, 90–96
chisel and gouge, 97–98
file, 98
peavey, 96–97
plow, 193–94
rake, 140–43
saw, 98–99
wood for, 89–90
Hard hat, wearing during felling, 30
Hardwoods, 16
Harrow, spike-tooth, construction of, 197–99
Hauling yoke. *See* Yoke
Hayfork. *See* Pitchforks
Hay rakes. *See* Rakes
Hazel, planting in coppices, 23
Heartwood, 16
Helving, of handles, 95–96
Hewing, of log, 183–84
Hickory, bark, use of, 16, 219
for bow saws, 84
for handles, 16, 20, 89–90
for mauls, 74
for wheelbarrow, 166
Hinge, in felling, 32
Hold-down, to hold wood on workbench, 116–17
Holly, 22
for spoons, 243
Hookaroon, for moving felled logs, 35
Hornbeam, for bow saws, 84
for mauls, 74
Humbolt undercut, in felling, 32

I

India stone, for sharpening, 12, 48, 69
Ironwood, for mallets, 74

J

Jig, to bend pitchfork, 156–57
to bend plow handle, 194

K

Kerf, location of, 29
Keys. *See* Wedges
Kindling, techniques for making, 45
Knives, description of, 4–7
sharpening of, 12–13

L

Lathe, 123–24
spring-pole, construction of, 124–30
use of, 130
Lilac, for rake tines, 16
Limbing, for felled tree, 32–33
Linden, for dough troughs, 253
Linseed oil, for finishing, 78, 291
Locust, for bow saws, 84
for sled runners, 184
Lodging, of felled tree, 29–30
Lumber, cutting methods, 19–21

M

Mallets, 7
carpenter's, 77
making of, 76–78
Maple, for tool handles, 90
for workbench, 108
Materials, 15–23, 293–94
Mauls, 7, 75–78
Mesquite, 22
for mauls, 74
Milking stool, construction of, 171–74
Mill file, for sharpening axes, 47–48
Miters, 117–18
Mortise and tenon construction, 112, 125, 281–89
Mountain ivy, for spoon making, 243
Mulberry, 22
for bow saws, 84
for mauls, 74

N

Notch, in felling, 32

Index

O

Oak, 16, 20
for baskets, 225–39
for bow saws, 84
harvesting times, 18
for mauls, 74
for pitchforks, 146
for plow, 191
for sled runners, 184
for tool handles, 90
in western states, 22
for wheelbarrow, 166
for workbench, 108
Obsedian, as material for knives, 4
Osage orange, for dough troughs, 253

P

Peavey, handle for, 96–97
for moving felled logs, 35
Persimmon, for mauls, 74
Pine, for wheelbarrow, 166
for whisks, 273–76
for workbench, 108
for yokes, 178
Pitchforks, 145–59
construction of, 148–59
wood for, 146
Plastic resin glue, for tabletop, 266
Plow, bull tongue, 191–95
wood for, 191
Pokes, construction of, 205–7
Polled axe, 44–45
Poplar, tulip. *See* Tulip poplar
Postholes, making of, 50
Posts, fence, pointing of, 50–51

Q

Quartersawn lumber, 20

R

Rakes, 135–43
construction of, 139–43
handles for, 140–43
wood for, 139
Rasp, for shaping handles, 93
Red alder, 22
Redwood, 16
Rhododendron, for making spoons, 16, 243
Ricks, for stacking wood, 38
Rivets, making of, 154
Roots, as woodworking material, 15
Rough locks, as sled brake, 188
Rust, removal from saw blades, 27

S

Safety, with bow saws, 85
when felling, 30, 33
in moving logs, 35
in spoon making, 245
in woodshed, 39
Sandbags, for holding wood on workbench, 117
Sapwood, 16
Sassafras, for bow saws, 84
Sawbuck, construction of, 55–57
use in woodshed, 38
Saws, 11
bow, construction of, 83–84
buck, construction of, 84–86
frame, 83
handles for, 98–99
turning, 83
construction of, 86–87
Scorp, description of, 7
Scroll saw, description of, 83
Seasonal factors, affecting wood's quality, 18
Seasoning, of wood, to prevent checking, 74–75
Shafts. *See* Handles
Shaving horses, construction of, 59–66
Shooting board, for guiding plane, 118
Shrubs, as woodworking material, 16
Single-foot plow. *See* Plow, bull tongue
Skidding, to move felled logs, 35
Slabbing, to split wood, 46
Slash-sawn lumber, 20
Sleds, 181–88
brakes for, 188
construction of, 184–87
half-soles for, 187
wood for, 184
Softwood, 16
Sourwood, for sleds, 184
Splint cuts, in felling, 32
Splitting, for baskets, 226
of logs, 39–46
Splitting maul, 40
Spokeshave, 70–71
sharpening of, 71
Spoon making, 241–50
woods for, 243
Spring pole, to control direction of felling, 30–32
Stock knife, description of, 6
Stone boat, description of, 188
Stool, milking, 171–74
Striking, tools for, 7–10
Stropping, of drawknife, 70
of knives, 13

T

Table, construction of, 263–67
Timber wedge, 28, 32, 101
Tine former, for making rakes, 140

Tools, 3–13
  for dough troughs, 254–55
  for felling, 26–29
  for woodshed, 38
Topping, of tree before felling, 32
Travois, for carrying bundles, 163
Tulip poplar, use of bark, 16, 217
  for yokes, 178
Turning saw, construction of, 86–87
  description of, 83
Tusk tenon. *See* Wedges

U

Undercut, in felling, 32

V

Vises, 119–21

W

Walnut, 16
Wattle hurdles, 33–34
Wedges, 10, 101–4
  gluts, 103–4
  key, 101, 103
  making of, 102–3
  tusk tenons, 101
  use in splitting wood, 43–44, 101
Wedging maul. *See* Splitting maul
Western states, wood common in, 22
Wheelbarrow, 163–69
  construction of, 166–68
  woods for, 166
Whetting, of drawknife, 69–70
  of knives, 12–13
Whisks, pine, making of, 273–76
Widow makers, 30
Willow, in coppices, 23
  for hay rakes, 139
Wood, bending of, 84, 154–55, 194
  finishing, 290–92
  seasoning of, 74–75
  splitting of, 39–46
Woodshed, 37–49
  splitting wood in, 39–46
  tools for, 38–39
Workbench, 107–21
  butt joint, 111–12
  half-lap, 111
  holding devices, 116–17
  keyed mortise and tenon, 112
  tabletop for, 113–14
  vises, 119–21
  wood for, 108

Y

Yew, Pacific, 22
Yoke, for carrying, 177–79